Higher Education and Community-Based Research

Higher Education and Community-Based Research

Creating a Global Vision

Edited by
Ronaldo Munck, Lorraine McIlrath, Budd Hall, and
Rajesh Tandon

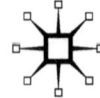

HIGHER EDUCATION AND COMMUNITY-BASED RESEARCH
Copyright © Ronaldo Munck, Lorraine McIlrath, Budd Hall, and Rajesh Tandon, 2014.

Softcover reprint of the hardcover 1st edition 2014 978-1-137-38527-7

All rights reserved.

First published in 2014 by
PALGRAVE MACMILLAN®
in the United States—a division of St. Martin's Press LLC,
175 Fifth Avenue, New York, NY 10010.

Where this book is distributed in the UK, Europe and the rest of the World, this is by Palgrave Macmillan, a division of Macmillan Publishers Limited, registered in England, company number 785998, of Houndmills, Basingstoke, Hampshire RG21 6XS.

Palgrave Macmillan is the global academic imprint of the above companies and has companies and representatives throughout the world.

Palgrave® and Macmillan® are registered trademarks in the United States, the United Kingdom, Europe and other countries.

ISBN 978-1-349-48120-0   ISBN 978-1-137-38528-4 (eBook)
DOI 10.1057/9781137385284

Library of Congress Cataloging-in-Publication Data

Higher education and community-based research : creating a global vision / editors, Ronaldo Munck, Lorraine McIlrath, Budd Hall and Rajesh Tandon.
    pages   cm
Includes index.

 1. Community and college. 2. Education, Higher—Social aspects.
 3. Education—Research. I. Munck, Ronaldo.
LC237.H54 2014
378.1′03—dc23   2014017347

A catalogue record of the book is available from the British Library.

Design by Integra Software Services

First edition: October 2014

10 9 8 7 6 5 4 3 2 1

Contents

Foreword   vii

1 Main Issues and Perspectives: An Introduction   1
  Ronaldo Munck, Lorraine McIlrath, Budd Hall, and Rajesh Tandon

Section I   Overview

2 Community-Based Research: Genealogy and Prospects   11
  Ronaldo Munck
3 The Problematic of Participation: Back to the Future   27
  Vanessa Liston
4 Community-Based Research, Health, and Social Interventions   39
  Jennifer Mullett
5 Majority-World Foundations of Community-Based Research   53
  Rajesh Tandon and Budd Hall

Section II   Experiences

6 "With or Without You"—The Development of Science Shops and Their Relationship to Higher Education Institutions in Europe   71
  Norbert Steinhaus
7 Research Engagement in the UK: Evolving Policy and Practice   85
  Sophie Duncan and Paul Manners
8 Emerging Policy and Practices on Community-Based Research—Perspectives from the Island of Ireland   101
  Lorraine McIlrath, Catherine Bates, Kenneth Burns, Ann Lyons, Emma McKenna, and Pádraig Murphy

9 Community-Based Research in Australian Universities: Reflections on National Policy, Institutional Strategy, and Research Practice 117
Michael Cuthill

10 Organizing Culture Change through Community-Based Research 133
Scott J. Peters and Maria Avila

11 Community Engagement as Fabric in Which to Weave in Teaching/Learning and Research 149
Ahmed C. Bawa

12 The Community-Based Research Tradition in Latin America 167
Jutta Gutberlet, Crystal Tremblay, and Carmen Moraes

Section III Perspectives

13 Community-Based Research: Searching for Its Foundations 183
Ronald Barnett

14 Higher Education and the Public Good: Precarious Potential? 199
Mala Singh

15 Knowledge, Action, and Hope: A Call for Strengthening the Community-Based Research Movement 217
Budd Hall, Rajesh Tandon, Ronaldo Munck, and Lorraine McIlrath

Contributor Biographies 219

Bibliography 223

Index 247

Foreword

Higher education internationally is currently facing a funding crisis and a crisis of perspectives. There is an increasing turn toward what we might call the commercialization or commodification of knowledge.

The turn toward the community or the discovery of a third mission alongside teaching and research may provide an alternative strategy for higher education, which might allow it to better fulfill its role as a public good.

This book addresses the community-based research strand of civic engagement, which we believe is now crucial to develop for deepening the social engagement mission of higher education. It takes different forms in different world regions but there is a common theme of knowledge democratization we seek to uncover.

It is our ambition that this volume will help to spark further debate around how best to take research into the community, for mutual benefit. We need to bring out models of best practice, seek the historical roots of current modalities of community-based research, and exchange ideas and practical experiences across disciplines and world regions.

This volume is very much based on experience (as advocated by the experiential learning philosophy of community-based research) but it also advocates a stronger critical theory-driven engagement with underlying principles and the politics of knowledge not always acknowledged by community-based research practitioners.

CHAPTER 1

Main Issues and Perspectives:
An Introduction

*Ronaldo Munck, Lorraine McIlrath, Budd Hall,
and Rajesh Tandon*

Community-based research (CBR) has become an integral element of the contemporary university's repertoire of activities. It may take different forms and respond to different priorities but it is no longer a marginal activity. It now joins community-based learning—which has a much longer history—as a key component of what is becoming known as the engaged university. We could say, then, that community-based learning and research has been mainstreamed, normalized, or brought into the field. CBR can even be seen as an activity that grants a competitive advantage to those institutions that promote it. It may serve to develop interdisciplinary research skills, provide students with "real world" experiential learning, promote the "public purpose" of the university, and even attract funding from philanthropic donors. These very real issues—especially salient in a period of economic and philosophical crisis—add a note of urgency to current attempts to generate local, national, and transnational platforms for community-based research as part of the broader engagement mission.

There is also an alternative community-based learning and research modality going back to the origins of adult education and a radical 1960s grassroots, bottom-up, or contestatory tradition. Here, education is seen not as an end in itself, but as a means of achieving individual and social transformation. A critical analysis of the world around us and an understanding of the structures of oppression are central to this alternative pedagogy. From this rich melting pot sprung interest in action research and participatory research in the 1960s, primarily in the global South, but which was also reflected in the imperialist heartlands as anticolonialism, antisexism, and antiracism came to the fore. Ever since, there has been what might be called a minority movement within the academy, whereby community links were fostered and social knowledge was valorized. Often on the fringes of the organization, these initiatives nevertheless kept alive a community-oriented teaching and research tradition. Sometimes this work is even recognized and promoted by a new generation of higher education managers and educational policy planners.

Rather than counterpose a mainstream and radical CBR theory and practice, we would be better served by acknowledging CBR's complexity. Against all forms of positivism, complexity recognizes that there are no linear laws or simple answers, and no inevitable outcome to social processes. Against all forms of structuralism, it also recognizes the importance of agency and the ability of human action to change things. So, a process such as community-based research is enormously variable as complexity would advise us, but we also need to recognize *contextuality* (e.g., knowledge is historically and geographically specific) and *contingency* (against teleological explanations, we accept the impact of conscious human agents). The university itself is also, of course, subject to complexity, contextuality, and contingency and cannot just have a linear teleological plan. If this complex university opens its research (and teaching) to the wider community, it will gain in legitimacy but also its integrity and impartiality as an institution are more likely to be recognized.

In Chapter 2, of Section I, Ronaldo Munck provides us with a wide-ranging genealogy of the term "community-based research" and some preliminary ideas around its possible prospects. He explores the Southern origins of the participatory research approach and the later manifestations of it in the very different context of the more affluent North. He argues that community-based research brings to the fore basic epistemological debates around the status of knowledge in the way it values experiential and grounded knowledge over abstract or universal knowledge. It thus feeds into a Southern perspective or epistemological standpoint that prioritizes subaltern knowledge. In the North we can see CBR as part of a response to the commercialization of the university and commodification of knowledge. Community-based research (and learning) poses another logic for staff and students alike, and they may become champions for a more socially robust form of knowledge fit for purpose in the complex world we live in. The overall message of this chapter is that "another knowledge" is possible and another university is possible.

In Chapter 3, Vanessa Liston discusses the way in which community-based research has dealt with the problematic of participation, particularly providing us with a strong definition of community-based research in which the researcher does not produce knowledge but, rather, helps participants to produce knowledge about themselves. Participatory rural appraisal and the iconic work of Robert Chambers are systematically explored to generate new learnings. This is not an uncritical reading, however, and participatory methodologies can, arguably, be seen as ineffective for empowerment and sustainability. Her conclusion is that participation as such is indeterminate in terms of its effects. Indeed, given that complexity is an inescapable condition of this type of research, we are more likely to see both advances and retreats, with learning and innovation always a precarious gain. If a health system, for example, can be seen as a complex adaptive system, then research might be seen as a form of complex adaptive participation.

Jennifer Mullett in Chapter 4 deals with the ways in which community-based research enhances community practices. This chapter is set in the context of the complex Canadian health system and social services but its lessons are more general. Community health requires, more or less inevitably, community and participatory forms of health promotion. There is no one agreed "cookbook" for participatory health research; rather, we tend to see flexible approaches driven by community priorities and not by outside experts. When the values of empowerment are to the fore, capacity-building interventions can have a tangible and sometimes durable impact on the community. Community-based research should promote collective well-being guided by a vision of a more just world. These approaches within the broad community health tradition can be attractive to government funders simply because they deliver results. At the same time, perhaps in a contradictory fashion, they also provide the opportunity for participants to make connections, develop a greater sense of self-worth, and make a contribution to their community. CBR, we are beginning to see, comes in different guises.

In Chapter 5, Rajesh Tandon and Budd Hall explore the majority world foundation of community-based research and challenge the Eurocentric bias of much contemporary scholarship in this area. Their point of departure is thus a historical corrective of the dominant discourse, which sees CBR emerging in the United States *circa* 1980. Both in India and in Africa, the engagement of research with communities has a longer and more complex history, which the authors trace and recover for current practitioners of CBR. From this rich experience they follow their own subsequent collaboration and creation of the first international networks to promote community-based research. They pose their long-term engagement with community-based research in terms of the relationship of knowledge to a more equitable world. The democratization of knowledge and knowledge democracy thus come to the fore in a debate that is often posed as a purely academic one. Clearly we can now move forward with community-based research that is oriented toward cognitive justice as a strand of activity within academia and beyond.

In Section II, we move toward more detailed case studies to exemplify the broad array of community-based research theory and practice.

The European science shops as mechanisms of community knowledge exchange are the focus of Norbert Steinhaus in Chapter 6. They represent a radical attempt post-1968 to "bring science to the people" in a practical way. The story of their evolution is of general interest because we can detect there the pressures from government, funders, and university administrators that CBR initiatives came under. The science shop movement—and that is what it was, and is still to some extent—showed the promise of an engagement by the community with the university. There was not, of course, one single model of the science shop that was slavishly followed but, rather, several variants around the same mission. Today the science shops are part of the European Union research funding strategy, but for some, they have lost their radical edge. Be that as it may, they are a required case study for any comparative international study of community-based research. Not least, they throw up the problem of scale: whether it is essential to have a locally embedded CBR initiative or whether it can be "scaled up" to city or, why not, a national level.

The United Kingdom (UK) experience of research engagement by universities is the focus of Sophie Duncan and Paul Manners in Chapter 7. While the UK has had many historical experiences of CBR reaching back to the Workers' Educational Association (WEA) and the Open University (OU), today we can discern a "tipping point" where societal engagement is about to become a major component in the strategy of universities in that jurisdiction. The authors are key drivers of the Beacons for Public Engagement initiative and thus well placed to situate this experience in its policy context and carry out their own reflexive analysis of its successes and contradictions. They establish a clear differentiation, as do other chapters, between "grassroots" or bottom-up CBR initiatives and those that are "top-down," reflecting the priorities of funders and policy-makers. In the UK it is now well established that engagement is, or should be, a core value for the university. How this might square with increasing moves toward commercialization, and even privatization, of the university remains to be seen.

Lorraine McIlrath, and colleagues, explores the distinctive Irish research-community interfaces in Chapter 8. What we see is a wide diversity of CBR philosophies and implementation practices. In Ireland, there has been an early replication of the European science shop model, but there is also a considerable influence of the US tradition of service learning and research. What is probably most noticeable is the development by the Irish government some years ago of a community engagement strategy. This has legitimized previous bottom-up initiatives to promote community-based learning and research. These activities benefit from the presence of a national civic engagement platform in the shape of Campus Engage, which is funded by the Higher Education Authority. The challenges faced by CBR in Ireland are many, as elsewhere, leading one to pose questions such as the following: Do the values of civic engagement conflict with current moves toward a more commercialized university? Will there be "buy-in" from an increasingly pressurized academic staff? Will cooperation overcome competition among CBR practitioners? Ireland is an interesting case study, falling as it does between the European and US "models," with a significant influence from Australia as well.

In Chapter 9, Michael Cuthill examines Australian university strategy and practice in regard to community-based research. As do other chapters, this one sets itself in the terrain of the Mode 2 knowledge paradigm (Gibbon et al., 1994) in understanding that the university is but one player today in a vastly expanded knowledge production process. This Australian case study is particularly valuable because it shows that the course of CBR does not always run smoothly. There is often a lack of collaboration skills or even of motivation, and what starts promisingly can grind to a halt. In other cases, especially where relationship development in diverse communities was a core focus, success was more likely. So CBR is not easy, but it is possible and immensely rewarding when got right. There are still many challenges—such as the fundamental question of whether academics are ready to work collectively and share power—but we have the technology and we can make CBR work, especially if we learn from international experience.

Organizing culture change through community-based research is the theme of Scott Peters and Maria Avila in Chapter 10, based mainly on US experiences, where there is a long history of CBR going back to the nineteenth-century land grant university. The authors recount two individual experiences, the first based on a land grant extension service program and the second based on community organizing and CBR practice, in Los Angeles. It is clear from these cases that CBR has the potential to facilitate learning and/or co-learning, solve some social problems, and advance knowledge. The challenge for the practitioners of CBR, and for those who seek to learn from, and theorize from, that practice, is to achieve the full potential of community-based research. An extremely interesting lesson that emerges from these dense studies is whether it is actually wise to blur the distinction between community and academic knowledge. Can CBR—in what we might call a populist mode—actually downgrade the properly applied intellectual knowledge of the experienced academic?

Ahmed Bawa in Chapter 11 takes up the challenge of describing and analyzing the rich experience of community-based research in postapartheid South Africa. Community engagement is posed as a fabric into which we can weave both teaching/learning and research. South Africa has a rich history of university-community engagement, which Bawa draws on to develop a grounded theory of community-based research oriented toward a progressive transformation of both knowledge and society. Community engagement has been "mainstreamed" in South Africa at national and local levels, yet it still has a long way to go in terms of capturing the imagination of most academics. Bawa provides an insider account of why this might be the case and advances some propositions for the future. What emerges is a conception of community engagement not as some rather under-specified "third pillar" alongside teaching and research but, rather, as a site for knowledge production in its own right. Also vital, moving forward, would be to critically address the power relations between universities and communities.

Latin America is widely seen as a region where university-community engagement had early roots, and it has provided global inspiration, not least through the work of Paulo Freire. In Chapter 12, Jutta Gutberlet, Crystal Tremblay, and Carmen Moraes capture some of the complexity and intensity of participatory and action-oriented research, particularly in Brazil. This has contributed significantly to the global construction of a postcolonial critical epistemology and methodology of considerably import. This approach, from the days of Paulo Freire to the present, has always been characterized by a marked political radicalism and cultural creativity. If we examine the CBR literature and practice globally, we will see to what extent participatory research—from rapid rural appraisal to social action-oriented research—has benefited from the work by Latin American theorists and practitioners. Indeed, it is the unity of theory and practice in *praxis* that is the most marked characteristic of the Latin American tradition on university-community engagement.

In Section III, we move toward a series of reflections or perspectives that take us back to some of the big issues raised in Section I in light of the rich tapestry of experiences outlined in Section II.

We start with Ronald Barnett in Chapter 13 and join him in a close critical engagement with the foundations of both community and research. He quite rightly questions not only the term community but what we mean by "base" in community-based research. Certainly, if we are to explore the meaning of what a community-oriented research practice would look like in a complex and global world, it would be different from CBR as it is most usually deployed in the literature. The very concept of CBR needs to be set in the context of the very complex relationships between universities and the wider society and hinges on the role of the university in terms of knowledge legitimation. These are fluid times and these relationships are constantly changing, but they are crucial in determining the challenges and the prospects for a sound and sustainable CBR practice. What Barnett advocates as a way forward is an "ecological university." That would represent a university that is directly attuned to its surrounding environment and able to play a key role in sustaining that environment but also, he would hope, improving it. This new type of university would take seriously its interconnection with the world around it and would be an effective home and driver of community-based research.

Mala Singh, in Chapter 14, takes up the underlying issue of the public good in a higher education setting. The current controversy over the future of the university is posed vey much as the new commercialization and privatization agenda against the classic understanding of education as a public good. The current ideological constraints and very real practical difficulties in moving toward a public good regime are outlined. The notion of public good is thus seen to have a very precarious potential in terms of constituting a new foundational basis for rethinking the contemporary university. A paradigm-changing approach would be to resist or remove public "bads" through the launching of more bottom-up public good interventions. Community-based research could be seen as precisely one such initiative that would serve to mediate the public "bads" people face in their everyday lives. It is a path that might guide the CBR practitioner, who moves between aspirations toward the grand narrative of the public good and the pessimism that sets in when we realize the barriers that the corporate university and neoliberal regimes put in our way.

In the final afterword (Chapter 15), the editors present a brief programmatic statement. This is not a statement that all the authors in this publication would necessarily share, but we do believe that most would share the underlying sentiments. We live in troubled times, and our interconnected world faces severe existential challenges. We do not believe that the university can answer all of these but we are convinced—not least by the rich history of engagement described and analyzed by the authors above—that the university has a role in democratizing knowledge, not least through community knowledge exchange. We thus pose a brief charter, manifesto, or statement that we hope might spark debate. Taking forward the tasks therein will be a collective effort. We certainly hope to inspire our readers through the rich tapestry of experiences presented in this volume.

Returning now to our opening remarks about complexity, in what direction does our wide array of contributions point us? Certainly they underscore the complex setting for CBR and diverse responses in different countries and different types of institutions. They all testify to the relevance of community-based research for any transformative educational system. We could go further, though, and argue that the current crisis of the university is also a period of opportunity. There is a funding crisis and a leadership crisis in many, if not most, university systems. Yet a crisis can also be a turning point, the start of something new. We need to reflect on the reasons for the current impasse and the ways in which that might be overcome. The diagnosis from a wide range of observers is clear, namely that the old model of the university is not working. Thus, we see many university strategists turning toward the market as savior, students as consumers, a global educational market, more efficient and cheaper delivery models, and the reduction of the academic to a cog in the great university of enterprise.

If there is one underlying foundation to the market turn, that would be the commodification of knowledge—it is to make something seemingly intangible, such as enlightenment, a commodity that can be bought and sold like any other. It is this assumption, the philosophy underlying it, and the university strategy that flows from it that are questioned by most forms of community-based research. They represent a move toward de-commodification in the sense that knowledge for social transformation is not sold to the highest bidder but shared according to social need. We might thus conceive of community-based teaching and research as part of a much wider counter-movement by society to protect itself from a market-driven commodification and commercialization of knowledge. In this wider context, the themes raised in this book have even greater significance if they are seen as part of a move to regain social and community influence in the mission of the university, which is now in danger of seeing profit as the sole mission.

SECTION 1

Overview

CHAPTER 2

Community-Based Research: Genealogy and Prospects

Ronaldo Munck

Community-based research (CBR) entails a different relationship between the research subject and the professional researcher than is customary in mainstream social science. People in the community, once subject to classification, experimentation, and regulation, are now viewed as owners of skills, knowledge, and expertise that may be useful to researchers and policy-makers. One variant of this approach is known as community-based participatory research (CBPR), which foregrounds the direct participation of the community and advocates an equal partnership between the professional researcher and the community subjects now redefined as "coresearchers." More recently, there has been emphasis on the mainstreaming of community research (CR), which is not directed at the empowerment of communities but is, rather, seen as a methodological tool often deployed to reach difficult-to-access populations through dedicated community researchers.

This introductory chapter will outline the basic genealogy of CBR and its various prospects going forward. Conscious of the very real diversity of experiences across the world in regard to university engagement with communities, we examine first some "Southern voices" such as the Latin American participatory action research (PAR) school and then "Northern experiences" such as the early US land-grant universities and the Dutch *science shop* movement of the 1970s. "Taking stock," we examine the very different epistemologies involved in community-based research, ranging from the instrumental to the transformative, which underpin the various modalities of CBR. "Moving on" then to the current situation where community-based research is very much mainstreamed, at least in some disciplines, we examine the options now opening up for universities to expand their community-based research as part of their civic engagement mission. Finally, in "Looking forward," we take a broader perspective posing some of the central current debates around the need to reimagine the university and the possible role of community-based research in terms of democratizing knowledge.

Southern Voices

Community-based research, particularly in its CBPR variant, is often traced back to the work of Orlando Fals Borda in Colombia in the late 1960s (Fals Borda and Rahman, 1991). Trained in the United States in a quantitative social science approach, Fals Borda began to find it inadequate to deal with the pressing issues of rural reform in Latin America. Social justice was beginning to come to the fore as a major concern for social researchers; Barrington Moore's (1966) comparative historical work, for example, influenced him strongly, and positivist methods within a Cold War political framework were not attractive from that perspective. For Fals Borda, PAR meant the following:

- Do not monopolize your knowledge nor impose arrogantly your techniques but respect and combine your skills with the knowledge of the researched or grassroots communities, taking them as full partners and co-researchers. That is, fill in the distance between subject and object;
- Do not trust elitist versions of history and science which respond to dominant interests, but be respective to counter-narratives and try to recapture them;
- Do not depend solely on your culture to interpret facts, but recover local values, traits, beliefs, and arts for action by and with the research organizations; and
- Do not impose your own ponderous scientific style for communicating results, but defuse and share what you have learned together, in a manner that is wholly understandable and even literary and pleasant, for science should not be necessarily a mystery nor a monopoly of experts and intellectuals.

(Fals Borda and Rahnema 1991)

PAR was ultimately a research philosophy that combined academic knowledge and the wisdom of communities. It was quite clearly overdetermined by the general effervescent political mood of the post-1968 period. Student radicalism, the war in Vietnam, the French May events of 1968, the

Cordobazo of 1969 in Argentina—all these influenced the debate among social scientists. As a Latin American "school," PAR was part of a much broader wave of critical thinking including the then emerging dependency theory but above all the not-unrelated work of Paulo Freire around *concientizaçaô* as a philosophy and practice of popular education. The *Pedagogy of the Oppressed* (Freire, 1970) had a huge influence beyond Latin America in promoting a humanist approach to education and research, which foregrounded the subjective experience of ordinary people. This reflexive-critical approach or method has now diffused across many disciplines, often taking the name of the "bottom-up" method. It can take different forms but it has very much influenced the flavor of non-positivist approaches to social research.

Another very influential CBR progenitor is the participatory rural appraisal (PRA) approach pioneered by Robert Chambers mainly in an African setting. This approach was at first adopted by radical nongovernmental organizations (NGOs) doing international development work but was eventually mainstreamed by the World Bank in the 1990s. Chambers, who acknowledges his debt to Paulo Freire, promoted a methodology committed to "putting the last first" (Chambers, 1983) by drawing out their vision of the world and their needs as rural illiterate communities. Chambers was committed to "the primacy of the personal" and eschewed citing political economy analyses of underdevelopment and its causes. This political vision was rather simplistic with a set of binary oppositions—core/periphery, white/black, male/female, old/young, teacher/pupil, senior/junior, donor/recipient—determining a simple moral view of the world and how it should be transformed.

It is not far-fetched to understand the Robert Chambers perspective as akin to a religious experience or, as one postcolonial critic put it, a form of "narcissistic samaritanism" (Kapoor, 2008, p. 63). Participatory action research becomes a messianic calling, and the path to salvation is centered around "empowerment" of the poor. Participatory research sessions sometimes take on the air of revivalist religious meetings with great mass fervor bent on discovery of the "truth." Sinners—the more powerful and better-off—can admit their sins and see the light. The ascetic selfless facilitator of PRA can exorcise bad thinking and help the "last become the first." It is at least doubtful whether this type of approach to community research will successfully remedy the admitted "democratic deficit" of mainstream top-down approaches. Put most simply, no one can "empower" another or a community for that matter.

If we stand back from the particular Latin American and African contexts—and their distinct local and international interlocutors—we find that the main debate is around the "participation" element in community-based participatory research. It advocates a "bottom-up" rather than "top-down" approach and prioritizes the "voice" of the poor over the international expert. It began as a radical critique of the development expert and the approach of bureaucratic organizations. Fairly rapidly, it gained acceptance in international development agencies, most notably the World Bank. What began as a radical critique of the mainstream approach to the objects of research (poor people) became transformed into an instrumental practice designed to gain access to communities and to give an air of legitimacy to policies that had gone through a process of consultation. When the World Bank articulates a strong commitment to participation and empowerment, it can be read, of course, in different and less benign or more instrumentalist ways.

The participatory approach can certainly be co-opted as we have seen above but it can also be critiqued in its own terms. There is now a growing feeling that "participation" can in fact be an imposition on those it is seeking to "empower." Those who have developed the argument that participation has become the "new tyranny" (Cooke and Kothari, 2001) point to the way in which the rhetoric of participation might mask the power relationships behind CBPR. Decision-making is still more or less monopolized by the international financial agency or NGO commissioning the research. The consultation exercises with the "bottom-up" ethos may even exacerbate local power differentials. We could also argue that the structural inequality issues that lie at the heart of international development and underdevelopment are effectively sidelined by a research and action perspective that prioritizes the process of participation and the articulation of "voice" without any effective mechanisms to redress real power differentials and inequalities.

In the global South, participatory research is today most often practiced by international development agencies from the World Bank to the NGOs. It is seen as a mechanism whereby "stakeholders" influence decision-making and the distribution of resources. This has given rise to a critique focused on the negative, instrumental, and extractive nature of it as a research approach. More radical definitions of CBR have also emerged in the South, emphasizing not just community involvement but the requirement that this should lead to the empowerment of local communities. One example that emerged in the mid-1990s is of regenerated Freirean literacy through empowering community techniques (REFLECT), an approach with a strong gender emphasis, which has led to increased community participation and action. We might conclude that we have now moved "beyond" the tyranny of participation (Hickey and Moha, 2004) in the sense that it is the context and the purpose of CBR that will determine whether it is empowering or disempowering.

There is the larger question of Southern knowledge in a world where science and technology is still concentrated in the North. As Santos and coauthors (2007) have put it, "there is no global justice without global cognitive justice" (p. XIX). Non-Western populations may view the concept of community and its relation to nature, knowledge, and memory quite differently from the dominant Eurocentric conception. A postcolonial approach to CBR would need to take this into account and not just assume one model is universal. What emerges then is a much greater diversity of CBR models and practices based on distinct epistemologies. Local, indigenous, or traditional knowledge in the South is now seen as central to the development process. For CBR practitioners from the Northern academia, it would be important to acknowledge North/South asymmetries and to see that a truly global CBR practice needs to go beyond a monocultural knowledge paradigm and recognize the complex global configuration of knowledges.

Northern Experiences

In the global North there are several background experiences that need to be taken into account in any genealogy of community-based research. We must examine the land-grant university experience in the United States going back to the late nineteenth century, which is surprisingly little known especially beyond North America. Sociology in North America had a clear interventionist intent at its inception, the most known of which is the 1920s Chicago school's commitment to using social science to address the social problems of an urbanizing and industrializing world. Albion Small, an early US sociologist, published his "Scholarship and Social Agitation" in 1896 in the *American Journal of Sociology* (Small, 1896) that challenged the claim that scholarship that "deals only with facts" was superior. Small advocated instead a scholarship that rejected the "do-nothing tradition" and was enriched by "the larger wisdom which comes from doing" and committed to "the control of forces in the interests of a more complete social and personal life" (cited in Peters, 2010, pp. 28–29). This is very much in the individualist tradition but it clearly promotes civic engagement as well.

Action research in both community and organizational settings has a long pedigree in the United States. For example, Kurt Lewin (1890–1947), who was a German-American psychologist, is claimed as the originator of the term "action research" in 1944, defined as comparative research on the conditions and forms of social action and research leading to social actions. Action research is oriented toward solving an immediate "social problem," a pragmatic approach that characterizes much of US social sciences to this day. For Lewin, to affect permanent social change, one needed to create the motivation for change, which in turn was strongly related to action. This behaviorist approach became particularly important in an organizational setting, where it became widely accepted that if people are involved in discussions that affect them, then they are more likely to adapt the new ways being proposed. In the workplace this shift can be summed up in terms of the move from Taylorism (time-motion study) to Elton Mayo's more humanistic approach to workers as individuals.

The land-grant universities in the United States carried out a concerted effort to place science at the service of social need. The national Cooperative Extension Scheme set up in 1914 was committed to promoting a broad and ambitious program of democratic agricultural modernization in alliance with the farming communities. This reform movement, as Scott Peters (2010) recounts, "embraced the view that academic professionals should play active roles, not only in addressing technical and social problems and challenges, but also in promoting and advancing... civic ideals" (p. 39). This movement fully accepted that communities held valuable local knowledge and that it did not just bring science to the people. This tradition found a reprise in Africa during the 1970s with a similarly ambitious rural extension program run by the more reformist international development agencies.

The interventionist stance of taking science into society was not of course unchallenged in the United States. The public intellectual tradition has continued, and "service learning" can trace its origins back to these early days. However, there is an equally strong tradition reacting against civic engagement, committed to separating science from social or political concerns. The true scholar should be concerned only with pure knowledge, which cannot be tainted by impure mixing with social need or, in the worst cases, social conflict. Mainstream US sociology largely rejected the tradition of C. Wright Mills (1959), foregrounding the sociological imagination and public engagement to become compartmentalized and professionalized, turning its back, on the whole, on society and social need. The service intellectual tradition carried on with engagement but, as Peters (2010) puts it, offering "the public a neutral, unbiased, dis-interested, and non-political source of scientific knowledge, information and expertise" (p. 53). This minimalist liberal vision of citizenship and the restricted role allocated to CBR is a world away from early land-grant universities' democratic commitment.

Western Europe in the 1970s was a very different place to the United States in the 1920s, yet a similar community-based research movement emerged. It sprung from within the universities as groups of students and younger academic staff reached out to communities of workers, squatters, environmentalists, mental health patients, and women's groups to address the research questions they deemed important. As Loet Leydesdorff and Janelle

Ward (2005) recount, "the terms of the debate were set by the science policy discourse about 'democratization', that is, access to higher education and university research as the scientific knowledge bases of society" (p. 6). There was a common political terrain between some of the new social movements and some university staff and students around the democratization of science. Interestingly, it was not mainly social scientists but rather engineers and natural scientists who drove this early wave of CBR through the so-called *science shops*.

The European science shop approach is quite distinctive and reflects a different understanding of science and society than, say, the US pragmatist problem-solving tradition. EU Science and Society Director Rainer Gerold argues that "There is a growing feeling that scientific research is aimed at abstract knowledge or profit and not sufficiently geared towards the needs and concerns of society" (Living Knowledge, 2013, p. 3). Much university research and business rhetoric are today couched in terms of social need. To better serve the community, science needs to get closer to society; thus, moves like the Science Shops are to break down university/community barriers. They provide much-needed social relevance to some disciplines or departments that have become remote from society or the "real world." That real world is also, of course, one based on private profit as the motivating force of the economic system, and it is not clear whether research is actually being conceived as a public good over and beyond the universal rhetoric of serving society.

In the 1990s, in the face of increased financial constraints and the general "marketization" of the universities, the science shops needed to adapt to the new environment. At first, the disadvantaged groups, which were their original clientele, were not turned away, but gradually "professionalization" and "marketization" undermined the original attitude of the science shops. Many of the science shops tried to become more market oriented and acted as consultancies or research institutes in the normal way; others were simply forced to close. The high tide of radical social thinking had subsided as neoliberalism and an emphasis on individualism and consumerism prevailed. As Wachelder (2003) puts it, "the attempt of the Amsterdam science shop [a beacon for the movement as a whole] to democratize science by turning into a professional agency failed, both in theory and in practice" (p. 261). Today's European science shop movement, with European Commission's financial backing, is seeking to recover some of the original democratic spirit, but whether it will be successful or not is still undecided.

Standing back from the specifics of the US land-grant universities and the Dutch science shops, what stands out is the question of CBR politics. The university and the production of knowledge are set within a political contest.

Power runs through the social relations within the university and its own relations with the wider society. Attempting to deny this political setting and that CBR has a political dimension is itself a political stance. From a bird's-eye view of CBR in Western Europe and North America, we can discern distinct radical, reformist, and instrumental underpinnings to the way universities and academics articulate their engagement with communities. Community-based research can take on very different complexions—from an instrumental to an emancipatory modality—and we cannot really hide behind an apolitical mask but simply be up-front about the type of political perspective we bring to our work.

Taking Stock

Community-based research brings to the fore some essential debates around "what is knowledge?" and necessitates some basic epistemological clarifications. It prioritizes local knowledge over universal knowledge and it values experiential over abstract knowledge. A parallel epistemological stance can be seen in feminist standpoint theory, which argues that the dominant Western model of what counts as knowledge is partial at best, not least through its gender bias. As Sandra Harding (1990) puts it, "the experiences arising from the activities assigned to women understood through feminist theory, provide a starting point for developing potentially more complete and less distorted knowledge claims" (p. 95). From a standpoint perspective, we might value differently the understanding of the world held by poor peasants, the urban poor, or the marginalized more generally in creating a science at the service of society.

If we were to represent in diagrammatical form the basic force fields within which CBR is situated, it would look something like this:

Knowledge paradigms	
Instrumental	Transformative
Positivism	Participation
Knowledge transfer	Knowledge transformation
Clinical/commercial use	Community use
Science	Society

So, in this admittedly polarized model, we see an overall distinction between instrumental and transformative approaches toward community-based knowledge. The first is underpinned by a positivist epistemology that sees facts as independent from the act of observation, versus a notion based on coparticipation in the production of theory and facts. The first approach adopts a "knowledge transfer" approach to university-community relationship, and its model of "translational research" is based on the clinical or commercial utility of research. In contrast, those who stress the participatory element in CBR see the university-community relationship as one characterized by "knowledge transformation," and their model of "translational research" is focused on social or community utility. Finally, as overarching determinants at each pole, we can place "science" and "society" as opposite attractors and basic foundations for both epistemology and legitimacy.

The knowledge paradigm grid outlined here should not be seen as a "bad" versus "good" set of attributes. Rather, it could be deployed to allow us to see how CBR might pull more toward an instrumental relationship with the community or a more transformative relationship. In an era where all universities are promoting the need for translational research, we can see how CBR might be deployed in a clinical setting or be driven by the "translation" of science into direct social or community applications.

Now, even if we might wish to advocate a transformative rather than instrumental view of CBR, we need to be reflexive and critical around the notion of "participation," which is certainly no panacea or guarantee of CBR appropriateness. To "participate" does not mean much in and of itself, if we do not consider who sets the terms of reference of that engagement with the subjects of research and who presents the results. It is, on the whole, the powerful who decide who is to "participate" and on what basis. Participation is not some unmediated process whereby the poor and powerless impact directly on research and its use. Nor is there really much in common between participation as spiritual duty (Chambers, 1983) and participation as articulated by the World Bank's *Participation Sourcebook*, where it is defined against its earlier "external expert stance" as now the bank wishing to place itself "inside the local social system.... [with] a willingness to work *collaboratively* with the other key stakeholders" (World Bank, 1996, p. 3). CBR is as much part of power/knowledge relations as any other modality of research or university/society/market relationship.

We also need to be reflexive and seek to deconstruct the notion of "community" contained within the community-based research (CBR) school or approach. In sociology, there is a long-standing myth around the notion of "community" constructed as a cozy, consensual milieu in contrast with the anomic characteristic of modern, industrial, bureaucratic societies. As Frances Cleaver (2001) puts it, "The 'community' in participatory approaches to development is often seen as a 'natural' social entity characterized by solidaristic relations. It is assumed that these can be represented and channeled in simple organizational forms" (p. 44). Power differentials within a given community—however this is defined—remain un-problematized as do the fluctuating processes of inclusion in and exclusion from "community" based often on gender, age, ethnicity, communalist, or political divisions. This does not mean we should do away with the term community, but it does imply we cannot use it uncritically as seems to be the case with many advocates of CBR.

In practice, knowledge generation is more "messy" than any simple either/or outcome or model. The changing knowledge paradigms produced by globalization and informationalization require us to understand the social contextualization of science. The latter is often set in terms of social or economic need, but this is quite weakly contextualized through various layers with some token social "consultation" mechanism. An example of strong contextualization would be the 1990s research into muscular dystrophy in France driven by a group of individual scientists and sufferers. It was the knowledge of the latter that framed the research question in a novel way. As Gibbons (2006) recounts, "patients, it seems, were unwilling to wait until muscular dystrophy came to the top of somebody else's research agenda" (p. 36). In practice, bottom-up and top-down research agendas often interact with one another, and the outcomes of CBR can be beneficial to communities and the powerful to varying degrees.

It might be useful to conceive of CBR (and its variants) as a type of "floating signifier," whereby the meaning of a concept is not fixed but can assume different connotations in different contexts and for distinct social groups. Democracy, liberty, and freedom can be seen as a "signifier" with a vague, contested, or even nonexistent "signified." Human rights might seem a totally clear and unambiguous concept from a Western perspective, but when deconstructed it is neither an "innocent" nor a univocal concept. Extending this approach, we could view CBR as a floating signifier that is filled with content and meaning in very different ways. Thus, in a development context, both the World Bank and a local community-based organization (CBO) may both deploy the term and method but with different intent. Likewise, in a Northern context, CBR may be used by government to research recalcitrant minority populations or by local community groups working with universities to create knowledge for empowerment.

For many observers, the Western university is "in ruins" (Readings, 1996) due to the rise of corporatism and what some analysts have called "academic capitalism." Be that as it may, from a CBR perspective, we can certainly advocate a university that is much more prepared to challenge and subvert the existing model(s). It does seem clear, over and beyond all the current rhetoric of universities of enterprise/excellence/learning/globalism/etc., that a crisis of mission is omnipresent. The so-called third mission of service (alongside those of teaching and research) is an oblique recognition that society and community are, or should be, part of the reinvention of the university. In a very specific way and relating to this supposed third mission, one analyst declared that

> For colleagues who, like me, work in applied or practice-based disciplines, being a good researcher might mean placing the requirement to make a practical and substantive difference to the "real" world beyond the confines of the academy above the requirements to satisfy the finance-driven metrics of research grants and publication impact factors.
>
> (Rolfe, 2013, p. 63)

That mood is now clearly growing in many different countries and disciplines.

Moving On

"There is a wind of change sweeping our research communities, there is a pervasive energy for something that is described variously as knowledge mobilization, knowledge exchange, knowledge translation, and knowledge transfer or knowledge application," state Hall and Bérubé (2010, p. 248). Research is seen to create knowledge, and that knowledge can be applied to address the "grand challenges" of humanity. For that to happen, knowledge needs to be "translated" or engaged in with society in mutually beneficial ways. There has thus been a revival of a form of "community research" (CR) that is not necessarily addressed to the empowerment of communities, need not be participatory, and may not even be community based. At a minimalist level, it is about "how to involve communities in the production of knowledge" (Goodin and Phillimore, 2012, p. 3), in health research for example or as a means to reach "hard-to-reach" social groups.

Recognizing that there is such a thing as community-based knowledge, the CR approach seeks to incorporate that knowledge into mainstream science. There is always some "local knowledge" that government departments or university research institutions cannot capture on their own. The professional researcher does not possess the "lived experience" of the marginalized and oppressed for whom social policies may be designed, for example. Academics working in health research, housing issues, educational access, or community development can access community knowledge—which combines local and experiential knowledge—only through intermediaries in these communities. This creates a "thin" researcher-researched relationship in contrast to the coproduction of knowledge between academic and community activists as advocated by the proponents of community-based participatory research (CBPR).

Another constraint on the current moves to foster community-based research is posed by the intense competition between higher education institutions for ever scarcer resources. This means that civic engagement—and thus community-based research—tends to be viewed pragmatically and not as a matter of principle for higher education and research institutions. In this context, it is not surprising to find that David Watson and colleagues (2011), in an extensive international survey of civic engagement activities, found that "community relations and public support are more of a positive by-product than a priority goal" of this activity (p. 209). There are many pragmatic reasons why higher education institutions might engage in civic engagement activities, such as enhancing the employability of its graduates. Thus, some may wish to encourage community-based learning and research on the basis of providing students with the opportunity for experiential learning. Others may simply wish to enhance their social responsibility credentials.

Having posed the constraints and limitations on community-based research in the current climate, I would like to explore the opportunities. To do so, I would like to open with a reprise of Michael Gibbons et al.'s well-known model of a transition to a Mode 2 knowledge production regime. Whereas in the Mode 1 regime, knowledge was pure, disciplinary, expert led, and university based, in the Mode 2 regime, knowledge is always applied, problem centered, heterogeneous, and embedded in diverse networks (Gibbons et al., 1994). This transition, roughly equivalent with the phase of marketization that led to "academic capitalism," opens up both a market-driven engagement with the corporate sector but also, we could argue, a turn to non-expert-led engagement with social or community research problems. Transitional periods pose options, and there is no strong reason why any one particular option will prevail.

What I would suggest is that for the "Mode 2 university," civic engagement and community-based research are an imperative and not an optional extra. It seems to me wrong to suggest, as Chris Duke (2010) does, that "It is not easy for a prestigious university to give more than token support [to civic engagement] while driving up intake scores, research outputs and financial investment reserves" (p. 45). This would mean accepting that civic engagement is the sole prerogative of the "soft left old liberal" scholar, as Duke puts it. If we accept, rather, that the old modernist nation-state-based Mode 1 knowledge regime is over, then we might pose with Michael Gibbons that society is now speaking back to and transforming science. Today, it is acknowledged that there is the need for "socially robust" knowledge and, also, that in a Mode 2 society, universities will need to broaden the base of their operations and thus that engagement should become a core value if they are to be successful (Gibbons, 2006).

It is important to also recognize the important current role of CBR in development research or research for development as it is put by progressive practitioners (see Laws, 2003). This is research serving the needs of pro-poor development in the global South. It faces the fact that research knowledge and skills are concentrated in the North and that highly paid academics and consultants are most often "parachuted in" as it were. These specialists "make brief visits to poverty-stricken areas and then return to their base, taking their data with them" (Laws, 2003, p. 15). The assumption is that only the expert holds the key to resolving development problems. Reversing this dominant model requires more than just a commitment to participatory methods to include a local and grounded development of CBR principles and practice. That objective will necessitate long-term commitment and partnerships between Northern and Southern higher education institutions, nongovernmental organizations, and far-sighted funders.

If we turn to best practices in the North, apart from the many examples in this book, we can mention by way of illustration how a group of social work academics in Germany, Finland, and Russia tried to "move from a tradition of research on the problem of social exclusion, to a model of research with excluded communities, in a way which promoted sustainable inclusion" (Bell et al., 2012, p. 89). Just by posing the research equation in this way, they moved beyond the positivist paradigm of objective facts not tainted by values or opinion, and also the "social problem" tradition, which foregrounds the policy priority, in this case "social exclusion." The project principles recognize the importance of situated or local knowledge and, instead of preaching detachment, work on the basis of respectful engagement. Empowering through dialogue, such as this variant of CBR practices, may well also be attractive to funders as the model may enhance the effectiveness and efficiency of service delivery, even if it also acts to transform the preexisting assumptions, models, and tacit ideologies of researchers in some cases.

Looking Forward

Looking forward as practitioners of CBR, we might ask whether our enterprise is essentially about what the critical realist philosopher Ray Bhaskar (2011) refers to as "reclaiming reality." We have argued above that, whereas a positivist approach to knowledge believes that facts are independent of social theory, standpoint and other epistemologies contest that view. For Bhaskar's (2011) critical realism, "positivism is a theory of the nature, limits and unity of knowledge. But it is not a theory of its *possibility*" (p. 64). It is an approach that ignores the social production of knowledge and what the Mode 2 knowledge theorists refer to as socially robust knowledge. Community-based research, in engaging with society and communities, goes beyond this pre-critical paradigm. The promises of participation and empowerment might sometimes be overstated, but CBR does at least acknowledge the *possibility* of "another knowledge."

A further underlying question for all those interested in community-based learning and research might be "what are universities for?," as posed by Stefan Collini (2012) most recently. The fact that this question is even being asked at all would signal that we are facing a crisis of perspectives at the moment in higher education everywhere. The global, market-oriented university is searching for a new niche to replace the once-secure nation-state-based role committed to secure European Enlightenment values. There are many self-proclaimed clichés around about the "excellent university" and the "world-class university" but also the somewhat desperate bid to accommodate the market forces by declaring for an "entrepreneurial university." Ronald Barnett (2013) bids us join instead the "imaginative university" committed to communicative openness, institutional self-criticality, trust, and a "societal transactionality" in which a university engages on mutual terms with its wider society (pp. 152–153).

We could argue that it is not the "spirit of enterprise" that is in short supply in the contemporary university but, rather, the spirit of imagination. In Ireland, at the very height of the Troubles, a group of Northern poets and playwrights came together in the Fifth Province initiative, which posited a fifth province of the imagination alongside Ireland's four geographical provinces. This fifth province metaphor alluded to a space that was neither physical nor political and had a language of its own. It posed a community of the imagination over and above the existing political, cultural, and religious divides. Its genealogy could be traced to the fifth province of Irish legend imagined at the Hill of Tara as a second center of gravity to the administrative authority (McCarthy, 2010). The Fifth Province was inclusive, and there were no experts, but only co-travelers seeking knowledge through a dialogic process not unlike CBR at its best.

Against all those who are pessimistic about the future of the university in an era of commodification of knowledge and marketization of courses, Gerard Delanty (2001) argues positively that "Universities are in a particularly strong position to exploit the advantages of new technologies and to make technology serve the requirements of citizenship" (pp. 127–128). To retreat behind a mythical notion of university autonomy is no longer an option, or at least not one that is likely to succeed. An engagement with market forces is inescapable, but so also, we might argue, is one with society, its needs and aspirations. So, for example, in relation to information technology and biotechnology, universities are engaging with the corporate sector. But, these technologies could be brought under social sway—the knowledge contained within them democratized or socialized—and this might quite clearly have a major impact on the quality of citizenship in the years to come.

The role of community-based research in reimagining the new globalized information-rich university could be considerable. It poses a clear link between university research and society, thus balancing the market-oriented knowledge with the transfer of the "university of enterprise." There is a great diversity of CBR activity across the higher education system as the national case studies in this book testify. There is also a wide range of motivations behind CBR initiatives from a grudging, instrumental approach to a joyous transformative engagement with its potential to change the university for the better. There is, arguably though, a shared commitment to a democratic (as against elitist) university, to greater access and widening participation, and to the democratization of knowledge committed to social advancement.

Finally, I would like to advance two propositions that might underpin a successful CBR movement: another knowledge is possible and another university is possible. Over the last few decades, there has been a recognition that Western development models and the Enlightenment paradigm are both dated and provincial (see Chakrabarty, 2007). A paradigm shift is underway with new forms of knowledge or recovered indigenous forms of knowledge coming to the fore, not least in Latin America (see Escobar, 1995). It has been referred to as an "epistemic decolonization," as local, gendered, and indigenous knowledges are recovered, reinvigorated, and revalorized. We see coming to the fore much more relational (and less individualistic and scientistic) modes of knowing, doing, and being. We could argue that the newfound interest in community-based research with all its variants and contradictions is part of this new wave of thinking.

Afterword

Stanley Fish—ex-Dean of the College of Liberal Arts and Sciences at the University of Illinois at Chicago—has proclaimed that "we are in the education business not the democracy business. Democracy, we must remember, is a political and not an educational project" (Fish, 2008). Leaving aside that this is, of course, a "political" statement, can we really say that the university, its staff, and students are not part of society, do not belong to communities, and do not have rights and obligations as citizens to promote democracy? When Fish proclaims in his book, entitled *Save the World on Your Own Time,* is this a message we wish to impart to our students? Is this what we might say to academics who engage with their local communities to address their concerns and deploy the knowledge of their disciplines to social need? The underlying epistemological divide between the public academic and the private citizen deployed by Fish to underpin his defense of the status quo is simply not defensible. Within the university we do, indeed, find very different political positions as we have seen in the pages above. But we do, I think, share a commitment to the democratization of knowledge. We do not live in a medieval era in which sages hold the monopoly of knowledge. Community-based research is but one of the ways we can take forward a shared mission to democratize knowledge whatever our position may be on the political spectrum.

There is, though, no need for us to be defensive, and this book provides ample evidence of the vitality of CBR despite all its limitations and contradictions. We are moving into a world where boundaries are breaking down, between nations, between North and South, between science and society, and between academic disciplines. Maybe this is not a post-national, post-conflict, postmodern world, but many barriers characteristic of the mid-twentieth century have broken down. This context provides a huge opportunity for all those who, for many different reasons, might want to go beyond traditional academy-community divides. Community-based research in all its different facets—and accepting its status as a floating and not fixed signifier—offers huge opportunities for experimental work designed to enhance community capacity and make the university fit for purpose in the twenty-first century.

CHAPTER 3

The Problematic of Participation: Back to the Future

Vanessa Liston

Introduction

The past two decades have seen a rapid growth in community-based research (CBR) as a response to the need for new types of knowledge in the face of complex health issues and socio-ecological crises. At both institutional and civil society levels, there are increasing calls for (1) more democratized, participatory knowledge to inform environmental and social policy (UNEP, 2009; Calheiros et al., 2000); (2) higher education (HE) institutions to become more engaged with the real and urgent social problems (Bawden, 2004); and (3) synergies with the transformations occurring in how people are using technology to create, share, and use knowledge for social change. A core driver behind these calls is the realization that current research methods, particularly those based in the positivist scientific method, are ill suited to addressing complex problems (Lidskog, 2008), are removed from the rapid pace of social change, and restrict understanding where multiple sources and types of knowledge are required for problem-solving (Levin, 1999).

The challenges to how knowledge is produced and the imperatives of social crises suggest a highly relevant and positive role for community-based research. Rooted in constructivism and critical theory, CBR recognizes the contested nature of knowledge, the importance of context-based approaches, and the complexity of social realities. Inquiry is a cooperative enterprise, richly informed by context, experience, and local knowledge in which communities participate at all stages of the research process for social change. It is argued that this approach can help to unlock "previously neglected knowledges and provide more nuanced understandings of complex social phenomena" (Kesby, 2000, p. 243). Furthermore, it can strengthen HEs to serve their larger social mission for social development, as collaborating directly with people has the potential to change power relations in the production of knowledge, opening up new avenues for innovation (Strand et al., 2003).

However, despite the potential advantages of CBR compared to standard research methods for complex problems, it is a highly contested concept. Critics argue that far from realizing any new knowledge or emancipatory function, participatory approaches are only weakly effective. At their worst, they can serve to entrench the status quo; lead to acquiescence that benefits vested interests and powerful groups at the expense of the marginalized; and close down alternative approaches to social change. Others highlight challenges in the design and implementation of participatory inquiry, citing trust, elite capture, and practical demands of research funding as constraints on achieving "strong" participation of communities.

These critiques are fundamental and go to the heart of the participatory epistemology. They suggest that the practical messiness of reality and unequal power relations resulting from participatory practice mitigate the realization of the democratic aspirations and empowerment ideals of community-based research. Does this imply that CBR is a temporary fad, that while morally justifiable, it is not practical as a method for generating knowledge in a way that can make a significant difference to social challenges? Or do these critiques suggest the need for new thinking on how we frame community-based research and the knowledge generated? Can we learn from them and innovate further?

These are the questions of concern in this chapter. To begin, I will set out a working definition of community-based research and then outline its origins in participatory traditions. I will then turn to critiques of participation that have been particularly influential in the participatory development sphere. Drawing on these fundamental critiques, I argue that far from spelling the doom of participation, critiques can be better understood in terms of a mismatch between our expectation of participation and how these play out within complex systems. The chapter then points to differences in how CBR is now being conducted through reflexive methodologies, and those that are based on complex adaptive systems. The chapter concludes with implications for how we understand the definition of community-based research and what this can mean for moving forward.

What Is (and Is Not) Community-Based Research?

Community-based research is defined as the "systematic investigation with the participation of those affected by an issue for purposes of education and action or affecting social change" (Green et al., 1995). Across the literature the definition is similar. Strand et al. (2003, p. 8) state that "community-based research is the systemic creation of knowledge that is done with and for the community for the purpose of addressing a community-identified need." In a strong interpretation, the researcher becomes a facilitator whose responsibility is not to produce knowledge but to help participants to produce knowledge about themselves. Ownership of the research is "shared with participants, who negotiate processes with the academic researcher" (Pain and Francis, 2003, p. 652). Core to the concept is the end goal of social change.

Techniques used to achieve these goals of empowerment and equal partnership in CBR are wide and varied. The most accessible are influenced by Freirean pedagogy (Freire, 1970), which enabled people to "see" and reflect on their realities and learn and act for transformative change. They include, among others, diagramming, ranking techniques, mapping, storytelling, and transect walks. Newer participatory techniques enabled by social communications technology include open source mapping and GPS-enabled sensors, which enable individuals to participate in the capture and sharing of local-level knowledge for policy-making. Strong personal contact and engagement (Sidaway, 2005) are also necessary for successful participation. Yet, while these techniques are necessary for enabling CBR, they are not sufficient.

The defining feature of CBR is the application of these techniques through principle-based participatory methodologies. These principles recognize multiple realities, prioritize the realities of the disadvantaged, promote co-learning, aim for empowerment, and embrace complexity (Mayoux, 2001). Examples of such participation methodologies include participatory action research, cooperative inquiry, and feminist research, among others. As Cornwall and Jewkes (1995) note, the difference with conventional research is the location of power in who defines the research problems, generates the data, performs the analysis, and owns and acts on the data (p. 1668).

Origins and Influences

In its emancipatory and empowerment philosophy, CBR has its origins in the innovations of radical thinkers on the determinants of oppression. The earliest influence is the Northern tradition of action research developed by Kurt Lewin in the 1940s. He was one of the first to promote a reflexive participatory mode of inquiry that involved planning, action, and examining the results of action. He resisted positivist approaches for which knowledge was objective and measurable, arguing that these methods separated knowledge producers from reality (Lewin, 1946).

In the 1970s similar ideas emerged in the South, most celebrated in the work of Paulo Freire (1970). He argued that objective reality did not exist but "includes the ways in which people involved with the facts perceive them... The concrete reality is the connection between the subject and the objective, never objectivity isolated from subjectivity" (Freire, 1982, p. 29). With a belief in the revolutionary possibilities of people, he led a popular education movement through which the oppressed could acquire self-awareness and *praxis* to achieve transformative change. Education for Freire was a form of de-socialization against domination, which has two moments: the struggle for meaning and the struggle over power relations (McKenna, 2013). Accordingly, Freire emphasized the importance of giving meaning to the politics of everyday life while affirming the importance of theory in opening up space for critique, possibility, politics, and practice (Giroux, 2010).

This understanding of knowledge and the radical possibilities of popular learning influenced the work of Robert Chambers (1994; 1997) in development. During the 1970s he began to combine techniques, such as mapping, with a set of human rights-based principles for participation. While a Freirean approach emphasized people educating themselves for social change, participatory methodologies aimed to challenge dominant paradigms in development and planning by empowering local people to assert their realities in a way that included research, framing of problems, and the identification of appropriate responses. Chambers advocated a "bottom-up" approach, which prioritized the "reality" of the poor over the self-constructed "professional reality" of the international expert. The goal was the empowerment of local people as a radical alternative to the dominant, ineffective top-down expert programs of the international community. The methods used were not rigid but constantly evolving based on critical reflexivity of those engaged in the participatory processes. Some of those that evolved from the 1980s included the following:

- participatory appraisal (PA), which describes community research and consultation that involves local people at all stages, from priority setting to implementation. It emphasizes education and collective action;
- participatory rural appraisal (PRA), which is derived from PA and used in development to resist top-down development research and practice;
- participatory learning and action (PLA), which develops from using participatory methods as an extractive process to one which is focused on sustainable learning between equal partners. It also emphasizes program and policy improvement as core parts of the learning process.

(Mayoux, 2001)

Based on the philosophies of education, empowerment, and action, participatory methodologies aim to overturn the standard approaches to research and social development in which participants are excluded in the process of knowledge creation and decision-making. The paradigm was highly influential and led to participatory methodologies becoming mainstreamed through development practice in the 1980s and 1990s. NGOs, donors, and governments demanded participatory methodologies at all stages of project development including problem identification, prioritization, implementation, funding, and monitoring and evaluation. Participation resonated with the democratic aspirations of citizens and with emancipatory ideologies. Therefore, mainstreaming participation through development research and practice could only mean liberation and empowerment of the poor, making *their* "reality count" (Chambers, 1997).

Critiques of Participatory Methodologies

It was a provocative book, *Participation: The New Tyranny?* by Cooke and Kothari (2001), that dramatically focused attention on the potential negative impacts of the participatory discourse. Contrary to established orthodoxy, these authors make a strong case for how participation can be tyrannical. Defined as "the illegitimate and/or unjust use of power" (p. 4), they identify three main types of tyranny: (1) the tyranny of decision-making and control, where participatory methods dominate and de-legitimatize local decision processes; (2) the tyranny of group influence, where participation can serve to strengthen those already in power in the community at the expense of the marginalized (Mosse, 2001; Hilyard et al., 2001); and (3) the tyranny of methods, where the discursive dominance closes out other approaches that might have advantages over participation.

For each type, the range of perspectives presented in Cooke and Kothari's book strikingly varied. Yet, in all cases, the fundamental questions relate to power and complexity. Authors are unequivocal that rather than being a tool for emancipation and empowerment, participation, as it has become codified into technique, becomes a form of co-optation to the goals and interests of the powerful. Hilyard et al. (2001) claim that participation can be used to justify exploitation, induce consent, and reinforce the status quo rather than produce radical change. Paradoxically, the focus on local knowledge to solve local problems (tyranny of methods) can distract from the more radical need to challenge macro-level processes and power structures, which are the strongest determinants of the poor's well-being (Cleaver, 2001).

A related line of argument draws out the implications of what is regarded as a naïve concept of community. Contrary to the use of the term, "communities" are not homogeneous and static (Minkler, 2005). They are complex, multi-scale, and characterized by shifting patterns of relationships and conflict. According to Guijt and Shah (1998), the prolific use of a simplified notion of community has significant implications for the objectives of participation. Idealized notions of "community" conceal power relations, lead to elite capture, and mask the diversity of needs based on, for example, different age groups, genders, and religions, leading to biases and opportunities for the more powerful. Similarly, participation can serve to hide the messy realities that define communities, and only those that are frontstage are taken to represent the reality of that community (Kothari, 2001).

A more nuanced critique is provided by Cooke (2004), who discusses the social-psychological dynamics of face-to-face engagement. He argues that group influences and process can have a distorting effect on decision-making. These distortions include the "risky shift," where people are more willing in a collective, than as individuals, to take risky decisions. Distorted decisions can also be the outcome of incorrectly second-guessing what others want (Albeine paradox), as well as strong normative pressures and coercive persuasion. The implications are that participatory decision processes may not be legitimate because of the processes used and the power dynamics at play.

In summary, the critical literature strongly suggests that participation is ineffective for empowerment and sustainability. The critiques are not just theoretical; they are supported by findings in strands of the critical empirical literature. Mansuri and Rao (2004) of the World Bank acknowledge that participatory programs have failed to deliver on expected social change. Even local knowledge, which was gathered through highly participatory events, was found by Mosse (2001) to be a "construct of the planning context and concealed the underlying politics of knowledge production and use" (Mansuri and Rao, 2004, p. 39).

These critiques have significant implications for the goal of community-based research, where authors are also keenly aware of similar difficulties, risks, and challenges. Lidskog (2008) warns of the co-optation possibilities of participation in his discussion of the democratization of science. Berkes (2004) notes that it is often difficult to find a cohesive social group to work with in the field: the notion of community being elusive and constantly changing. Pain and Francis (2003) find that practical barriers to participation limited what they could do in their study of homeless youth. Wallerstein and Duran (2006) identify the issue of co-optation of communities and caution against pursuing community-*placed* rather than community-*based* research. Minkler (2005) asks:

> What is community participation? Who is participating? Who is not participating? What interests are being served or not served? If community members

are participating, in which aspects are they participating and in which decisions is there little participation?

However, instead of drawing a pessimistic conclusion that participatory methods should be abandoned as suggested by Cooke and Kothari (2001), they strike a positive and optimistic tone. Reaffirming the moral and epistemic needs of empowerment and local knowledge, the authors suggest that difficulties with participation can be addressed through a dialogical and reflexive approach to research, open communication, and a flexible research design. These echo Chambers, whose work has consistently emphasized the need for participatory approaches to be guided by reflexivity and learning (1997; 2010). This argument, however, does not go unchallenged. Cooke (2004) potently claims that this response is endogenous to the participatory discourse and therefore cannot result in the fundamental problems, enacted through participation, being overcome.

A Spanner in the Works

Given what is quite a fundamental critique of participation as it is practiced, and being left with no alternatives by the authors of *the New Tyranny?*, what are the implications for community-based research? Is it possible to proceed in a way that builds and finds strength in these critiques? Can we innovate and move participation forward in a way that builds conceptual resilience? To address these questions, we need first to try to clarify how participation has been conceptualized by these authors. Without reducing and oversimplifying the incisive and sophisticated critiques, we can tentatively conclude that while participation started out as a radical concept for emancipation and empowerment, its codification into technique and subsequent mainstreaming by development organizations resulted in a number of unexpected negative effects. While the language of participation identified the complexity and situatedness of people's realities, its codification into practice reflected the interventionist paradigms of the time, which were situated in linear and rationalist project interventions. The focus was on "mechanistic" (Kay and Schneider, 1994) and managerial processes in which outcomes would be measurable and predictable. In this way, "Radical ideas [were] co-opted, reduced to technique and applied for non-emancipatory ends" (Cooke, 2004, p. 46).

The question posed in this chapter is about the extent to which these critiques are relevant to community-based research. A review of some strands of the CBR literature suggests that there are lessons to be learned. Where there is a tendency to replicate the "linear" or "managerial" approach to participation,

CBR can be regarded as susceptible to the same criticisms of participation as raised by the critics of participatory development. To illustrate, a common research approach is to begin with a collaboratively defined project question or one that is accepted by the community as important. The research findings describe the methods (collaborative) to address the issue, progress of the research (reflexive, reciprocal learning), and findings that relate to whether the goal was reached or not (see, for example, van Olphen et al., 2003; Israel et al., 2010). Authors advise that researchers should identify "the points of policy impact before the research begins" and careful attention must be given to the potential side effects of participation (Kelly et al., 1988, pp. 8–9 quoted in Minkler, 2004). Pain and Francis (2003) advise careful planning for the start, appreciation of the context, scale of intervention, and actors in order to *predict* the best routes to effect change. As Resnicow and Page (2008) note, implicit in this approach is the assumption that the change process is largely under conscious control. For the purposes of this argument, I call this a *flexible linear* approach, because the research project is understood as having a visible end point, toward which activities are oriented, with latitude for change, reflexivity, and community direction in between.

Methodologically, there have been a number of advances that aim to support this research approach. Wallerstein et al. (2010), in "What predicts outcomes in CBPR?," propose a linear conceptual model of CBR. System and capacity changes listed are those that are observable and related to the topic of the research. Sandoval et al. (2012) present a logic model of the state of CBR research, an evaluation framework for partnership effectiveness, and collective reflection with the aim of defining what constitutes successful CBR. They note that there are few measures to estimate the impact of CBR on a range of indicators and in response have developed a matrix of those used in the literature. The similarities with the mainstreamed participatory paradigm are notable. As such, there is an opportunity to look further, to find paradigms of ways of thinking that can shift participation in a direction that makes it more robust to these fundamental critiques.

We do not need to look far. Despite the transmutation of the concept of participation to linear/*flexible linear* practice frameworks, elements of alternative ways of thinking about participation remained embedded in the discourse—notions that rationalist methodologies, positivist science, and expert-driven solutions could not address community/social issues because they were complex and unpredictable. The problem is that, paradoxically, participation in practice was expected to provide predictable and replicable outcomes—better health, better sanitation, and improved well-being.

With hindsight, and in the face of wicked and complex problems, the full implications of participation in knowledge production and adaptation are emerging. Rather than being seen as a pragmatic tool for achieving desired ends of particular social change goals, defined collaboratively at the outset of a project, participation is being approached as indeterminate. This notion, while it seems self-evident, is important for the way social change is understood in the very definition of community-based research.

Through the Looking Glass

To sketch this approach, we return to the initial premise that is driving increased interest in CBR, the widespread acknowledgment that communities, ecological systems, and urban health issues are complex adaptive systems. While there is no agreed definition yet on the concept, they are generally characterized by nonlinear effects, uncertainty, and unanticipated outcomes. Their properties are linked and interdependent, they are highly context specific, and they do not have predictable generalizable responses to stimuli across different times and circumstances (Keshavarz et al., 2010). These properties lead to the emergence of patterns at different scales (Roux, 2011).

Responding to the challenges in "standard" research methods for studying these systems, there is increasing interest in using complex systems thinking across the study of health care (Miller et al., 2010), public health interventions (Keshavarz et al., 2010; Resnicow and Page, 2008), education (Davis and Sumara, 2005), and ecological public health (Morris, 2010). It is also the foundation of innovation systems theory that is being applied in agricultural research (Klerkx et al., 2012). In contrast to the standard (though flexible) knowledge production methods, complex systems thinking focuses on understanding the system under research at various scales, becoming more exploratory and responsive by constantly raising new questions. Unexpected events become an opportunity for learning and shifting research trajectory. Schut et al. (2013) develop a typology for what they call *dynamic research configurations*. Advocating complex systems thinking, Resnicow and Page (2008) argue that public health practitioners and researchers incorporate nonlinear concepts into the design and analysis of their interventions. They advocate adjusting expectations for prediction and quantification of the change process.

New methodologies for studying complexity systems have emerged that are directly relevant to the objectives of community-based research. The diamond schematic and an adaptive methodology for ecosystem sustainability and health integrate complex systems theories into sustainable development projects (Waltner-Toews and Kay, 2005). Other developments include assessing the characteristics of a community in which a research engagement is planned. For example, Kurtz and Snowden (2003) categorize systems into simple, complicated, complex, and chaos systems. Keshavarz et al. (2010), in their study of health programs in schools, set out by analyzing the extent to which the "community" under study was a complex system. Building on the work of Babbie (2006), they analyze the school communities under study according to whether they demonstrated the properties of emergence, nested systems, distributed control, constant adaption, and unpredictability. They argued that understanding these features provided richer information for deciding on approaches to implementing healthy schools policies. Similar approaches include starting with conceptual mental models of the system (Sterman, 2000), and formal models and simulations of social systems. Stringer et al. (2006) "unpack" what participation can mean for the adaptive management of social-ecological systems.

As CBR is a nascent field, CBR scholars, uniquely positioned to innovate in research on and with complex systems, are expanding the literature in this space. The results and implications of the findings are exciting. Cundill et al. (2005) assess conceptual models in two community-level assessments as part of the Millennium Ecosystem Assessment. Their study highlights the multiple pathways in complex systems research, the challenge of comparability of findings, the importance of scale, and approaches to reconciling different epistemologies. McCarthy et al. (2012) focus on building adaptive capacity among local communities through collaborative geoinformatics. They affirm other authors' findings that instead of change being pursued as an objective, building the adaptive capacity of communities can lead them to better anticipate change and be ready to innovate.

> By embracing the complexity of linked social and ecological systems and acknowledging the key role of uncertainty and disturbance within a system, communities can better anticipate change, prepare for a crisis and be ready to innovate. By nurturing diversity and fostering the integration of a diversity of knowledge systems, communities will be prepared, and have the tools, to develop innovative responses to change.
>
> (p. 309)

The conclusion of these authors is that where complexity is an insurmountable challenge to research, it is in its essence "trial and error" that leads to innovation, evolution, and learning. Authors across disciplines are developing approaches *a priori* that support a systemic understanding of the "community" of research at different scales; theoretically reasoning why particular research or intervention could have a positive impact; and evaluating the probability of that happening and the various levers of change. However, while these are current views, they also take the researcher as a starting point. Alternative views could see complex systems research being initiated and driven by the community with the input of researchers. Science shops, discussed later in this book, could give a valuable platform for exploring these possibilities further.

An exhaustive account of complex adaptive systems for community-based research is beyond the scope of this chapter, but as a paradigm it provides a new way forward for our understanding of participation as it relates to community-based research. While current literature focuses on the benefits of complex adaptive systems thinking to addressing complex problems, I will focus here on what it means for understanding *participation*. I suggest there are at least three ways that systems thinking can help move CBR beyond the fundamental critiques of participation, which help researchers and communities work "with the grain": first, instead of communities being idealized, simplified to stakeholder groups, and prone to elite capture, communities and their dynamics are conceptualized at multiple levels and scales. This *expands* and *alters* the concept of community, avoids normative and idealized claims, and requires reflexivity on its own impact.

Second, a systems view also opens new possibilities for how social change is achieved. Instead of expecting a particular predefined output, systems thinking leads to change approaches that support innovation and adaptive capacity. A direct and linear link between research objectives is not expected; rather, we see *indirect, counterintuitive* (Hall and Clark, 2010), and *emergent* effects. Participation is seen not in instrumental terms for achieving a definitive end, which is prone to failure due to random changes and indeterminacy in the system, but as an activity from which change can emerge. This is particularly relevant in the context of complex issues. As Wallerstein and Duran (2006) argue, current research methods are "rarely the structural framework for change," and they suggest that a complex systems approach to inquiry and action may lead to stronger effects. In the field of public policy, Uyarra and Flanagan (2013) suggest that acknowledging complexity and system dynamics and being less ambitious might lead to more useful regional innovation policy analysis.

Finally, power dynamics remains an issue. However, at the macro level, a systems approach at least helps avoid the charge that participatory methods reinforce the status quo. As participation is indeterminate, there is no fixed end goal to which participation is orientated. Participation becomes *revealing* of how the system operates and its levers, options, and capacity for adapting and innovating. Taking participation as indeterminate can liberate it from some of the fundamental critiques raised against the linear participation methods. Therefore, it can support greater freedom in knowledge and learning and provide a more flexible approach to realizing the Freirean ideals of learning and emancipation.

Conclusion

There is growing consensus across a broad range of disciplines on the need for new approaches to inquire into complex systems, an understanding that is well established in the principles and reasoning of community-based research. The challenge remains in realizing new methods of questioning and inquiry that "go with the grain" of the system of interest and work *with* its self-organizing processes (Kay and Schneider, 1994). Looking back to participatory development, it may be argued that participation did not "go with the grain." It was codified in ways that suited the systems and realities of donors and bureaucracies but not those of the communities of interest.

Looking to the future, we should therefore be encouraged by the despair expressed so pointedly by the authors of *The New Tyranny*? We can be optimistic that far from spelling the death knell for participation, the values and epistemology have never been stronger or more relevant. If opportunities are born from crises, so too do the lessons learned from these critiques point us to a clearer realization that the potential of participation for social change depends on us, in some sense, letting participation and social change speak for themselves. The perspective is touched upon in Chambers' more recent writings (2010), wherein he refers to communities as complex systems and for participation to be understood as "adaptive participatory pluralism."

This is where opportunity lies. Complexity thinking, growing across a wide range of disciplines, has participation and co-learning at its core. By looking back to the origins of participation and learning lessons from how the concept was applied in practice, we can get new insights into what it can mean for the future. The need for confidence and innovation in this area has never been greater. Complex and wicked social challenges demand collective will, intelligence, and creativity to steer a course to sustainability. It therefore seems plausible that CBR in its moral and epistemic orientation, at the coalface of the challenges that are driving new research methods, could underpin new roles and significance for higher education. However, this potential demands continued creativity and systematic reflexivity—not only in methods—but in the shifting kaleidoscopes of reality and what they say about the fundamental meaning of research, participation, and social change.

CHAPTER 4

Community-Based Research, Health, and Social Interventions

Jennifer Mullett

Introduction

Health systems and social services are becoming increasingly more complex and more beleaguered, with greater numbers of clients and fewer resources. In the health sector, managers and clinicians are being asked to demonstrate greater efficacy and greater efficiency, to "do more with less." Meanwhile, in the social services sector, more services are being delegated to community agencies through direct service contracts. Historically, nonprofits were funded through a combination of fund-raising, grants, and government contracts. Over the past 20 years, however, there has been a fundamental shift.

In the 1980s, a trend developed in public policy across the industrial world toward a new public management and the implementation of a "managerialist" ethic in the public services, as an attempt to improve efficiency through new methods of accountability. Competitive contracting was introduced and may have increased the purchasing power of government: however, competitive contract funding arrangements had negative effects on the community nonprofit agencies and the ability of health authorities to fund innovative programs.

Competition may be healthy in the private sector but in the nonprofit sector it undermines the *raison d'être* of most community agencies, which is to provide support to community members through an integrated and cooperative approach. In some cases community agencies were empowered with a clear mandate, but the managerial shift, with a greater emphasis on accountability and demonstrated effectiveness, has led to increased bureaucratization and professionalization, which diverts scarce organizational resources from core service provision (Common and Flynn, 1992; Reading, 1994) and undermines the capacity for flexible and innovative approaches to serving clients (Wistow et al., 1994). But rather than lament the emphasis on managerial and financial sophistication, community-based researchers could use the opportunity to demonstrate to government funders and policy-makers new forms of knowledge that accommodate community development initiatives, health promotion, and innovative prevention practices. Through relevant and empowering research, higher education has the opportunity to support voluntary agencies in their role as agents of human and social change and promote innovative science. This chapter offers two examples of the ways in which community-based research (CBR) can play a role in enhancing community practices and engaging funders in a new dialogue, one of development rather than efficiency. At the same time, the examples will illustrate the constraints, implicit and explicit, exacted by the funding structures on the capacity of nonprofits and community practitioners to facilitate significant change. Roles of the researcher working with community groups are likewise reshaped to be that of facilitator, ambassador, mentor, craftsperson, narrator, and friend striving to build capacity through knowledge sharing.

Health Promotion and Community Development

Since the Ottawa charter (1986), there has been an increased interest in the social determinants of health, a concept that emphasizes environmental conditions including social, economic, and cultural factors as significant in achieving health. Health promotion and multidisciplinary collaborations have emerged as key strategies to address the social determinants of health at the community level. Campbell (2004) outlines three main approaches to health promotion: information provision, self-empowerment, and community development. A self-empowerment approach aims to enhance motivation to change behavior by providing information along with new skills. Community development approaches, rather than focus on individual behaviors, seek to create community contexts that support and enable change (Campbell, 2004).

It is this latter approach to health promotion that is closest to a CBR approach. Community-based research is a set of methodological principles that aim to build capacities within the community by involving community members in guiding the research process (Reason, 1988; 1994; Heron and Reason, 1997), helping to select the research methods, analyze data, and implement information to enact system change and effect policy. These principles are paralleled in community development, community psychology, participatory action research, the healthy communities' movement, and health promotion and public health. Across these fields, the shared principles include a democratic participatory process that is driven by community priorities rather than by outside expertise, a focus on the strengths of the community rather than on the deficits, and a flexibility of approach.

Theory, Community Work, and Funding Structures

If the role of the researcher is to explain, elucidate, and illustrate, which theories might accommodate or be congruent with the work of community development, capacity building, and education for the purpose of coming to share in the social consciousness (Dewey, 1916), the development of consciousness and the "self" was articulated in the sociocultural theories of Lev Vygotsky, George Herbert Mead, and Paulo Freire as the internalization of social interactions, dialogue, and social relations. The fields of community development and health promotion, concerned as they are with "the learning and living of adults in natural settings," might be regarded as the pragmatic strategies that enhance the processes of development and education, they being the focus of these theorists.

However, as noted earlier, many community developers and health promoters are publicly funded, and their "existence is dependent on accountability through evaluation" (Harris, 1992, p. 64). Harris suggested that the dominant evaluation tradition is an applied version of that used in mainstream research, one concerned with measurement and statistical tools. New paradigms for evaluation have evolved since Harris' criticism such as empowerment evaluation (Fetterman, 1994) and developmental evaluation (Patton, 2011), and also various participatory evaluation frameworks have been developed by international health agencies. But these remain overshadowed by the prevalence of a demand for "evidence-based practice," a research of effectiveness, subjugated by financial constraint and risk reduction. However, evolution in the practice of evaluation toward more participatory approaches has stirred debate. Two opponents have supported competing paradigms. Fetterman (1994) has argued that empowering, participatory, utilization-focused evaluations are more worthwhile, more moral in their quest to contribute to self-determination, while Stufflebeam (1994) has argued against that approach, claiming it is insufficiently scientific, and destructive to the credibility of the field of evaluation. While practitioners can be unaware or unconcerned with the high-level debate, they can often find themselves unwittingly wrestling with these issues in their practice as they try to balance the competing demands of their two masters: the funders and the clients. While practitioners are concerned with maintaining their own personal values and integrity in the service of their clients, they also worry about the sustainability of their program without "scientific evidence" (i.e., empirical or quantitative) of effectiveness for future funders. This dilemma highlights a significant role for community-based researchers—namely to bridge the gap between professional research protocols and the value placed by communities on experiential knowledge. The challenge for the community-based researcher is to find research methods that can balance the goals of human flourishing inherent in health promotion and community development with the restrictions of traditional funding requirements. In their attempts to fulfill evaluation criteria, nonprofits often inadvertently render their clients into objects of investigation rather than participants, or practitioners struggle to explain how their developmental processes do not fit the deterministic version of rationality presupposed by evidence-based decision-making (Webb, 2001). In the following sections, three cases will be described where community-based research was used to provide evidence that is more congruent with the developmental, reflexive, indeterminate practices of community workers. At the same time the examples will illustrate the relevance of the sociocultural theories of Mead, Vygotsky, and Freire, given the constraints described above.

Case One: Creating Language-Rich Environments

The first case is a community development project designed to enhance early childhood learning. In the community of Nanaimo, British Columbia, there was a waiting list of up to one year for access to clinical intervention from speech pathologists at the CBI Health Centre. At the same time, a study by Hertzman (2004) identified children in Nanaimo as being more vulnerable and less ready for school than children in other communities.

Based on this evidence, the Vancouver Island Health Authority supported two speech pathologists in Nanaimo to expand their normal clinical services to include teaching, mentoring, modeling, and information provision. Community development activities focused on enhancing the capacity of other community members, for example, teachers, librarians, childcare workers, etc., who regularly interacted with children, to support speech development and create "language-rich environments." The speech pathologists taught, mentored, modeled, and consulted with colleagues in health units, day care centers, school district programs, drop-in centers, and preschools. They used the media, health fairs, and all means of accessing the public and service providers to raise awareness even using billboards on the roadsides to get the message out to "sing, talk and read."

As is often the case when a new approach is tried, the speech pathologists were not without their detractors. Some practitioners and policy-makers felt that waiting lists at the Health Centre would increase while the speech pathologists were operating in the community. There was also a view that the teaching and modeling could be done by someone other than a clinician—childcare workers, for example. I was asked to use a participatory approach to determine the effectiveness of the activities in promoting community capacity for intervention and prevention. The research was aimed at identifying the activities and agencies that were involved in developing comprehensive supportive environments and with what impact on practice. Research methods included a documentary analysis of ten months of diaries, observations of capacity building, and interviews with practitioners and parents. From an analysis and synthesis of the three types of qualitative data, a conceptual framework was created to illustrate the multilevel intervention.

The collaborative team of speech pathologists and researchers began by reviewing the documentation accumulated to date: research that indicated the need for the intervention, goals and objectives, and detailed logs (daily diaries) of the speech pathologists. As documents to guide the initial implementation activities, these were adequate but they were not sufficient to explain the context and the long-term value of these activities to policy-makers concerned with waiting lists. The task then for the research partnership was to create a framework that captured the essence of their work, with a rationale for activities and a coherent concept of their community empowerment approach. While the speech pathologists continued with their logs, I began observing their work in various settings, analyzing their logs, and engaging with community agencies.

Meetings were held regularly, every two weeks, to review the data and to develop three models that represented their work. The diary accounts evolved from a simple listing of events to a coherent presentation of the goals of the initiative linked with the emerging changes in attitudes and practices in the community. A model was developed by the team of researchers and speech pathologists to illustrate how the program expanded beyond treatment services at the Health Center to include preventative initiatives in the community. Changes in thinking and behavior with regard to the development of language skills were documented throughout the community; for example, practitioners said that they now knew more ways of talking with children and had more ideas to stimulate language acquisition and development.

The results of all the activities of the speech pathologists were an increased awareness of the importance of language development and an increased ability to facilitate the development of language by all sectors. This means that the services are now better able to support parents in providing an understanding of, and an ability to enhance, language development. An inherent value of CBR is knowledge democracy. Through the sharing and demonstrating of knowledge by the speech pathologists, the parents and community practitioners developed a level of expert knowledge to be able to engage in health promotion work themselves. This led to a reduction in labels of pathology and reliance on experts for minor problems. A diagram of the community agencies that incorporated the techniques for stimulating dialogue is shown in Figure 4.1.

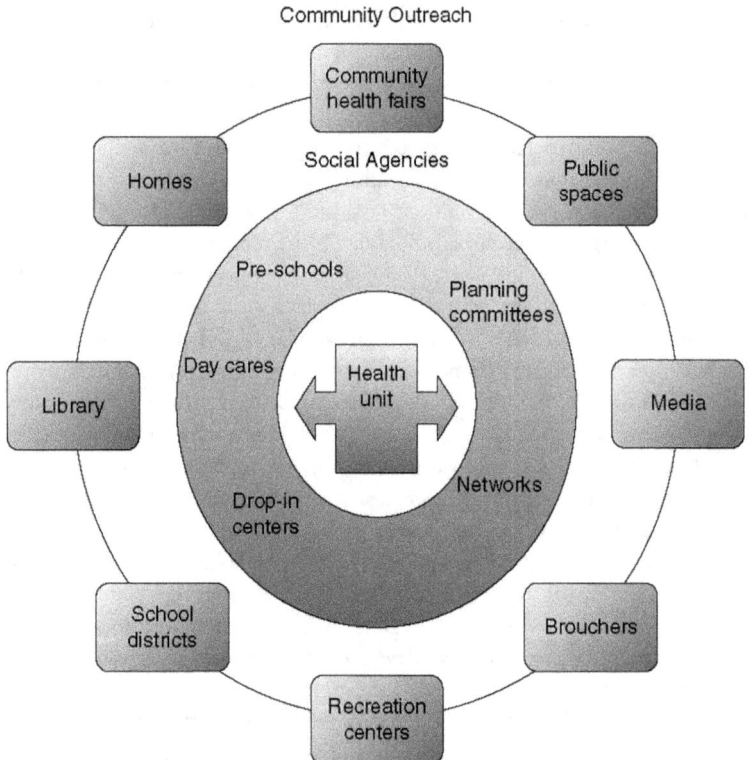

Figure 4.1   Community wide intervention to create language rich environments

Reflections

The research provided the space and opportunity for the speech pathologists to regularly reflect on their community practice and, through discussion, realize the full impact of their work. Interviews with parents and community members and practitioners afforded them encouragement while reflection, analysis, and dialogue stages engendered a visual representation of community work that advanced the knowledge of the practitioners and the researchers. This type of CBR, with its focus on reflection in practice where cycles of data gathering inform implementation of community development work, provides the opportunity for the development of theory and illustrates how theory informs practice. In this case, CBR provided the opportunity for all of the partners to build their skills in community work. The speech pathologists, their managers, and colleagues learned how to build a conceptual framework for their work, while the researchers learned how to implement an ecological approach to child development. The research process provided the opportunity for parents and community members to define success in a community-wide intervention, and it resulted in the creation of a model for others to follow. Rather than focus on clinic waiting lists, the managers changed policy to devote resources to community development activities.

The results of the research were applauded by the speech pathologists' supporters and criticized by their detractors as not addressing the fundamental issue of waiting lists. The most wounding criticism claimed that the speech pathologists were doing work in the community that could be done by others while children in great need went without clinical help. The greatest difficulty lay in the fundamental difference between the goals of the speech pathologists and those of the funders and the government departments. The government funds are aimed at identifying deficits or lack of development and providing clinical services to address those deficits. The speech pathologists' goals were future oriented. To paraphrase Leont'ev (cited in Wertsch, 1985), they were not as concerned with assessing where a child is now but striving to discover how a child can become what he or she not yet is. Their approach aligns with Vygotsky's (1934) theory that higher mental functions are developed through the internalization of social processes. Speech has a social function, an external inter-psychological process that becomes transformed as it is internalized to become intra-psychological processes. Through this inner dialogue, thinking develops. Hertzman, a prominent researcher in the area of readiness for school, proposed five domains of development and concluded that a child's competent use of language mediates four of the five domains (Hertzman, 2004). The speech pathologists are thus not just encouraging speech; they are engaged in helping the child to develop the higher mental functions necessary to succeed in school and later in society.

Outcomes

Parents were able to "drop in" to places like community centers, the mall, and other nonclinical venues to chat with the speech pathologists about their concerns. Relationship building was an important skill that the coordinators and the speech pathologists had honed. The ability to develop trust and build rapport was essential. Many vulnerable clients had been through other programs and were wary at the beginning or felt that there was something wrong with their child's development. The skills of the coordinators illuminate areas of new competencies required for community engagement by the universities: relationship building, facilitation, and collaboration. Researchers can learn much from the strategies used by community development workers to enhance their skills in building relationships. Designed to support projects that would play a preventative and a supportive role, the funding enabled many of the participants to achieve personal empowerment, which, Laverack and Wallerstein (2001) wrote, is evidenced when "participants gain power as a result of a change in control over decisions in the inter-personal relationships that influence their lives" (p. 182). It is clear from the community projects and the speech pathologists' interventions that the participants learned skills, the confidence to identify problems, find solutions, and implementations—the essence of gaining power (Laverack and Wallerstein, 2001).

Community-based research is a process through which these subtle and overt changes can be demonstrated. At the same time CBR reveals the complexity of the community work with vulnerable people that has to be balanced with reporting to funders. An alternative to the linear model of evaluation is introduced to community workers and funders with CBR, and engagement with CBR builds capacity for reflection and problem-solving. Community-based research offers teams of researchers and community workers the option to fulfill accountability requirements in a participatory and critical way without turning clients into "subjects." It also provides the opportunity to highlight the potential for government agencies to invest funds in prevention work that complements or relieves government services. Community practitioners, by engaging in partnership with researchers, build their capacity for future research endeavors while benefiting from the evidence that articulates, explains, and justifies their health promotion and community development activities. Partnerships with higher education generate the opportunity to introduce what Heron and Reason (1997) called "propositional knowledge," theoretical or known, to be combined with practical, experiential, and representational forms of knowledge.

Case Two: Developing Community-Based Evaluation Plans

In British Columbia, the Ministry of Children and Families invested $2 million in community intervention projects aimed at reducing the number of families and children requiring support or care from the government. This provided an unusual opportunity for community workers and members to submit proposals for community interventions. I assisted the successful candidates (hereafter called coordinators) to develop community-based evaluation research plans that reflected the intent and values of a collaborative process designed by a steering committee of community members and academics. Part of the criteria for funding included a prescription to, "if appropriate, involve in the development, implementation and evaluation of the project, those affected by the initiative." In effect they were being asked to do community-based research. For the most part coordinators embraced this form of evaluation enthusiastically as it was aligned with their values. I became the broker of a bidirectional knowledge development process, reporting regularly to the Steering Committee and contacting the coordinators monthly throughout the two years of the project. The practitioners developed skills for CBR, and the Steering Committee learned of new ethical and practical dilemmas of CBR. The evaluations of the community projects were to demonstrate progress on goals and outcomes, and key lessons learned in the development and delivery of the interventions.

From the community projects, this case and case three which follows best illustrate the problems coordinators encountered while implementing community-based evaluation research with vulnerable people. These were around issues of power, stigma, fear, and literacy. Coordinators were trying to remain true to the principles of participation and empowerment and protection of clients' vulnerability while assessing or documenting clients' progress in the project.

In this case a project was designed by a community agency to teach parenting skills and safety to mothers whose children were, or had been, in government care. The mothers were all mandated to attend sessions, and, for some, this was the only time they saw their children, under supervision of the coordinators. Half of the funding came directly from government, and these funds required a questionnaire to be completed by the mothers to indicate their progress toward becoming a better parent with a greater ability to keep their children safe. The coordinators running the program were unhappy with the questionnaire as it did not represent their goals but did not know how else to report progress. They approached the mothers from a Freirian perspective, as in they created opportunities for the mothers to reflect on their powerlessness and to engage in dialogue about their role as mothers. Their goal was not to make them "good mothers" but to enable them to overcome their circumstances (e.g., domineering boyfriends, unsafe environments, and/or negative family dynamics) to become empowered individuals with the consciousness to reflect on and change their living situations in order to keep their children safer. In this way, as Freire (1970) suggested, they would develop the power to see how they exist in the world in which they find themselves and to see that world "not as a static reality but as a reality in process, in transformation" (p. 64). Education was gentle dialogue embedded in activities. Interactions were observed, for example, over lunch, and used to engage the parents in discussions about options for dealing with their child's behavior. However, this was not explicitly seen by the parents as teaching or learning. Standard evaluation questions such as "What was the most important thing that you learned in this program?" would get the response "I didn't learn anything; I just had lunch with my child at the program and talked." The community-based evaluation was designed so that (a) it would act as a further intervention for learning and (b) it would help the mothers appreciate and reflect on what they had gained in the project. It also took account of the low literacy level of some of them.

The solution to this dilemma was a group format that allowed the synergy of the group to create a collective memory of knowledge. Government questionnaires created fear, and the group approach dispelled the fear of being tested and gave the mothers a chance to demonstrate their knowledge of safe child rearing and circumvented the literacy issue. Staff who had developed a relationship with the mothers asked the questions, each of which was written on a separate flip chart sheet. After each question was asked, discussed, and documented, it was taped to the wall in the group room. Participants were urged to add any thoughts to the posted questions at any time during the rest of the session and during breaks. This allowed for processing and discussion time. Mothers could also engage with interactive colored posters detailing "hot zones," which were unsafe environments for their children (e.g., drug-involved boyfriends in the home), and "cold zones," which were safe environments. Group discussion of examples provided the opportunity for critical reflection on relationships that negatively affected their children.

According to Freire (1970), these types of problem-posing educative strategies recognize the individual as in a state of becoming, and the process affirms women and men as beings who transcend themselves, who move forward and look ahead, for whom immobility represents a fatal threat, and for whom looking at the past must only be a means of understanding more clearly what and who they are so that they can more wisely build the future.

(p. 65)

In this case, the problem posing allowed the women to focus on the future rather than the shame and guilt of the past.

Case Three: Youth and Ecological Restoration (YER) Project

In a third example, an intervention that sought to reconnect troubled young people with their community was designed by a community member who had been trained in ecological protection and restoration. Her belief in the interconnectedness of all living organisms led to the development of a program that introduced troubled youth to the outdoors and the satisfaction of contributing to the sustainability of the local ecology. The Youth and Ecological Restoration (YER) Project linked restorative justice and ecological restoration, both introducing healing relationships—one with the human world and the other with the natural world. Restorative justice involves transforming and strengthening relationships between individuals, families, and communities, while ecological restoration requires taking responsibility for restoring the land. The project used the need for ecological restoration work in the watersheds of the community to provide an opportunity for young people (under 19 years of age) to feel meaningfully involved in the community. They signed a contract committing to 20 hours of restoration work and to giving a slide show presentation to a community group at the end.

The goals of the YER were to build future employment skills in ecological restoration and scientific research; enhance skills in cooperative working, conflict resolution, leadership, and social development; support cross-cultural experiences and sense of belonging in community; motivate youth to take responsibility for the environment and develop future land stewardship ethics; raise community awareness and positive perspectives of youth and their issues; provide youth with inspiring and positive role models through association with community volunteers; and develop problem-solving, communication, analytical, and strategic thinking skills. Upon completion of the program, the young people received a certificate, a badge, a letter of reference, and several photos of themselves engaged in work.

This project far surpassed the expectations of the funding committee, which was initially apprehensive because the coordinator was simply an individual with an innovative idea. She was not part of a larger program, and, while they liked the innovation, they were taking a risk in allocating funds to a completely new approach. The committee was enabled to recognize the success of the project because of the participatory research that the coordinator provided to them. The young people were interviewed at various stages of the project to indicate changes in attitude and progress in capacity-building; photographs of intergenerational team work documented the process; and daily journals by both the coordinator and the youth provided a dialogue of reflections. Empowerment, a major value in CBR, was achieved in this project by providing the opportunity for participants to give to others and to make a contribution to their community, providing feelings of connectedness, self-worth, and achievement. One youth said:

> When you give your energy to help your community, it makes you feel good inside and warms your heart.
>
> (Kotilla, 2012)

Furthermore, it helped them to find a place in their community and the world:

> Everything is connected, everything I've learned in this program has taught me that we are all connected and every choice we make impacts everyone and everything around us.
>
> (Kotilla, 2012)

The coordinator and I, the researcher, had many conversations at each stage of the project, and while the dialogue was ostensibly to build coordinator research capacity, the process actually reflected Freire's ideas on the development of critical consciousness through dialogue. The coordinator posed a problem, and through dialogue and discussion the author and the coordinator gained knowledge of all of the issues.

Reflections

In these later two cases, we see how CBR can contribute to the work of increasing empowerment at the personal, relational, and community level. In the second case, participants were socially marginalized through poverty, lack of education, and unemployment or were discriminated against for various reasons. Nelson and Prilleltensky (2005) suggest that social marginalization is "a major human problem, undermining the essence of humanity" (p. 300). They argue that being engaged in human life requires the ability to enter into and critically negotiate social relations. For the examples here, it is key to consider Mead's (1956) view that the self develops through social relations and patterns of social interaction. Empowerment at the community or societal level would entail a more deliberate incorporation of the liberatory practices of Freire (1970). However, within the limits of their mandate, the community workers in partnership with CBR researchers helped participants in their projects to achieve a more positive view of themselves and to be more engaged in their community.

Laverack and Wallerstein (2001) point out that participatory approaches do not have the agenda of empowerment to emancipate and affect political change. However, in this chapter, the examples indicate the value of those approaches in contributing to the social movement of knowledge democracy (see Hall and Tandon's description of this movement in Chapter 5) and helping the next generation to become fully engaged citizens. As one youth said: "This program helped me to be a citizen, helped me to work with the community" (Kotilla, 2012).

Conclusion

For community practitioners and for the academy and institutions of higher education, CBR provides interesting real-world problems for critical reflection and exposes unique ethical issues. Community-based research is a platform and a process for bidirectional knowledge sharing. New perspectives that can be gained by the community include the value of critical reflection, the development of reflective practice, the dialectic of developing theory from action and action from theory, the iterative processes of action research such as planning, implementation, and reflection, and a research process that helps to ensure the outcomes are achieved rather than research that examines the binary question of whether or not they were met. The process of CBR offers a way of systematizing work in the community, and helps to solve community issues while creating collective knowledge about and for change. When important activities that contribute to the development of the community are not documented or not articulated, the effects of these activities are often regarded as "unexpected outcomes" or "side effects" when in fact they are a direct result of the community process.

Furthermore, the participatory nature of community-based research necessitates several stages of reflection and dialogue. Watkins (2003), reflecting on the developmental theories of Mead, Vygotsky, and Freire, suggested that we commit to the nurturing of dialogical capabilities as the current hierarchies of our society do not invite deep dialogue and result in silenced voices.

She wrote that the nurturing of dialogue turns us toward "the processes of non-violent communication and reconciliation" that are needed to nurture our communities. Although glimpsed only briefly in the examples here, these developmental theories help us to reflect on the significance of the community work. While the funders see empirical evidence as an indication that a program is producing outcomes, the community coordinators, immersed as they are in the social interactions of community, are focused on something deeper and more sustained, the restoration of the personhood of the marginalized.

CHAPTER 5

Majority-World Foundations of Community-Based Research

Rajesh Tandon and Budd Hall

Introduction

This chapter explores the majority-world foundations of community-based research with a particular focus on the rise of participatory research (PR) in social movement and civil society settings in the global South and its subsequent spread to the North, eventually finding its way into universities. The authors were involved in both the creation of the discourse and the spread of the initial ideas through the International Participatory Research Network. In the 1970s, Rajesh Tandon came to his initial thinking about participatory research while working with tribal peoples in Rajasthan, India. Budd Hall was working at the Institute for Adult Education in Tanzania during those days. The chapter challenges the Eurocentric bias of much contemporary scholarship in the field of community-based research (CBR). It closes with three challenges to contemporary scholars.

Ancient Roots

We quite comfortably accept that some majority-world scholar-activists of the twentieth and twenty-first centuries have made contributions to the mainstream literature of, what we call today, community-based research. But we also generally accept the Eurocentric fallacy that knowledge-based institutions such as universities and sophisticated knowledge systems are the product of mostly white male intellectuals, with scholars from the United States adding their bits and pieces a bit later in the game. The point of departure for the thinking of these authors is the historical corrective that posits that the first universities and the first systematization of socially relevant knowledge systems were created in what we can call the majority world. The majority world is that part of the world where most of our people live. It covers Asia, Africa, the Arabic-speaking world, Latin America, the Caribbean, and the Indigenous Peoples of the planet. It is the home of our oldest intellectual traditions, but it also contains the largest number of people living in poverty. Africa is the place where human life is generally said to have originated. The indigenous African knowledge that gave us the ability to survive and indeed eventually flourish as human beings, we would argue, can still be drawn upon (Wangoola, 2002; Odora-Hoppers, 2002). The world's first known university was not founded as we often see in Bologna, Italy, but 1,400 years earlier in Taxila. The university in Taxila was founded in the former India, now Pakistan, in 700 BC. At its peak, it had nearly 8,000 students in residence and 1,800 scholars engaged in research and teaching. The leitmotif of this university was "service to humanity." We posit here that Taxila is the earliest known source of community-based research.

The Abbasid period of Islamic history (750–1258 AD) is sometimes referred to as the "golden" era of Islam. During this period, Islamic scholarship and dedication to education was leading the world. Islamic scholars established centers of elite scholarship, where the very foundations of contemporary mathematics, astronomy, physics, and geography were created. One of these early universities, Al-Azhar University (969 AD) located in Cairo, is still active. But the Abbasid Caliphate also supported the first expansion of mass education, with schools created wherever there was a mosque. In contrast, the push for the common school in Europe did not come until the late nineteenth century. The Abbasid period also has a claim to being among the foundational sources for CBR, as there was much focus on applied research resulting in new agricultural systems, water transportation methods, and other tools.

Moving forward centuries, we approach contemporary times where in the 1930s, as part of the need to create a set of political cadres who would work for the independence of India, Mahatma Gandhi urged the New Delhi-based Islamic intellectuals to create the Jamia Millia Islamia, a large and profoundly community-based research-oriented university. Jamia Millia Islamia is the site of the launch in December 2012 of the UNESCO (United Nations Educational, Scientific and Cultural Organization) Chair in Community-Based Research. Gandhi also urged his supporters to create the Gujarat Vidyapith with a focus on mother tongue scholarship and politically effective community-based research. A third university that Gandhi named as one of the three decolonized universities in India of the 1930s was, in fact, already in existence. It was the Shantiniketan, a university in West Bengal founded by the Nobel Prize-winning poet and intellectual, Rabindranath Tagore. If we had the space, we could document both institutions and knowledge systems in China, the indigenous empires of the Inca, the Mayans, and the Aztecs, and many other parts of the majority world that substantiate our claim that the questions about knowledge and social change were originated in the majority world. It is troubling that attention to these diverse roots has remained invisible in our late-twentieth-century and early-twenty-first-century discourses. Perhaps this will change as economic and political power on a global basis shifts with time. But let us turn now to the more contemporary majority-world foundations of community-based participatory research as seen through the eyes of these two authors.

"Poor People Don't Use Money for a Weapon"

This is something that late President of Tanzania Julius K. Nyerere said often in support of his vision of a participatory nation based on African concepts of family hood (*ujamaa*). He said that instead of money, ordinary people used knowledge and leadership. In saying this, he underscored the belief that people living subsistence lives in rural areas or in cities created knowledge that could be used to transform their lives and the lives of all in their communities. Tanzania was the place where the words "participatory research" were first expressed in the early 1970s. They arose in a context of dialogue and debate among a circle of researchers working in civil society, the government, and the University of Dar es Salaam, who wanted to see their research linked to the aspirations and engagement of a nation that was said to be in transition to socialism, an African form of socialism.

The most profound early influences were the ideas, strategies, and programs of the Tanzanian government of the day, articulated most effectively by late President Julius K. Nyerere. Nyerere, himself a former teacher, had written much about the capacity of education in an independent nation to unchain people just as it had been used by the colonial powers to enchain a people. The philosophy of *ujamaa* and self-reliance, concepts of what we would call today Afrocentric development and local economic development, were open challenges to the way that the rich countries saw the world. Tanzania and Tanzanians were in so many ways telling the world that the "emperor has no clothes." Nyerere and a generation of articulate and gifted leaders such as Paul Mhaiki, who went on to become the Director of Adult Education at UNESCO in Paris, challenged all who were working in Tanzania, nationals and expatriates alike, to look through a different lens to understand education, agriculture, development, history, culture, and, eventually for some of us, even research and evaluation methods. We were all encouraged to "meet the masses more," and while on a day-to-day basis this was difficult to understand, over time many of us were profoundly transformed.

In September of 1971 there was a visit by Paulo Freire, the Brazilian intellectual, to Tanzania. Budd Hall was responsible for organizing that visit and for working with him during his stay. One of the things that Freire was asked to talk about were his ideas about research methods. Most readers will remember chapter three in *Pedagogy of the Oppressed*, wherein Paulo writes about what he called thematic investigation. In his account he began to talk about understanding research as engaged practice, not a neutral dispassionate act but an act of solidarity and active support. This talk was edited and published in 1971 as *A Talk by Paulo Freire*. Some passages from that 1971 talk are as follows:

> First of all I must underline the point that the central question that I think that we have to discuss here is not the methodological one. In my point of view . . . it is necessary to perceive in a very clear way the ideological background that determines the very methodology. It is impossible for me to think about neutral education, neutral methodology, neutral science or even neutral God.
>
> I think that adult education in Tanzania should have, as one of its main tasks, to invite people to believe in themselves. It should invite people to believe that they have knowledge. The people must be challenged to discover their historical existence through the critical analysis of their cultural production: their art and their music. One of the characteristics of colonization is that, in order for the colonizers to oppress the people easily, they convinced themselves that the colonized have a mere biological life and never an historical existence.
>
> (Freire, 1971, pp. 1–5)

The work of Marja-Liisa Swantz was another early influence. Swantz was a Finnish-born social scientist attached to the geography department of the University of Dar es Salaam. She and a group of students from the University of Dar es Salaam including Kemal Mustapha, who was later to become the African coordinator for the participatory research network, were working in an engaged way with women and others in the coastal region of Tanzania. Through this practice she and the others began to articulate what she called participant research. In an early paper published in 1974, she notes:

> Research strategies, which developing countries such as Tanzania have followed, have generally been patterned in the Universities of developed countries. In planning research on a subject related to development one has to first answer some questions: Who are the beneficiaries of this research? What are the aims? Who is going to be involved? What approach and methods of research should

Majority-World Foundations of Community-Based Research 57

be used so that the research would bring the greatest possible gains for development? Research and researcher can become agents of development and change in the process while the research is being done ...

(Swantz, 1975, p. 47)

In 1975, Budd Hall spent a year as a visiting fellow at the Institute of Development Studies at the University of Sussex. It was at that time that he began to find that people in many other countries were thinking along similar lines as those in Tanzania—Francisco Vio Grossi in Chile, Rajesh Tandon in India, and even researchers in England and Europe. The connection between research, politics, and action had been opened up, never to be closed again. It was during that period at Sussex that Hall edited a special issue of the journal *Convergence* (1975), on the theme of "participatory research." This was the first time that the term was used because it seemed to be the best common description of the various approaches that were described within the issue.

The first inkling that something like an international network might be possible or welcome came with the response to the publication of the special issue of *Convergence*. The adult education community and related community development activists bought out all the copies of the journal for the first time in the history of the journal. Requests for copies poured in from all over the world, and the small item in the lead article inviting persons who were interested in exchanging information about their activities went from a trickle, to a stream, to a river. It was clear that many people in the majority world and people working with, or for, marginalized persons in rich countries were actively engaged in research projects that were very different from the standards of the day, often contradicting the dominant research paradigms of the university world of the day.

The next source of energy towards a network in this field came via the First World Assembly of the International Council for Adult Education, which took place in Dar es Salaam, Tanzania in 1976. As Hall was serving as Conference Secretary, he arranged for one of the sessions of the conference to deal with a questioning of the then orthodox research methodologies. Helen Callaway of Oxford University and Kathleen Rockhill of the United States both presented papers putting forward more qualitative and more ethnographic approaches to adult education. In the debates and committees which arose from the Dar es Salaam conference, a recommendation was made to the world adult education community that, "adult educators should be given the opportunity to learn about and share their experiences in participatory research" (Hall and Kidd, 1978). Important for the next steps in the eventual development of the International Participatory Research Network was the fact that Ted Jackson, an activist adult educator from Canada, was a participant at the Dar es Salaam conference as part of a study-travel course organized by the Ontario Institute for Studies in Education (OISE) in Canada.

By then Budd Hall was living in Toronto and working full time as the Research Officer for the International Council for Adult Education (ICAE). Roby Kidd, the Secretary-General of the ICAE, had agreed that in return for organizing the Dar es Salaam World Assembly, he would support the development of, what was initially called, the Participatory Research (PR) Project. The PR Project was begun by Hall, Edward Jackson, and the late dian marino, the latter two PhD students at the University of Toronto. The first decision taken was that they were not going to support or create an international network without being engaged in the practices themselves. They took very seriously the critique that researchers in the rich countries created careers through projects in the majority world without ever taking the responsibility to analyze and take action in their own countries first. They noted that the first goal was to become engaged in a variety of participatory research projects or struggles in their own community and their own part of the world. Links with the global South would be made on the basis of shared values, shared understandings of knowledge and power, and shared political engagement.

The Cartagena Conference of April 1977

Orlando Fals Borda, the Colombian activist-scholar, had made plans to hold a conference on his approach to action research. Hall was invited to present a paper based on the work that had begun in Tanzania and which was now picking up energies from Chile, India, Brazil, and elsewhere. The April meeting in Cartagena was to become a critical piece of the foundation of the participatory research movement. Working as scholar-activists, these Latin American intellectuals had amassed a set of important experiences. Fals Borda through his links with the International Sociological Association had met others elsewhere who shared these visions. So to Cartagena came radical intellectuals from many parts of the world to debate new directions for the late 1970s and the 1980s. Fals Borda's profound vision of a science of the common people was at times sharply criticized by colleagues, who felt that a more orthodox Marxist understanding of the role of an intellectual vanguard was the way to work. For those of us from the rich minority world, what we saw was a sophisticated, committed group of activist scholars or militant intellectuals who totally and efficiently dismissed for once and for all the pretention of detached positivist science. The work of Fals Borda himself, of persons like Paul Oquist (writing on the epistemology of action research), of Ton de Wit and Vera Gianotten of Peru and the Netherlands, of Xavier Albo of Bolivia and so many others gave Hall and, through him, others in their group a huge burst of energy and enthusiasm. Hall met with Fals Borda on a chair in one of the large halls and asked him for his support for a network that would respect the values and energies that had brought so many to Cartagena. Fals Borda was gracious and generous in his support but wanted to make sure that the countries of the majority world would be given the dominant role in driving the network that Hall and his colleagues had proposed to call "participatory research." Orlando had preferred the use of the term action research (AR) up until then, but after some reflection with others in the Latin American group, he shifted his discourse to "participatory (action) research." Sometime later, perhaps through interaction with the Latin American network of participatory research, he began to refer to this kind of work as "participatory action research" (PAR). He was the first person, to my knowledge, to ever use that precise combination of words.

Founding of the International Network

Upon return from Cartagena and a subsequent visit with Francisco Vio Grossi, whom Hall had met while at the University of Sussex in 1974 and who was living in Venezuela, Hall returned to Toronto to start organizing a series of events that would provide a platform for the founding of an international network. The most important of the early meetings took place in Caracas, Venezuela, in 1978 at the Universidad Nacional Experimental Simón Rodríguez where Francisco Vio Grossi was teaching. It was here that Rajesh Tandon, the person who was to found the Asian network and eventually lead the International Participatory Research Network, first met with others from Europe, North America, and Africa. This also marked the beginning of a 35-year period of collaboration between Hall and Tandon.

Among the most important political principles of the network was the insistence that each node or networking group, working in the various parts of the world, would be autonomous and self-directing. They would each be committed to building an international network but the Toronto group would not be in charge. The Toronto PR Group, as it became known, was to be one among equals engaged in a variety of community development, participatory research action, and reflection activities. The early principles of participatory research, many of which can be seen in the formulations of contemporary community-based researches, that were elaborated upon in the late 1970s include the following:

1. PR involves a whole range of powerless groups of people—the exploited, the poor, the oppressed, and the marginalized.

2. It involves the full and active participation of the community in the entire research process.
3. The subject of the research originates in the community itself and the problem is defined, analyzed and solved by the community.
4. The ultimate goal is the radical transformation of social reality and the improvement of the lives of the people themselves. The beneficiaries of the research are the members of the community.
5. The process of participatory research can create a greater awareness in the people of their own resources and mobilize them for self-reliant development.
6. It is a more scientific method of research in that the participation of the community in the research process facilitates a more accurate and authentic analysis of social reality.
7. The researcher is a committed participant and learner in the process of research, i.e. a militant rather than a detached observer.

(Hall, 1984, p. 5)

The participants deliberately chose the concept of a network for their organizational form. This was long before the "network" concept, so ubiquitous today, was in common usage. They wanted a structure that was horizontal in power terms, which allowed for and encouraged autonomous locally or regionally accountable nodes, which took the cues from the grass roots rather than the center, and where power flowed according to the tasks at hand rather than funding, tradition, or imperial world divisions. They were also very much aware that the "international" was a context, which they could use to strengthen their local work and increase visibility for their ideas in the settings where they lived and worked every day.

By 1978 there were five nodes in the network: (North America) Toronto; (Asia) New Delhi—Rajesh Tandon, coordinator; (Africa) Dar es Salaam, Tanzania—Yusuf Kassam, coordinator; (Europe) The Netherlands—Jan de Vries, coordinator; (Latin America) Caracas, Venezuela—Francisco Vio Grossi, coordinator. They organized a series of meetings to increase awareness of ideas, to deepen understanding, to build support for others who were trying such work, and to show people in various locations that these ideas had world resonance and relevance. And in all of the work, they honored the facts that the majority world was the intellectual source for these exciting new ways of working and that it continued to inspire. They also recognized that these ideas were as relevant in Europe and North America as they were anywhere, that people wanted to use research as a contribution to changes in power relations. Their definitions of participatory research were explicit politically, were seen as valid in all parts of the world where unequal power relations persisted, and highlighted the use of cultural approaches to knowledge creation.

Rajesh Tandon and the Founding of the Society for Participatory Research in Asia

Rajesh came to the Venezuela meeting of the International Participatory Research Project in 1978. He had come in contact with Budd Hall when he was trying to finish writing his PhD thesis at Case Western Reserve University, Cleveland, in 1977. He was doing fieldwork in rural Rajasthan, India, trying to understand the dynamics of development in the context of government programs. As he began to understand that dynamics, it also became clear to him that the illiterate tribal communities were not really ignorant; they were knowledgeable about many aspects of their life and living.

> In my encounter, I had read and heard contradictory opinions about the wisdom of a villager. Some had seen a reservoir of untapped wisdom in the village-folk. Others considered them almost stupid. In my encounters with them, I found the villagers very wise in the ways of the world. They were mature in their understanding about life and living; they had time-tested wisdom, which governed their day-to-day behaviour. They were insightful and astute in their judgements. Their views about the social and political order reflected their wisdom.
>
> (Tandon, 1978, p. 7)

The period 1978–1979 was essentially used to sharpen, deepen, and systemize our collective critique of conventional social sciences research and begin to articulate elements of, what was then thought of as, characteristics of participatory research. It saw the formation of various regional networks that became the building blocks of the activity for practicing and supporting participatory research for social transformation. The definition of participatory research even then had an alternative vision of society but it focused on separate elements of investigation, education, and organization. The political economy of research and questioning the basic objectives of research enterprise had only begun to be articulated during that period.

The regional coordinators met in October 1978 in Venezuela and then in the summer of 1979 in Sweden. It is in the second meeting that the idea of an international forum of participatory research was mooted and planned. In April 1980, in Yugoslavia, the forum took place, involving more than 60 participatory researchers from different parts of the world. Spread over a period of a week, with case studies, theoretical papers, and debate, this event marked a major step forward in the articulation of the meaning of participatory research as well as strengthening regional networks. It began to raise the issues of links between participatory research and people's struggles and organization. It asked the question of whose interest does research serve and it debated issues around the production of knowledge and the appropriation of knowledge of the experts by ordinary people. This was also the first event where members of various regional networks came together to meet across regions and establish links and bonds of solidarity. Many of us who attended that forum felt rejuvenated, affirmed, and supported.

As Tandon began to promote the network of participatory research in Asia, it became clear that a larger institutional framework was needed to pursue this methodology for social transformation. In consultation with the then network partners, Participatory Research in Asia (PRIA) was set up as a not-for-profit civil society organization with the motto "Knowledge is power":

> The alternative institutional framework of PRIA was challenged on several accounts. As an effort to make it a part of the wider, voluntary non-government movement in the country and the region, PRIA was seen as a different "animal" because it was not engaged in grassroots work on its own. PR was promoting the idea of knowledge as a basis for social transformation. Learning was an integral component of organizing, and capacity building was a necessary step in bringing about a just and egalitarian order.
> (Tandon, 1998, p. 190)

The initial years at PRIA were spent in practicing and innovating this methodology of participatory research. In partnership with local activists, knowledge from people's perspectives and experiences was generated in a wide range of issues around forests, land, occupational health, women's livelihoods, etc. While practitioners found great resonance in this process of enquiry, academia initially ignored it, and then criticized it:

> One of the clear implications of this was rejection by the academic enterprise within the country and the region. Our pursuits were labelled as unscientific and our phraseology was seen as contradictory. Some academics would call the phraseology of Participatory Research, Popular knowledge and Empowerment as a political ideology, while others would look at it as a community development tool. Our desire to link knowledge with participation of the excluded and the marginalised was challenged as they were seen as independent initiatives. Top down knowledge production could be utilised for bottom-up participatory processes was the message given to us in the early 80's.
> (Tandon, 1998, p. 188)

However, the practice of participatory research expanded through its new "avatar" of participatory rural appraisal (PRA). Robert Chambers was able to promote tools of PRA in a wide variety of development organizations. His seminal contributions included "Whose Knowledge Counts?" (1995) and "Who Counts?"(2007).

The streams of participatory research began to diverge in the 1990s. The practice of PRA, PAR, PR, and AR became somewhat separated from each other. It was in this context that Orlando Fals Borda convened a second Cartagena conference in June 1997 to bring together these diverse streams for a multi-logue. The conversations in Cartagena turned out to be significant in expanding and deepening the discourse on participatory research among practitioners and academics. One of the streams became known as "practice research engagement." An early manual of practice research engagement traces the roots, principles, and practices of four well-known participatory research approaches: participatory research (PR), participatory action research (PAR), action research (AR), and participatory rural appraisal (PRA):

> The inspiration for this manual came from a World Congress on Participatory Action Research held in Cartagena, Columbia, (June 1–5, 1997) where people from over 30 countries gathered to discuss participatory approaches to research, education and social development. The experience for most of those present was an eye-opener. It revealed that although the term "participation" has varied connotations and participatory approaches or methodologies have been developed in response to different contexts and situations, yet the opportunities for convergence—to discuss, to share and learn from each other's experiences—are immense.
>
> (PRIA, 2000, p. 5)

As the field began to develop in different ways, the tension between the world of practice and the world of research seemed to grow. By the turn of the millennium, the gap was ever wider between universities and practitioners. Experience suggests that practice research engagement (PRE) is not always successful. The interests and perspectives of practitioners and researchers diverge as their methods become more sophisticated and specialized. The dominance of positivist research traditions in social sciences has often hampered their engagement with the complexity and uncertainties of many practice traditions. In spite of these tensions, some efforts to bring researchers and practitioners together have led to action research in the service of organizational change, participatory research that has raised awareness of oppressed groups, and participatory rural appraisals that have improved understanding of grassroots realities. But PRE is not easy—too often the parties find themselves mired in misunderstandings, split by conflicting incentives and procedures, and unable to use their differences constructively, even with the best of interests (Brown, 2001, p. 31).

Contemporary Networking

During the mid-1990s and early 2000s, Hall had lost hope that the university world where he had moved after his 20 years with the International Council for Adult Education was going to be a welcoming space for the ideas that he had been so closely linked to since the 1970s. During these years, Hall and Tandon maintained their close friendship, but, given the lack of support from the Canadian university world for CBR, a more productive series of projects was not possible. It was not until the University of Victoria created the Office of Community Based Research in 2006, with Hall as the founding director, that he was to have a base once again for more intensive collaboration. Tandon continued moving his work, and the work of his colleagues, forward through the innovative structures of the PRIA. He was named as the Chair of the External Advisory Committee of the Office of Community Based Research (OCBR) in 2007. The OCBR organized the third Community University Exposition (CUExpo) in 2008 at the University of Victoria in Canada. Tandon and Hall took the opportunity to launch a global network called the Global Alliance on Community-Engaged Research (GACER). A wide range of international networks have emerged around this broad theme in the twenty-first century, and GACER attempts to bring them together on a common platform, bringing the world of practice and the world of research together in a shared network. The convening of "big tent" conversations among the networks by GACER became an instrument for promoting research for social transformation, carried out in partnership with activists, civil society, and community agencies (www.gacer.org).

The creation of the UNESCO Chair in Community Based Research and Social Responsibility in Higher Education in 2012 and the subsequent appointment of Budd Hall and Rajesh Tandon as joint holders of the chair was a landmark in the promotion of community-based and participatory research. The chair demonstrates South-North and civil society-higher education collaboration and co-construction through its very form. In its new perspective, it has begun to find a meaningful place in the world of academia. The promotion of social responsibility in higher education is now being linked to the discourse on knowledge democracy.

Reflections

In some ways, we feel that we have made substantial progress in gaining academic credibility for community-based participatory research. When

Budd Hall gave a talk at Stanford University in 1975 on the subject, a room full of social scientists, who claimed that research is a neutral exercise, universally condemned him. Hall's claim that even our very methods of research were ideological was labeled naïve and wrong-headed, and that it risked throwing out the research baby with the bathwater. Now in 2014, while the climate in the university world vis-à-vis community-based research varies widely, the Haas Center at Stanford University, the place that tore a strip off the young participatory research advocate 35 years earlier, has over 20 scholars engaged in what they refer to proudly as participatory research, research engaged in social change. In Canada at the University of Victoria and scores of other universities in North America and Europe, there are offices, centers, and university-wide administrative structures to facilitate community-university research partnerships (Hall et al., 2013). Funding for "partnership research" can now be obtained from many of the government granting councils in Europe and North America. There is still a struggle for recognition of this work in terms of career advancement, but the foot is more than just in the door; it has reached a little bit into the room.

But have we perhaps also lost something? In the 1980s and 1990s when the International Participatory Research Network was at its peak, the leadership of the global South was evident in the field. But in spite of fairly active publishing agendas of persons such as Tandon and Hall, and scores of Latin Americans such as Fals Borda, Brandao, and Vio Grossi constantly raising the visibility of the origins of participatory research in the global South, if you were to ask most North American or European scholars, they are not aware of the origins of CBR as described here. Ernest Boyer, the American foundation president, who wrote in the 1990s, is most often seen as a patron saint of our field!

Additionally, the fact that the doors of academia have opened to the discourses of participatory research and related areas does not mean that the communities and the movements where the roots lie have been allowed to enter. We have not seen broad recognition of the knowledge-creating roles of civil society or the community or social movements or traditional indigenous intellectuals or persons labeled disabled. Has the university once more done what it has done so well over the years? Has it taken on the critical discourse, but stripped out the action component? Our community groups in Africa, Latin America, Asia and the Arabic world, and within most of Europe and North America have seen sharp declines of funding overall and, with some encouraging exceptions, they have seen no funding to build their own autonomous research and knowledge creation capacities. We have a struggle on our hands in the universities to make sure that academics who practice community-based research are able to advance in their careers. But we have virtually no struggle to create positions for community-based scholars to enjoy the stability of university funding for their work.

Knowledge Democracy

The development of the discourse of knowledge democracy has been emerging in recent years to help us to understand the relationship of knowledge to a more equitable world. This discourse is important for, at least, two reasons. First, we have found the use of the concepts of knowledge economy and knowledge society to be wanting from the perspective of justice, and, second, we have seen a more general loss of confidence in the capacity of Western white male Eurocentric science to respond to the profound challenges of our times. As Tony Judt writes in the first sentence of his book *Ill Fares the Land*, "Something is profoundly wrong with the way we live today" (2010, p. 1).

As Cristina Escrigas, the Executive Director of the Global University Network for Innovation, has said, it is time to "review and reconsider the interchange of values between university and society; that is to say, we need to rethink the social relevance of universities." She goes on to say that humanity "Is now facing a time of major challenges, not to say, serious and profound problems regarding coexistence and relations with the natural environment. Unresolved problems include social injustice, poverty and disparity of wealth, fraud and lack of democracy, armed conflicts, exhaustion of natural resources and more" (Escrigas et al., 2014, p. xxviii).

Knowledge democracy refers to an interrelationship of phenomena. First, it acknowledges the importance of the existence of multiple epistemologies or ways of knowing such as organic, spiritual, and land-based systems, frameworks arising from our social movements, and the knowledge of the marginalized or excluded everywhere, or what is sometimes referred to as subaltern knowledge. Second, it affirms that knowledge is both created and represented in multiple forms including text, image, numbers, story, music, drama, poetry, ceremony, meditation, and more. Third, and fundamental to our thinking about knowledge democracy, is understanding that knowledge is a powerful tool for taking action to deepen democracy and to struggle for a fairer and healthier world. Knowledge democracy is about intentionally linking values of democracy and action to the process of using knowledge.

Ecologies of Knowledge and Cognitive Justice

Boaventura de Sousa Santos, a Portuguese sociologist and legal scholar, has a narrative that begins with his observation that in the realm of knowledge we have created an intellectual abyss that hinders human progress.

Abyssal thinking, he notes, "consists in granting to modern science the monopoly of the universal distinction between true and false to the detriment of... alternative bodies of knowledge" (2007, p. 47).

The global dividing line that he is referring to is the one that separates the visible constituents of knowledge and power from those that are invisible. Popular, lay, plebeian, peasant, indigenous, the knowledge of the disabled themselves, and more cannot be fitted in any of the ways of knowing on "this side of the line." They exist on the other side of the "abyss," the other side of the line. And because of this invisibility they are beyond truth or falsehood. The "other side of the line" is the realm of beliefs, opinions, or intuitive or subjective understandings, which at best may become "objects or raw material for scientific inquiry." De Sousa Santos makes the strong link between values and aspiration: "Global social injustice is therefore intimately linked to global cognitive injustice. The struggle for global social justice will, therefore, be a struggle for cognitive justice as well" (2007, p. 52).

He sees a way forward in the concept of "ecologies of knowledge." Post-abyssal thinking is linked to the notion of subaltern cosmopolitanism, or what he also refers to as an "epistemology of the South," ecology of knowledges centered in the knowledges from the "other side of the line" and based on the idea that the diversity of the world is inexhaustible. If the diversity of the world is inexhaustible, then we need a form of epistemological diversity, which allows this diversity to be acknowledged. The contribution of knowledge, he suggests, is to be measured through knowledge as intervention in reality rather than knowledge as representation of reality. "The credibility of cognitive construction is measured by the type of intervention in the world that it affords or prevents" (2007, p. 57). The achievement of post-abyssal thinking will depend according to de Sousa Santos on the achievement of a radical copresence of all knowledges with an understanding of the incompleteness of knowledge.

Shiv Visvanathan, an Indian intellectual linked to environmental movements of India, contributes to this discourse with the concept of "cognitive justice." He notes that

> The idea of cognitive justice sensitizes us not only to forms of knowledge but to the diverse communities of problem solving. What one offers then is a democratic imagination with a non-market, non-competitive view of the world, where conversation, reciprocity, translation create knowledge not as an expert, almost zero-sum view of the world but as a collaboration of memories, legacies, heritages, a manifold heuristics of problem solving, where a citizen takes both power and knowledge into his or her own hands.
> (2009, p. 5)

John Gaventa, a founding member of the original International Participatory Research Network when he was based at Highlander Center in the United States, who is now heading up the Coady International Institute in Canada, says:

> Any visions of democracy that include meaningful participation of people in decisions that affect their lives, also must consider their participation in the production of knowledge itself. Without consideration of how, why and for whom it is produced, knowledge is not necessarily a force for democracy.
> (Gaventa and Bivens, 2014, p. 46)

Edward Said, the Palestinian-American scholar, underscores the choice facing us, noting,

> I think the major choice faced by the intellectual is whether to be allied with the stability of the victors and rulers or—the more difficult path—to consider that stability as a state of emergency threatening the less fortunate with the danger of extinction, and take into account the experience of subordination itself, as well as the memory of forgotten voices and persons.
> (1996, p. 35)

We close with three challenges for contemporary researchers:

- Inform ourselves of the true global roots of community-based research by acknowledging the foundational roots from the majority world.
- Provide visibility and support for the thousands of contemporary community-based researchers working today in the majority world.
- Recognize the central role that social movements and civil society organizations, totally independent of universities, play in the creation of transformative knowledge.

SECTION II

Experiences

CHAPTER 6

"With or Without You"—The Development of Science Shops and Their Relationship to Higher Education Institutions in Europe

Norbert Steinhaus

Introduction

Society's participation in developing research agendas, in the research process itself, and in the debate about its findings will be key factors when determining the success of the transformation process. In order to support it, cooperation between, and much closer integration of, a range of scientific disciplines and policy is essential. But next to institutionalized scientific advice for policy-makers, it needs research centers that are closely linked with civil society organizations, as the latter play an increasing role in empowerment of civil society.

Research and education have a key role to play in the current societal transformation process. In cooperation with policy-makers, business, and society at large, the scientific community is tasked with developing visions for society, exploring various development pathways, and supporting sustainable technological and social innovations. Education should help to create problem awareness and promote systemic thinking, thus empowering people to participate in, and shape, the transformation process.

Perhaps one of the most effective efforts to address some of these issues has been the emergence of community-based research. In this type of research, lay people work with professionally trained scientists in a community-driven process and have the opportunity to collaborate with professional researchers in defining a problem, conducting the research, interpreting results, and using the results to effect constructive social and environmental change (Fischer, 2000).

Citizens and Science Shops

Science shops are not "shops" in the traditional sense of the word. They are often, but not always, linked to universities, where students conduct research as part of their curriculum. Most science shops are small entities that carry out scientific research in a wide range of disciplines, usually free of charge and on behalf of citizens and local civil society. There is no one standard model for science shops because they function within different sociopolitical, cultural, and organizational contexts (Mulder et al., 2001). There are, however, some important shared features among the many different types of science shops. By focusing on these parallels, an international group of organizations identified themselves as science shops, with the following definition:

> A Science Shop provides independent, participatory research support in response to concerns experienced by civil society.

There are many differences in the way science shops meet the above definition, but they all have a general mission statement in common. They all seek to

- provide civil society with knowledge and skills through research and education;
- provide their services on an affordable basis;
- promote and support public access to and influence on science and technology;
- create equitable and supportive partnerships with civil society organizations;
- enhance understanding among policymakers as well as education and research institutions of the research and education needs of civil society;
- enhance the transferable skills and knowledge of students, community representatives and researchers.

(DeBok and Steinhaus, 2008)

Science shops appear all over the world but operate in many different ways. What they have in common is their demand-driven and bottom-up approach. Also, they all share commitment to an interactive dialogue with the community and direct community involvement in research. How they are organized and operate is highly dependent on their context. The term "science" is used in its broadest sense, incorporating social and human sciences, as well as natural, physical, engineering, and technical sciences (Mulder et al., 2006).

Awareness and understanding of scientific information and knowledge is an essential step toward greater public participation in decision-making processes. The many requests science shops receive clearly show that providing information on its own is not sufficient to raise citizens' understanding, and that additional efforts are needed to bridge the gap between science and society. The INTERACTS case studies (Jørgensen et al., 2004) show that the knowledge requirements of nongovernmental organizations (NGOs) and citizens who approach science shops can be categorized as follows:

- scientific analysis of a problem;
- enhancement of knowledge around a certain topic;
- research on the impact of governmental projects;
- development of solutions;
- evaluation of NGO or community services/projects.

In practice, science shop work starts with a first contact between a civil society organization and a science shop on a specific problem. Then, in a cooperative search for a solution, new knowledge is generated, or at least existing knowledge is combined and adapted in true partnership without the "science" dominating. Through their contacts, however, science shops also provide a unique "antenna function" for society's current and future demands on science (Hende and Jørgensen, 2001).

The History of Science Shops in Europe

The establishment of science shops in Europe happened in waves, with many ups and downs, but constantly moving forward. During the first wave, science shops were established in the Netherlands in the 1970s—at the chemistry faculty in Utrecht in 1973 and at the University of Amsterdam in 1978 following the students' movement there (Leydesdorff and Besselaar, 1987; Farkas, 1999; 2002). The institutionalization of the Dutch science shops can be considered to be a result of the political program of the left-wing coalition, which won the elections of 1973 with the motto "equal distribution of income, wealth, and knowledge." The science shops that first emerged in the Netherlands are now important actors in community-based research. They have evolved and become institutions with a rich experience and advisory competence with respect to societal needs and issues. One of their major achievements is that they have developed functional structures for good interactions between civil society and science—structures other institutions (e.g., those in the field of participatory technology assessment) can build on, even in times when many science shops have gone through a crisis or have been closed (Banthien et al., 2003).

In the 1980s, a second wave of science shops developed in Germany, France, and Denmark, as well as two shops in Belgium. These shops are seen as having emerged from alternative movements such as the *Bürgerinitiativen* (citizens' initiatives) in Germany. The environmental movement of that time also had a strong impact on these developments, which were mainly based on collaborations with emerging university departments in environmental sciences. Some of these science shops still focus exclusively on environmental issues. During the 1990s, a "revival" of the science shop idea occurred, and that can be linked to a change in the discourse about science and society. The Information and Communications Technology (ICT) revolution impacted on the relationship between science and the public to such an extent that a call for a new social contract for science was voiced. In the course of that debate, there was a renewal of interest from policy-makers in the concept of science shops. A new model was emerging where the public is considered, not just as a receiver of scientific knowledge or as an interactive conversation partner, but as a stakeholder with his or her own knowledge interests.

In this favorable atmosphere, a third wave of science shops was initiated in Austria and the United Kingdom (UK) during the 1990s. The Austrian shops were, at least partly, triggered by the Dutch example (Steinhaus, 1999), while the British initiatives were launched by government agencies and the Nuffield Foundation, a charitable trust one of whose aims is to increase research capacity in science. Though the term "science shop" is not in use in Spain, some Spanish institutions have developed self-standing science shop-type initiatives. In a fourth wave, science shops were established in the East European accession countries in the period from 1995 to 2000, modeled on the Dutch example and realized in cooperation with Dutch science shops. Although the initiative eventually failed in the Czech Republic, eight science shops have been successfully established in Romania (Mulder, 2000; INTERACTS, 2003).

The debates around science shops have resonated at the European level and led to the development of an action plan by the European Commission to enhance the networking of science shops and provide funding to several projects (Fischer et al., 2004). European funding programs continue to move in the right direction, opening up a "third sector for knowledge production." Strands such as "research for the benefit of civil society organizations" within the European Union (EU) Seventh Framework Programme (FP7) are to be welcomed. There have been many examples of funding schemes, both in Europe and beyond, which have, at different times, worked to encourage researchers and civil society groups to collaborate. European science shops have invited citizens into universities and taken academics out into the communities to create new research projects. The Canadian Social Sciences and Humanities Research Council supported a network of "community-university research alliances." And since 2005 in France, the Partenariats Institutions-Citoyens pour la Recherche et l'Innovation (PICRI) initiative in Île de France has brought together citizens and researchers to support research across areas of common interest (Stilgoe, 2009). In the UK, the Beacons for Public Engagement have been doing the same.

The most recent wave of development has led to intense international cooperation under the umbrella of Public Engagement with Research and Research Engagement with Society (PERARES) as the latest of a series of projects that focused on the establishment of civil society-research interfaces, following the methodology of science shops. PERARES is a four-year project, funded under the EU FP7, which started in 2010 bringing together science shops, Civil Society Organizations (CSOs), and universities from 16 European countries. The PERARES project aims to strengthen public engagement in research (PER) by involving researchers and CSOs in the formulation of research agendas and the research process, both at the institutional level (including higher education institutes) and at regional and transnational/European levels. Under PERARES, partners are setting up and advancing science shops in Cambridge (UK), Dublin (Ireland), Lyon (France), Grenoble (France), Crete (Greece), Stavanger (Norway), and Sassari (Sardinia, Italy), and in Cyprus, Estonia, and Israel. All have done feasibility studies, and set up provisional structures and advisory boards, which include CSO members. Pilot projects involving students and CSOs have started. The new science shops are mentored by staff from established science shops. Summer schools for "beginners" (those interested in establishing science shops) are offered at public events and conferences.

Community-engaged research and learning are developing fields in Ireland, and members of the network see an opportunity to support further embedding, both at the level of individual higher education institutes (HEIs) and at policy-making level. The policy context for the development of this area of work in Ireland is encouraging—the recent National Strategy for Higher Education to 2030 set a policy context where research, teaching, and civic engagement are the three main strategic priorities for HEIs in Ireland. This is the first time that civic engagement has been formally identified as a key pillar in higher education in Ireland. The challenge now is to ensure that this strategic priority is translated into action (*Living Knowledge Newsletter* no. 40).

Decline and Revival

The history of science shops in Europe has not been a continuous success story. During the 1990s, as new science shops were developing, some of those in the early founding countries faced decline. Germany was one example where the attempt to develop the "Dutch model" of university-based science shops failed. There was not a great deal of support for the concept in the German universities of the 1980s. This lack of support led to Germany's first science shop at the University of Essen closing as early as 1983. More successful were the science shops that were established as nonprofit organizations, of which there were 25 in Germany during the 1980s. But, dependent as they were on volunteers and with a lack of permanent subsidy for their work, many closed (Mulder et al., 2006). There was a decline to only three in the late 1990s. However, there is a new science shop movement happening in Germany, and today there are 11 operating, of which six have been established within the past five years, five of them non-university-based.

The Stifterverband für die Deutsche Wissenschaft (Donors' Association) found that in Germany there is neither a tradition nor a generally shared understanding of a civic mission for universities outside of research and teaching (Stifterverband, 2013). But a growing interest within German higher education institutes for structures to link with civil society can be noted, not least because of the EU's commitments. The universities are increasingly seeing the value of their role in civil society and the social engagement of their institutions. In 2011, funding was provided through collaboration between Stifterverband and the Stiftung Mercator foundation, the US-based Carter Foundation, the Robert Bosch Foundation, and the Stuttgart-based Agentur Mehrwert agency, to support a process of self-understanding as civil society actors in universities, "More than research and teaching" and "Do it!" The consortium provided funding to six German universities to support community-related activities (from social learning to community-based research). These six were chosen from among a total of 78 (25 percent of the total number of universities in Germany) that had made applications for the funding (Stiftung Mercator, 2011).

In France, there were about 15 science shops operating by the end of the 1980s, but this was followed by a period of decline. During the period 1985–1995, interest in science shops as a policy instrument tended to fade because of the increased focus on entrepreneurship, privatization, and commercialization (Irwin, 1995; Sclove, 1995; Clark, 1998). However, there are now again five science shops operating in France. In a study on Dutch science shops,

Wachelder (2003) cites the reasons for their decline as being the decline of state funding, a change of the political climate, a stricter academic regime for students that makes it harder for them to participate, and more pressure on academic staff to publish, thus making them more reluctant to engage in science shop projects.

It is difficult to assess the exact number of science shops in Europe today. It is particularly problematic in the context of constant movement, with the generation of new shops on the one hand and the closing of established ones on the other. Furthermore, shops may still exist "on paper," but no longer be active. Also, as discussed earlier, the term science shop is not universally used in Europe, and so not every institution or program that fits with the mission of science shop calls itself one. For example, in Denmark there are programs at three universities that are called "project agencies" but that share all of the characteristics of science shops. Germany has "cooperation offices" that work with trade unions as their client group, and in the UK there are programs called "community exchange programs" (Hall and Hall, 2002).

International

In the international network of science shops, "Living Knowledge," more than 60 science shops from 24 countries, with different backgrounds and forms of embedding in HEI and research systems, cooperate (www.livingknowledge.org). The exchange of information and specialized knowledge and the cooperation between the science shops creates synergies during processing social and ecological problems. From a modest extension of a university service on a voluntary basis, their number has today mushroomed to professional organizations in several countries across the world (such as Videnskapsbutikken in Denmark, Wissenschaftsladen in Germany and Austria, Intermediu in Romania, Science Shop in the UK, Community Based Research Center in the United States, and Shopfront, at the University of Technology, Sydney).

Since the start of the international networking of science shops, there have been increasing demands from science shop start-up initiatives and from newly established science shops for support in the development of structures, procedures, and materials.

Science Shops and Higher Education Institutes

Government reforms in higher education across many European countries (including university mergers) are impacting on HEI-based science shops. The prevailing view is that in order for science shops to maintain their position in HEIs, they need to contribute to the core activities of teaching and research (Martin et al., 2011). In 2003 the European Commission published a communication "The Role of the Universities in the Europe of Knowledge," which laid out some of the new challenges facing European universities:

> On the one hand, we have the increasing diversification and specialization of knowledge, and the emergence of research and teaching specialties which are increasingly specific and at the cutting edge. On the other, we see the academic world having an urgent need to adapt to the interdisciplinary character of the fields opened up by society's major problems such as sustainable development, the new medical scourges, risk management, etc. Yet the activities of the universities, particularly when it comes to teaching, tend to remain organized, and more often than not compartmentalized, within the traditional disciplinary framework... The universities have a major role to play in initiatives under the "Science and Society" action plan, designed to foster the development and improve the coordination of national activities and policies in areas such as scientific opinion and dialogue with the people, ethics, science education, and "women and science".

Since many science shop projects are of an interdisciplinary nature and since science shops contribute to the university curricula and research through the involvement and participation of students, supervisors, and researchers, science shops are ideally placed to contribute to the development of interdisciplinary teaching and research. Also, since their beginning, networking and cooperation and the exchange of practice have been central to the mission of science shops. The development of interdisciplinary teaching and research as implemented through science shops supports universities in playing a role in "the dialogue with the people" (European Commission, 2003). Within the last decade, the European Commission has decided to make science shop development one of the key actions in Directorate General (DG) Research's Science & Society policy. This is mentioned in Action 21 of the commission's Science & Society Action Plan (European Commission, 2002). The EU has financed studies on science shops (SCIPAS [Study and Conference on Improving Public Access to Science] and INTERACTS) and financed projects such as Improving Science Shop Networking (ISSNET), Training and Mentoring of Science Shops (TRAMS), and, as outlined earlier, PERARES. The reasons for the commission's support were summarized by their former Director for Science and Society, Dr. Rainer Gerold (European Commission, 2003):

1. The trust of citizens in science is helped by Science Shops
2. By contacts between the European Science Shops and the commission there will be shorter communication lines between the citizens and European research policy

3. When they approach a Science Shop, people are open to a scientific approach (Raising Public Awareness)
4. Science shops have their influence on young researchers & research institutes (Raising Science's Awareness)
5. The themes of research by Science Shops fit well with European ideals.

All HEIs have strategic documents on a range of issues. At the highest level, there are mission statements and strategic plans, below which come strategies, such as those for teaching and learning, for research, and sometimes for engagement with business and society. Below this again, science shops have been included within curricula and plans of particular academic departments. Long-standing science shops attribute their success in part to this inclusion in policy and strategic planning both within and beyond their HEI, for example, in government policies. Successful science shops also work directly with HEI funders and governments where possible, to ensure the support of external agencies for the embedding of science shops within HEIs (Martin and McKenna, 2013). When examining whether, or how, science shops are embedded within HEIs, there are a number of factors to consider. Is the science shop located within an academic department and therefore specialist within one discipline? Or is it based within the administrative function of the university, servicing students from many disciplines? How does it link to the HEI strategy? Is it written in at senior management level, at operational level, or not at all? Does it link to research, teaching and learning, or civic engagement policies?

There is huge variation in where science shops are located within HEI structures. A small-scale survey undertaken for the PERARES project indicated that of the science shops that responded, 13 were based within academic departments while 18 were based within administrative units of the university. The longest-established science shops are more likely to be located within academic departments but, given that most of these science shops are Dutch, this could reflect the fact that they operate within a national context where specialization within an academic discipline is the norm. Typically, these types of science shops complete smaller numbers of very high-quality projects, often with graduate students. In many cases they are not staffed full-time but rather are staffed by individuals who also have an academic role within their particular department. There was greater variety in the case of newer science shops, with roughly half being located within academic structures and the other half being located within administrative or support service structures. For those science shops that were established more than five and less than 15 years ago, more were located within administrative or support services than within academic structures. It is also noteworthy that for those science shops located within administrative structures, there was no clear "home." They were to be found in departments such as communications, student affairs, research, strategic affairs, cultural affairs, and science communication. This indicates the flexibility of the model and the different ways in which it can be placed within different organizational contexts (Martin et al., 2011).

The values of community engagement and community-based research are not universally prioritized in higher education institutions. The priorities are often focused on other "higher-level" objectives such as research funding, student retention, income-generating initiatives, and the research needs of business and governments. Economic context is an issue here in that, in times of economic constraint, HEI energies and resources are more likely to be diverted to income-generating areas and less facilitative of initiatives that do not generate their own incomes. Times of crises and uncertainty can also create opportunities: it is still possible to be creative by working on submissions to strategic planning processes; organizing public lectures on community-based research, networking, and making each community-based research initiative as effective as is possible; making a contribution to communities; and highlighting the impact on the lives of community and voluntary groups, as well as on the participating students and academic supervisors. Finally, to embed engagement practices or science shop structures and activities, coordinators are required to garner support at all levels in the HEI: course team, department, school, college, senior management, and committees (Martin and McKenna, 2013).

Impact of Science Shops on Higher Education and Research

Higher education institutions have many relationships with society. Science shops have a special place in linking the three university missions: education, research, and knowledge transfer to society (outreach). Science shop projects prepare students in a flexible way, not only by teaching them how-to "knowledge," but also by teaching the competence "to apply knowledge in context, in a rapidly changing society." In science shop projects, students learn valuable skills, such as communicating with nonexperts and solving problems in context. Additional impacts can be created by using science shop cases as examples in "regular" courses. There are examples of science shops developing methodological courses and contributing to restructuring of curricula (Fokkink and Mulder, 2004). The analyses of science shop case studies in the INTERACTS project show that through cooperation with civil society, students may enhance or develop the following (employable) skills and competencies (Teodosiu and Teleman, 2003):

- social competencies (real-life experiences);
- communication and cooperation skills, also with nonscientists;
- new knowledge and perspectives;
- knowledge and expertise within transdisciplinary research; and
- skills to connect and bring together the needs and demands of different groups, including those with more theoretical scientific backgrounds.

Science shops can change or add to the focus of the research agenda and can create dialogue within research. They introduce participatory research methods, and some even develop into participatory research centers (Hende and Jørgensen, 2001). One example, that of the science shop for pharmaceutics in Groningen in the Netherlands, illustrates the antenna function of the science shop, in which emerging themes led to focused scientific attention. Several small questions on medicine use in the tropics, posed by an NGO, led to two larger PhD projects. The resulting publications were best sellers at the bookshop of the Royal Dutch Tropical Institute (Mulder et al., 2006). In Denmark several requests from NGOs through the science shop at the Technical University of Denmark (DTU) resulted in the establishment of organic food as a research and teaching area at the university (Hende and Jørgensen, 2001).

In the UK, as in the Netherlands, and more and more other countries, science shops can be seen as relating to the third mission of the university—knowledge transfer to society (outreach). There was a recognition by the UK universities engaged in the INTERACTS project that active engagement between universities and society was now on the agenda of government, and many expressed commitment to developing those links, and promoting university staff expertise to external bodies. Universities are becoming more aware of the fact that teaching and learning can be combined with community outreach and further justify public funding (Jørgensen et al., 2004).

Closing Remarks

Scaling up the efforts described in this chapter means thinking about collaborative research between universities and the third sector in much the same way as with the private sector. Innovation systems around the world have endeavored to bring universities and companies together. Science parks, public-private partnerships, and research networks have tried to get industry and academia working together, with some success. If our intention is broad public benefit and our targets are global challenges, we should start building imaginative new partnerships between university researchers and civil society. Such initiatives can help place academic research at the heart of civil society.

They may open new avenues for research and chip away at the "ivory tower" culture of universities.

As can be seen, science shops today work in many different ways and with a variety of structures and organizational models that differ from country to country but they have consolidated their bridging function between universities and society. What they have in common is their commitment to supply custom-oriented knowledge, facilitate community partners working with universities, and offer—where linked to universities—project-oriented learning experiences for students. Thus, they contribute to participative education, which addresses issues of relevance to society's transformation processes. The science shop method supplies the next generation of scientists with a vehicle to complement and improve their scientific training. In most cases, students are able to do science shop research projects as part of their curriculum. Here they can learn skills that are otherwise hard to obtain. Through this feature, science shops have a synergy with education renewal and can therefore fit within the education, research, or engagement elements of HEI mission statements.

Research and education—in cooperation with policy-makers, business, the scientific community, and society at large—are tasked with developing visions for society, exploring development pathways, and supporting sustainable technological and social innovations by creating problem awareness and promoting systemic thinking, thus empowering people to participate in and shape the transformation process. Here we see a powerful change, because civil society has the impression that the science system does not take on the pressing societal challenges such as climate change, resource scarcity, urbanization, or affordable health in an aging society—the "grand challenges"—in sufficient numbers and with adequate means. To come to practical solutions, to develop responsible research and innovation (RRI), public engagement and participation on all levels is vital, involving participation of citizens not only in generating research, but also in monitoring or performing research, in data collection, and in scenario development. A structured public engagement and involvement of CSOs in research and innovation (R&I) therefore has the potential to shape an innovation-friendly culture. Only by integrating all forms of knowledge, including, what has up to now been insufficiently considered, local knowledge and practical experiential knowledge along with expert and scientific knowledge, will we be able to build a truly knowledge-based society. Society's participation in developing research issues, in the research process itself, and in the debate about its findings will be an important factor in determining the success of the transformation process (Steinhaus, 2013).

The new "Science with and for Society" funding scheme in the EU Horizon 2020 program emphasizes the role of civil society and its organizations in future research processes. To date, workshops and conferences under the scheme have focused on, and explored, the role of philanthropy in the promotion of responsible research in innovation, building public engagement in Horizon 2020, and research and innovation and community university engagement, just to mention a few (*Living Knowledge Newsletter* no. 40). There are exciting times ahead, and science shops—with or without structural links to universities—will play their role in addressing the societal challenges spelt out in Horizon 2020: building capacities and developing innovative ways of connecting science to society.

CHAPTER 7

Research Engagement in the UK: Evolving Policy and Practice

Sophie Duncan and Paul Manners

Introduction

In this chapter we tell the story of how UK research policy and practice have slowly evolved in response to the increasing imperative to demonstrate the social relevance of higher education (HE). This pressure has been building in the HE research sector in the UK for a number of years, with both grassroots practices (such as community-based research and patient involvement in health) and top-down policy initiatives (like knowledge exchange and research "impact") gaining increasing traction.

We believe that the UK research system has now reached a "tipping point" where these different developments are aligning, opening up the prospect of a significant paradigm shift that places societal engagement at the core of how universities imagine and enact their research, rather than as an "optional" or peripheral activity. Although our interpretation of these developments is optimistic, we recognize the very significant risks and challenges inherent in realizing the full potential of this alignment, and some of the issues that a more engaged research culture raises.

How we think about research, the roles of researchers, its funding, and its purposes are all deeply conditioned by existing cultures and practices within universities, and the impact of previous policies and funding arrangements. Views are strongly polarized and contested. For many, this kind of societal engagement carries with it serious risks, to the independence of researchers for instance, opening up the specter of research being increasingly constrained by the expectation that it meet short-term, instrumental, and politically motivated ends. These concerns need to be taken seriously.

It is also important to recognize that the necessary changes to culture and professional practice cannot be imposed—they need to be negotiated. To begin to unravel these different viewpoints, and to imagine different models and approaches, requires everyone to make the space to reflect, to explore what is at stake, to "own" the implications for their own practice, and to contribute to reimagining policies and practice. This process of culture change is one that is core to our work at the UK National Coordinating Centre for Public Engagement (NCCPE).

What we try to provide in this chapter, therefore, is a summary of how we are currently making sense of the complex dynamics of change, and a framework of questions that have arisen out of the work to date. We hope these will trigger productive dialogue and engagement with the topic wherever people are seeking to embed more effective arrangements to support "engaged" research.

Universities in a Changing World

The world around HE is changing dramatically. We are living through a profound shift in the dynamics of the wider political sphere. Many commentators have described both the nature and urgency of change that universities need to grasp. A recent report by the UK think tank Institute for Public Policy Research, *An Avalanche Is Coming: Higher Education and the Revolution Ahead* (2013), argues that the gap between HE and the rapidly changing society is increasing so fast that only a revolution in the sector can address the gulf:

> Our belief is that deep, radical and urgent transformation is required in higher education as much as it is in school systems. Our fear is that, perhaps as a result of complacency, caution or anxiety, or a combination of all three, the pace of change is too slow and the nature of change too incremental.
>
> (p. 3)

Craig Calhoun, president of the London School of Economics, also identifies that universities are living through a period of "deep transformation" in their relationship with a society that itself is undergoing profound reorganization and change ("The University and the Public Good," 2006):

> Universities have flourished in the modern era as central public institutions and bases for critical thought. They are currently challenged by a variety of social forces and undergoing a deep transformation in both their internal structure and their relationship to the rest of society. Critical theorists need

to assess this both in order to grasp adequately the social conditions of their own work and because the transformation of universities is central to a more general intensification of social inequality, privatization of public institutions, and reorganization of the relation of access to knowledge.

(p. 7)

These "social forces" are clearly not unique to universities; all public institutions—whether governments, public services, charities, media organizations, or businesses—are being required to navigate and negotiate dramatically shifting public expectations. In the UK, these pressures are particularly intense in five areas, and all reflect an increasing level of scrutiny, distrust, and impatience with elite or unresponsive forms of governance and professional practice:

- Trust: increasing challenges to the "moral authority" of public figures, increasing scrutiny of their activities, and declining trust in "experts" and authority figures;
- Accountability: increasing expectation that those who receive public funding should be held to account for that funding;
- Relevance: both an expectation that those in receipt of public funding should make substantial efforts to align their work with society's needs—and increasing innovation from "alternative providers" who find new, creative, and efficient ways to offer services better tuned to the needs of the public;
- Community: questions about how the values of public institutions align with the values of the communities they aim to serve—and how authentically they live up to the values they espouse;
- Impact: finding a way to effectively evidence and articulate the "difference" we make that has credibility and meaning to a host of stakeholders—not just our peers (see Benneworth, 2009).

All of these pressures demand new forms of responsiveness from universities. They are demanding rapid innovation in how they develop their teaching to ensure they prepare graduates for this rapidly changing world, and they are requiring universities to reframe the relationship between their research activity and how it contributes to and aligns with the world outside the campus.

Developments in Research Policy and Practice

Mobilized by these rapid changes in the context in which universities work, it is interesting to note how engagement is moving into mainstream thinking and policy in the UK. It is increasingly being recognized that "engaged" teaching and research provide a necessary route to accommodating these external pressures and expectations, and a means to better aligning university activity with society. For instance, Universities UK (UUK), the group representing UK vice-chancellors, conducted a review in 2011 of the future trends most likely to impact on HE. This project concluded by identifying two possible scenarios (*Futures for Higher Education: Analysing Trends*, 2012, p. 29):

> UK HE currently faces a number of possible futures. The most positive of these would see the increasing integration of institutional interest with the wider public good, placing universities at the heart of economic and social advancement...

It identified the critical role of engagement in realizing the aspiration for deeper integration, "ensuring that universities continue to remain fully engaged in society at all levels, understanding its needs and developments" (p. 29).

Community-based research (CBR)—the main focus of this book—provides one significant example of the kind of purposeful and powerful dialogue that is possible between researchers and communities outside the academy, and which can generate the kind of responsiveness that UUK identify as critical to a thriving HE system. But there are many other examples of how researchers and policy-makers are developing "engaged" practices that allow powerful and productive dialogue with wider society. It is important to position CBR within this wider paradigm of research engagement, if we are to fully grasp the dynamics of the current evolving landscape.

To make sense of these different developments in engaged practice, we think it is helpful to distinguish between practices that have evolved from the "grass roots"—in response to researchers and their collaborators seeking to develop effective practices to coproduce knowledge—and those that have been triggered by "top-down" interventions from funders and policy-makers. Examples of grassroots engaged practices include community-based participatory research. This approach to research is characterized by a commitment to working with community-based organizations, has strong links to the community development movement, and draws on many of the conceptual and professional resources developed in that field. Other fields of practice have also developed "engaged" research methodologies, for instance, practices in health and in design, or in arts and culture. The NCCPE conducted a review of the academic literature in the field in 2012 (*Towards a Knowledge Base for University-Public Engagement*) and identified a huge breadth of activity:

Publications appear in a wide range of fields, including: Higher Education studies, Philosophy, Communications and Cultural Studies, Community Arts, Regional Development, Institutional Change, Social Work, Learning Sciences, Science and Technology Studies, History of Ideas, Participatory Design and Community Studies, to name but a few. Journals dedicated to engagement dynamics are also emerging, such as "Co-Design," which focuses on arts and design based participation, "Public Understanding of Science," "Community Engagement" and "Evidence and Policy," but tend to remain specific to particular disciplines or sectors of the public. New courses are also being established, often mirroring the concerns and research present in these journals.

(2012, p. 4)

What emerged from the review was a picture of a rich tapestry of engagement practices in the research activity of universities, many of which have developed over many years, but which still exist in relative isolation from each other. One commentator described these different communities of engaged research as "cottage industries":

It is becoming increasingly urgent, therefore, for those seeking to conduct an informed debate about the public value of the university as well as for those working to create new university-public relationships on the ground, to find better ways to share and build insight in this area.

(Facer et al., 2012, p. 3)

This is a point we will return to later in the chapter.

In tandem with the development of these expert engaged research practices, there have been numerous top-down interventions by funders of HE in the UK aimed at fostering greater external engagement by researchers. We have chosen to identify three distinct "waves" of policy that have sought to incentivize this in the UK.

Investments in the "Third Mission" of Universities

Coined to spotlight the necessity to reconnect university research to wider societal demand and need, this broad category of investments encompasses knowledge transfer and knowledge exchange, but is not limited to interaction with business and the private sector. The framing as a "third mission" was intended to raise the importance of societal engagement to a par with research and teaching (the first and second missions).

The Higher Education Funding Council for England commissioned a review of the outcomes of their investment in this type of activity in 2012. Public and Corporate Economic Consultants' (PACEC's) report *Strengthening the Contribution of English HEIs to the Innovation System:*

Knowledge Exchange and HEIF Funding offers a conceptual framework to describe the different ways in which university knowledge and research can contribute to their communities:

- **Facilitating the research exploitation process** through, for example, supporting the contract research process, consultancy activities and licensing/spin-outs through technology transfer.
- **Skills and human capital development** of academics, students and those external to the HEI through, for example, continuing professional development (CPD), training for academics and students, providing entrepreneurship and employability training etc.
- **Entrepreneurship and enterprise education**, including social enterprise activities.
- **Knowledge networks/diffusion**, including the stimulation of interactions between those in the HEI and those in the economy and society through, for example, the development of networks, and holding events that bring academics and external organisations together to share ideas and knowledge.
- **Exploiting the physical assets of the HEI** through, for example, the development of science parks, incubators, design studios, hiring of specialist equipment, as well as museums, exhibition space and so forth.
- **Supporting the community/public engagement** through, for example, outreach and volunteering, widening participation programmes and so on.

(2012, pp. 73–74)

While the term third mission has now largely disappeared from the policy landscape, more and more universities are reframing their strategic plans to prioritize societal engagement as either a cross-cutting theme or as a goal in its own right. The University of Manchester, for instance, identifies three goals in its 2011 strategic plan (Manchester 2020). The third of these—after teaching and learning—is "social responsibility":

> The University will contribute to the social and economic success of the local, national and international community by using our expertise and knowledge to find solutions to the major challenges of the 21st century, and by producing graduates who exercise social leadership and responsibility.

(2011, p. 15)

Investments in "Science and Society"

Another key cluster of policy interventions to promote engagement with research has occurred under the umbrella of Science and Society policy. The mid-2000s saw a series of scares about public attitudes to cutting-edge scientific research, perhaps most vividly seen in the debates about "Frankenstein foods" and the powerful public backlash against research into genetically modified organisms (GMOs). Until that point, the dominant framing for thinking about the relationship between scientists and the public had been "public understanding," a movement, triggered back in the 1980s, by the work of bodies like The Committee on the Public Understanding of Science (COPUS), which had been set up in 1986 to interpret scientific advances and make them more accessible to nonscientists.

What the genetically modified (GM) food debate brought home to the science community and its funders was that the intense social and ethical sensitivity that existed around research could not be accommodated simply by explaining the science and why it was justified. The public expected to be engaged in a debate about the frontiers of science policy. If scientists and policy-makers did not open up this conversation, and bring this social intelligence into the research and policy-making process, then similar breakdowns in trust were likely to happen again.

As a consequence, the Royal Society (2006) commissioned an influential survey to investigate the cultural and professional barriers within the science community that inhibited effective engagement with the public. In tandem, efforts were made to engineer a shift from "public understanding" to "public engagement" in science policy, most notably through the government's establishing the Sciencewise project, now the Sciencewise Expert Resource Centre. This initiative sought to facilitate engagement with members of the public to explore the social sensitivities around emerging areas of science policy, and to ensure that this feedback was used to influence policy and research priorities.

While Sciencewise addressed the mechanics of policy-making, the Royal Society survey teased out the cultural and professional norms that shaped how scientists approached their relationship with the public:

- 64 percent of those polled said the need to spend more time on research was stopping them getting more engaged (the top response);
- 20 percent agreed that scientists who engage are less well regarded by other scientists;
- 3 percent cited peer pressure as a barrier;
- the Research Assessment Exercise (RAE) was cited as a key driver influencing the academic community in the UK and as having a negative influence on science communication and, more broadly, on all non-research activities, such as teaching;
- science communication was viewed as "altruistic" and not a central part of academic life.

Clearly, engagement, and those who chose to engage with the public, would not flourish well in this culture:

> In the qualitative interviews, several researchers highlighted that public engagement activity was seen by peers as bad for their career. A further message that emerged was that public engagement was done by those who were "not good enough" for an academic career; and that public engagement was seen as "light" or "fluffy," and risked reinforcing negative stereotypes for women involved in such activity.
>
> (p. 11)

The origins of the Beacons for Public Engagement program, of which the NCCPE is a part, can be traced back to a concerted attempt to address these cultural challenges. Established in 2008, the aim of the Beacons project was to "create a culture within UK HE where public engagement is formalized and embedded as a valued and recognized activity for staff at all levels, and for students" (HEFCE, 2014). Six pilot Beacon projects were funded, where universities and civic partners worked together to meet this challenge, and the NCCPE was set up to draw together and share the learning from across the project. It is important to note that this initiative was working across all disciplines, not just science. What emerged during the lifetime of the Beacons project was a challenge to the assumption (shared by many people) that there was little engagement activity happening in universities. In fact, the different traditions, practices, and policy investments have resulted in a research "ecosystem" that in many ways bears little resemblance to the stereotype of the "ivory tower." There is a significant amount of engaged research practice evident in the system—but the evidence suggests that too often it is undervalued and under-supported.

This was evidenced in research done by the UK Innovation Research Centre. Their 2009 report, *Knowledge Exchange between Academics and the Business, Public and Third Sectors*, describes the findings of a uniquely large-scale survey of academics in the UK, with over 22,000 responses. What it revealed was just how extensive the amount of engagement is:

> This report shows that academics from all disciplines are engaged in the knowledge exchange process—it does not simply involve those from science and technology based disciplines, but also includes academics from the arts and humanities and the social sciences. And the knowledge exchange mechanisms are wide and varied—it is not simply about the codified transfer of science (patents, licences, etc.) but includes many people based, problem solving and community driven activities.
>
> (2009, p. 7)

The research revealed that—despite much of the policy discourse focusing on incentivizing greater interaction with business, and the generation of patents and intellectual property—there was a much broader tapestry of engaged practice that covered a diverse range of partners, communities, and publics:

> Academics are engaged with a range of partners—and in the private business sector the range is not confined to the high-technology manufacturing industries but includes services and many so-called low technology sectors. Furthermore, many academics are interacting with the public and third sectors—and on many metrics the level of interaction is higher with these sectors than with the private sector.
>
> (p. 7)

While the report offers convincing evidence that researchers themselves are often very "engaged" in their practice, it also confirms the early experiences of the Beacons. There is little evidence of how the universities are embracing a strategic approach to engagement. The 2009 report identifies a number of ways in which—despite the extent and quantity of activity reported—this kind of "engaged" practice still struggles to be properly recognized, rewarded, and resourced within universities.

The Beacons project sought to address this over a four-year period, and the work led to a deeper understanding of how to affect institutional cultures to embed engagement (see McIlrath et al., 2012, chapter 13). As a consequence of this work, over 60 universities in the UK have signed up to the NCCPE's "Engaged University" manifesto (see NCCPE, 2012b), a commitment to embed engagement into their culture and practice; the UK research funders have launched a Concordat for Engaging the Public with Research (see RCUK, 2014) that sets out their expectations of the organizations that they fund; and a Catalyst project (see NCCPE, 2013) has funded eight universities across the UK to take the learning from the Beacons and adopt it into their own practice.

The Impact Agenda

In tandem with the work described above, which addresses the cultural factors that inhibit more engaged research practices, there has also been a major shift in how research is funded in the UK. The so-called impact agenda has resulted in a new set of incentives and accountability measures for research funding, which explicitly incentivize research that delivers impact "beyond academia." The origins of "impact" can be traced back to the mid-2000s and the so-called Warry Report (*Increasing the Economic Impact of the Research*

Councils (2006)), and traced through a complex consultation process and significant "battle" with the sector (at one point, a petition of over 18,000 signatories was delivered to the Prime Minister, calling for the abandonment of the plans).

All Research Councils grants now expect applicants to complete a "pathways to impact statement":

> At the application stage we do not expect applicants or peer reviewers to be able to predict the economic or societal impacts that research will achieve. However, we want to encourage applicants to consider and explore, in ways that are appropriate given the nature of the research they are proposing to conduct, potential pathways to impact, for example through engagement or collaboration with partners.
>
> (RCUK, 2011)

In parallel, the new Research Excellence Framework (REF), which retrospectively assesses the quality of a research unit's work, includes an assessment of the impact of the research beyond academia. This is a radical departure from the previous Research Assessment Exercise, which focused only on the quality of research outputs as judged by academic peers.

Underpinning both schemes are similar typologies that provide prompts to explain the types of impact that might be expected. For instance, in the Arts and Humanities, the REF guidance (REF, 2012) provides what could be argued to be a rich palate of such triggers. Researchers are invited to evidence how their research has enriched "Culture and Society" in the following domains (p. 89):

> **Civil society:** Influencing the form and content of associations between people or groups to illuminate and challenge cultural values and social assumptions.
>
> **Public discourse:** Extending the range and improving the quality of evidence, argument and expression to enhance public understanding of the major issues and challenges faced by individuals and society.
>
> **Cultural life:** Creating and interpreting cultural capital in all of its forms to enrich and expand the lives, imaginations and sensibilities of individuals and groups.

Possible indicators that might be used to evidence "impact" in such domains are also offered, including specific guidance about accounting for the impact of public engagement.

Given the importance of the REF to the culture of academia, this inclusion of impact will no doubt result in profound changes to the academy. With researchers able to draw down funding to support their pathways to impact plans, and a recognized need to evidence the impact of their research on society, it is likely that engagement will become more important as a valued part of what it means to do research.

Collectively, what these three waves of top-down policy initiatives add up to is a concerted effort by policy-makers to incentivize more engaged, socially responsive types of research practice. From early attempts to fund "knowledge transfer" (a rather linear one-way view of how research could be commercialized and applied), a more sophisticated model is emerging, embodying a relatively nuanced understanding of how knowledge "diffuses" within society and how solutions can be cocreated through engagement.

Frontiers: The Future of Research Engagement in the UK

While there is convincing evidence that the HE sector is slowly embracing the strategic necessity of engagement, and beginning to evolve to bring that commitment more fully into the mainstream of its culture and practices, what the previous section shows is that progress toward "mainstreaming" this practice is still gradual. It is also important to acknowledge that there is spirited resistance to many of the developments outlined above, from a range of different directions.

While it is possible to interpret the impact agenda as a welcome invitation to the sector to value its external engagement, and to increase its commitment, to this type of research, for many the agenda is a deeply troubling development. One example is the formation of a significant alliance, known as the Council for the Defence of British Universities (CDBU), which lays out its stall firmly in opposition to impact, and to other recent policy changes promoting a marketization of the sector. CDBU draws up battle lines between "academic values" and the political forces ranged against the freedom universities have long enjoyed. This challenge is an important one. In considering the future of engaged research in the UK, we need to address these and other concerns if the current momentum is to lead to lasting and sustained change and improvement.

Universities are, of course, always full of argument and contestation: this is very much in their DNA. As Clark Kerr wrote in 1963 in his book *The Uses of the University*:

> These several competing visions of true purpose, each relating to a different layer of history, a different web of forces, cause much of the malaise in the university communities of today. The university is so many things to so many different people that it must, of necessity, be partially at war with itself.
>
> (2001, p. 7)

Considerations about engaged research should be no different. The challenge is to develop a framework for properly debating the value, purposes, and methods of engaged research, which will help us to develop a coherent discourse to talk about engaged theory and practice. In this final section, we will identify some of the key pressure points that we think require significant work if the promise of engaged research is to be fully realized.

A first challenge concerns finding an appropriate balance between "engagement" and "detachment"—the so-called critical distance that has played such an important part in establishing the credibility and legitimacy of the institution of the university and of its research. This point is developed by Craig Calhoun in "The University and the Public Good":

> If its walls are too strong, it risks becoming irrelevant or having those who control its resources decide externally on how it should change. But if advice simply to break down all the walls is heeded, universities risk losing their capacity to organize long-term intellectual agendas instead of short-term responses to immediate questions, the possibility for academics to speak with authority within specific fields of competence, and the basis for the internal public discourse aimed at the continual correction of errors and improvements of understanding that gives participants an incentive to put the pursuit of truth ahead of the mere desire to use knowledge in other enterprises.
>
> (2006a, p. 35)

This returns us to our introductory remarks: there needs to be intense debate and deliberation to weigh up these different perspectives and expectations. Engagement crucially needs to be understood not as an end in itself, but as a means to an end: a healthily "connected" HE system that is generating value for society that is widely felt and understood, but which is also sufficiently independent and detached to allow it to "pursue truth" independent of undue external influence.

In an attempt to identify the theoretical and political "frontiers" of our current thinking about engaged research, the NCCPE recently undertook a scoping study, a review, to try to distill the theoretical challenges. Our publication, *Towards a Knowledge Base for University-Public Engagement* (2012b), was built upon an extensive literature review of research exploring the dynamics of engagement, and on conversations with a range of people working actively in this space. The review noted that despite this rich tapestry of engaged research practice, a number of significant challenges remain in building a robust knowledge base to underpin these approaches, including the dispersed nature of the activity across different disciplinary and practice domains:

> This activity on the ground has the potential to serve as a powerful resource for informing our understanding of the potential of the university to contribute to

Research Engagement in UK: Evolving Policy & Practice 97

the public good. Even its advocates admit, however, that such activity is poorly researched, highly fragmented and dominated by small-scale evaluation and advocacy. At present, the networks for sharing knowledge about what works and who benefits from these activities are fragmented and the robust, longer term and critically reflective research base is far from secure.

(p. 3)

Emerging from the literature were three broad thematic areas that provide a helpful framework for critical debate and for further research.

The first of these concerned *how well we understand engagement processes themselves*. As we have seen in this chapter, a rich tapestry of engagement practices have evolved within HE, but often operating in silos and not sharing and developing a broader professional scrutiny of the dynamics of university-public engagement. The review argued that we urgently need to deepen our knowledge about "what is going on" in the dynamic and diverse encounters when researchers and communities engage. In particular, it identified how important it is to deepen our insight into the profound ethical questions raised by these new forms of engaged research practice, but also to share our insights into how we understand processes such as how knowledge develops, how people make meaning, how change happens, and how knowledge-based institutions themselves develop.

The second "frontier" addressed the *governance and political economy of engagement*. As we identified earlier, it is easy to imagine a future in which universities are increasingly controlled by politicians and by the most powerful actors in society. So how can we adapt our governance processes to ensure we are tuned in and listening—but retain sufficient detachment to develop knowledge that is of lasting value to society? What new approaches to accountability need to be developed that allow us to find effective ways of balancing the needs and expectations of an increasingly diverse range of stakeholders, in an increasingly unequal society?

The third area we identified concerned our ability to talk authoritatively and coherently about the *quality, value, and impact of the engagement activity*. We are still a long way from being able to evidence whether, and in what ways, engagement generates "better" research; to articulate and measure public good beyond the economic; and to develop methodologies that allow us to evaluate these activities over time. For example, when and where in research processes does public engagement have most public benefit? What methods and processes are beneficial for which groups? Which methods and processes exclude and encourage which forms of encounter and why?

The picture that emerged from the review is of a thriving but still nascent field: there is much work still to be done to critique and debate the role of engaged research. The questions outlined above—and the conversations needed to address them—provide, we believe, a vital resource in realizing our ambition to maximize the ways in which research can enrich society. They also help us to negotiate the space and freedom to work in ways that make the pursuit of knowledge and its long-term custodianship as purposeful and secure as possible.

Conclusion

So where does this leave "engaged research" in the UK? The review to date demonstrates a very mixed picture.

While there are significant amounts of engaged research happening, it is also clear that it is often, still, on the periphery and not fully mainstreamed and supported. There are powerful voices and deeply engrained cultures within HE that challenge the value and significance of this work. These attitudes are slow to change, and the challenge they mount is robust. It is also fair to say that there is still much work to be done to articulate rigorously how engaged practices generate vital new forms of knowledge that are distinctly different to those generated by more conventional arrangements. Often, engaged practice is promoted as a self-evident good, and more needs to be done to create a reflective, critical discourse with which to progress and deepen our shared understandings.

The discourse around engagement is also bedeviled by "grandstanding." Universities are easily seduced by grand narratives that position them as "heroes" solving society's problems. The language of engagement is increasingly being adopted by managers and strategists in the sector—but the risk is that this is just as a rhetorical device to "wish away" the really tough and critical questions that need to be asked if genuine mutual benefit is to be achieved.

To realize the paradigm shift we outlined in the introduction to the chapter, there are therefore significant challenges still to be addressed. There are genuinely difficult intellectual and political choices inherent in working out the ideal "balance" in how universities respond to or detach themselves from societal issues. We need to move from just accepting that engagement is a "good thing" in its own right and seek to open up a richer and more robust dialogue about the purposes, processes, and impact of engagement.

What we have endeavored to do here is to outline a platform for focused ongoing conversations about the role of the university and its contribution to the public sphere. These conversations need to be held within the sector, with our communities, and with our politicians: multiple conversations at multiple levels, hopefully creating a greater collective sense of purpose—and much greater self-consciousness about excellence and how to support it. This attitude toward engagement is captured succinctly by the definition offered by the Association of Commonwealth Universities in 2001 in their consultation document "Engagement as a Core Value for the University":

> Engagement implies strenuous, thoughtful, argumentative interaction with the non-university world in at least four spheres: setting universities' aims, purposes and priorities; relating teaching and learning to the wider world; the back-and-forth dialogue between researchers and practitioners; and taking on wider responsibilities as neighbours and citizens.
>
> (2001, p. 6)

This optimistic and muscular vision—of a finely balanced and responsive system that delivers on the promise of "social relevance" but through robust debate—is a helpful place to pause. We look forward to ongoing dialogue on this topic.

CHAPTER 8

Emerging Policy and Practices on Community-Based Research—Perspectives from the Island of Ireland

Lorraine McIlrath, Catherine Bates, Kenneth Burns, Ann Lyons, Emma McKenna, and Pádraig Murphy

> In recent decades, much ground has been lost in terms of the public realm; that shared essential space of scholarly discourse and contestation of an independent people free to participate and change their circumstances, to imagine their future—be it in Ireland, Europe or at global level has to be reclaimed by generous and open scholarship... The challenge is to ethically reconnect economy, culture, science and society and in the process of so doing, to recover or reinforce an ethos of emancipatory scholarship. Independent thought, from home and abroad, and scholarly engagement with our current circumstances are crucial.
>
> (Higgins, 2013 p. 1)

Introduction

It is our shared understanding that one of the core roles of higher education is "to reconnect economy, culture, science and society" as argued by the President of Ireland, Michael D. Higgins, and, in doing so, evolve scholarship that creates positive social change through the fostering of collaborative partnerships with community and the wider society. Higher education is going through a period of rapid change as globally the economic recession has caused a shift in conceptual thinking from economic foci toward engagement with community and society (Escrigas et al., 2014; Inman and Schuetze, 2011). It is widely agreed, in principle, that higher education institutions can play a pivotal role in terms of societal well-being through their three core activities of research, teaching, and service (also called engagement or outreach). Watson (2007) argues that it is through an intentional civic or community engagement strategy and practice that higher education can impact positively upon community and society.

There is a multifaceted rationale for the development of community and civic engagement strategies and practices within higher education. For example, in Northern Ireland (as part of the United Kingdom), engagement or public engagement with research has gained traction as a result of a concerted effort by research funders to seek impactful research that resonates with, and is responsive to, society, while in the Republic of Ireland, engagement is seen as central to economic and social development and recovery in a period of fiscal crisis. As the "value added" role of higher education in community engagement gains recognition, on the island of Ireland a range of approaches have developed to foster greater civic and community engagement, including community-based research (CBR).

In this chapter, we articulate understandings, principles, and characteristics of CBR and discuss its position within an all-island Irish context, examining both national and local policies and practices. We then highlight five vignettes of institutional practice that have evolved across the island of Ireland to support and develop an institution-wide approach to CBR. Opportunities and challenges to community-based research are explored with regard to both Northern Ireland and the Republic, which have different higher education systems, policies, structures, and funding arrangements. As part of this analysis, we discuss networks that support this work across Ireland, in particular Campus Engage, a platform to support the development of civic engagement activities across Irish higher education. This development is framed against a new Irish higher education policy vision whereby "engaging with the wider society" is "one of the three interconnected core roles of higher education" alongside teaching and learning, and research (Department of Education and Skills (DES), 2010, p. 5). In the UK context, the Department for Employment and Learning (DELNI) produced a strategy, *Graduating to Success: A Higher Education Strategy for Northern Ireland* (2012), that emphasizes the importance of research, teaching, and engagement. We conclude the chapter with a concise overview of possible future developments in CBR practice and policy implementation.

Community-Based Research: General Principles and Local Flavors

CBR seeks to connect communities and civil society organizations with higher education institutions (HEIs) through student, and also through staff, research activities. The starting point of CBR is a research question or puzzle generated by, and of significance to, the community. Community in this sense could mean local cooperatives, voluntary or not-for-profit organizations such as mental health charities, community gardens, services for persons with disabilities, and local communities identified by a clear geographical affiliation. It could also mean communities of interest around a shared topic of concern such as the local economy, health, housing, or crime, all of which are seeking collective social action (Strand et al., 2003). These groups of engaged citizens seek a way to partner with their local HEI, and CBR initiatives are vehicles for this matching service (known as science shops in some countries: see Chapter 6). CBR initiatives can involve both academic staff and students. Academics can engage through supervising student researchers, or through collaborating with communities in their personal research activities. Students can be involved in CBR from undergraduate to PhD level, and are matched with community groups to work on their research questions as part of the students' course work.

CBR can be placed within what is known as the Mode 2 form of knowledge production (Gibbons et al., 1994), a mode that centralizes participation, democracy, and social accountability in academic research. Mode 2 is differentiated from Mode 1 knowledge production, which has, traditionally, privileged the lone researcher in his/her lab, is hierarchical in nature, and may work under public patronage, and from which innovation arises in a linear way. It represents an epistemological change as much as a procedural one. CBR can be positioned therefore within the participatory paradigm that centralizes the importance of action and collaboration. It is not characterized by a particular method (McDonald, 2009); rather, it is the *principles* informing this approach to research which are its hallmark. While there is a common set of principles that distinguishes CBR across different countries, the local CBR initiative often derives its *flavor* from the local culture, disciplinary background of the participants, policy frameworks, and available resources. The Community Health Scholars Program defines community-based research as

> A collaborative approach to research that equitably involves all partners in the research process and recognizes the unique strengths that each brings. CBPR [community-based participatory research] begins with a research topic of importance to the community and has the aim of combining knowledge with action and achieving social change...
> (2001, cited in Minkler and Wallerstein, 2003, p. 4)

In seeking to promote equitable relationships between HEIs and the wider community, the "flow" of resources and knowledge is not just from HEIs to the community. The community brings its own strengths, knowledge, locally derived questions, and capacity to the research relationship, and contributes to the training and civic engagement of student researchers and the HEI. Also, CBR promotes equity by seeking to facilitate access for community groups that may feel excluded from the HEI in their locality. The CBR knowledge production process has an explicit goal of translating the findings and research process into action for change at community and/or national level. This action seeks to transform communities and society for the better. This transformation can include tackling environmental issues such as soil and water quality, addressing and highlighting social justice concerns, and developing technological solutions to support communities and citizens.

While CBR projects are commonly underpinned by a participatory ethos that emphasizes equality of power relations, highlights shared ownership of data, and uses collaborative research design and processes, there is variety in the degree of participation among community and voluntary groups in the CBR process. While some groups are content to provide a question and receive a research report at the end of the process, others share full responsibility for the study and operate as equal partners in the design, decision-making, and data collection (see Biggs, 1989). The degree of participation can be influenced by a range of factors, including, but not limited to, HEI research cultures, demands on community groups, perceived levels of skill, and the ability of the CBR initiative to mentor and support a fully participatory process. Many structural, practical, skills and power components can be negotiated throughout the research process, to facilitate the desired level of participation and collaboration by partners.

On the island of Ireland, a number of HEIs have been implementing the principles and practices of CBR through HEI-wide facilitation units that support the development of CBR as an intentional research activity. Some of these units have evolved from a grassroots or bottom-up approach, with academic staff evolving the CBR activities; in other instances the units exist due to a top-down commitment from senior administration of the HEI; while others bear the characteristics of both top-down and bottom-up approaches. The most evolved initiative is the science shop at Queen's University Belfast, established 25 years ago, while the Dublin Institute of Technology, University College Cork, Dublin City University, and the National University of Ireland, Galway, are at varying degrees of evolution and establishment. Though there are now a number of initiatives in train throughout the HEIs, in this chapter we focus on five examples of CBR emanating from our own practice, based in five different institutional locations, including an academic department, careers, teaching and learning, and access and widening participation. The following vignettes give a flavor of the history, the *modus operandi*, and some of the types of CBR activities supported. These vignettes are shared with the reader to stimulate thinking on the challenges, opportunities, policy context, resources, and creativity that can lead to the setup and maintenance of CBR activities.

Community-Based Research Activities on the Island of Ireland

The Science Shop at Queen's University Belfast

This was established in 1988, based on models from the Netherlands, where the name literally translates as knowledge exchange. The science shop works with civil society organizations (CSOs) to develop research projects based on their research needs that are suitable for students within the university to carry out as part of their degree programs. Science shop research projects are therefore examples of cocreated research, with community organizations bringing their specific needs and knowledge, and students bringing their research training and skills. Organizations typically benefit from a piece of research that they do not have the resources to carry out, while students get the experience of doing research in a real-life situation, which benefits both their learning and their career development. The science shop is based within Academic and Student Affairs, and has 2.2 full-time equivalent (FTE) staff. Since 2007, this science shop has been funded by the Department of Employment and Learning through the Higher Education Innovation Funding (HEIF) scheme. It is funded by the department "[given] the absence of a dedicated Higher Education Active Community Fund in Northern Ireland and also the fact that the NI Science Shop . . . was widely regarded as an EU exemplar of best practice in Higher Education" (Department of Employment and Learning, 2010). During the last three years of HEIF funding, 320 projects were developed with 110 CSOs, of which 200 were completed. Over 400 students in total were involved in completing these research projects. A further round of funding for 2013–2016 was recently confirmed. While the science shop works with students right across the university, in practice more projects take place in environmental and social science disciplines than any other. To give an example, a group of undergraduate Social Policy students worked with the Forum for Action on Substance Abuse on potential links between substance abuse and suicide. Their report was brought to the Northern Ireland Assembly's Inquiry into the Prevention of Suicide and Self-Harm. Another example was a group of MSc Environmental Management students who worked with Belfast Hills Partnership to examine options for restoring quarries while minimizing the impact on biodiversity. Their conclusions will be used to prepare a funding case for restoring a quarry for mountain biking with potential for income generation. The science shop at Queen's University Belfast has also been involved in developing the field of public engagement with research at both UK and international levels. It has provided support and mentoring to CBR initiatives across Ireland, both informally and through European Commission (EC)-funded projects such as the Public Engagement with Research and Research Engagement with Society (PERARES) project.

Students Learning with Communities (SLWC) at Dublin Institute of Technology (DIT)

This program at DIT was set up in 2008 on the basis of a successful funding application to the HEA (Higher Education Authority)'s Strategic Innovation Fund (SIF). Two full-time coordinating staff were appointed for three years to develop the program. It built on a previous DIT pilot project, called the Community Learning Program. SLWC is based in the Directorate of Student Services, as part of the DIT Access and Civic Engagement Office. In 2011 the staffing level was reduced from 2.3 FTE to 1.3 as the three-year SIF funding came to an end. SLWC staff secured some additional funding from the EC as part of the four-year PERARES project, which aims to increase the involvement of civil society in research.

SLWC supports community-based learning, or service learning, which is process focused rather than outcome focused, as well as community-based research, which has a research output as the focus of the work. SLWC staff collaborates with a wide range of community partners in developing research ideas and concerns. Community research ideas are framed as broad questions, categorized by disciplines, and advertised to students and academic staff through the SLWC website (www.dit.ie/ace/slwc) and in regular e-mail updates. Individual students can apply (with the support of their supervisor) to undertake research in response to these community research ideas. A three-way meeting between the academic, student, and community partner is facilitated by SLWC staff to discuss and agree the detail of the research question and approach. Academics can also decide to work with a cohort of students on research questions from one or more community partners. As an Institute of Technology, DIT has programs in many applied subject areas, and students' research projects with communities can lead to a product concept or design as much as to a traditional thesis or research report. Since 2008, over 140 research projects have been undertaken by DIT students in response to questions from community partners. Examples of CBR projects in DIT include a PhD project in Product Design, jointly supervised with

Enable Ireland, to research and develop a design framework for user-centered collaboration by designing an alternative computer input device for people with disabilities; two master's thesis projects in Higher Education and Child, Family and Community Development in collaboration with AONTAS (the National Adult Learning Organisation), investigating supports needed by community and adult learners in order to access higher education; Chemistry undergraduate students comparing the relative effectiveness of different methods of testing for alcohol in breath and urine, with the Garda Road Safety Unit; and Tourism undergraduate students working with Slane Community Forum to research opportunities to regenerate the local community through tourism.

Community-Academic Research Links (CARL) at University College Cork (UCC)

CARL was established at UCC in 2006 and commenced student and community project work in 2010. It is based on the science shop community-based research model. and began as an academic-led volunteer initiative, largely within the School of Applied Social Studies. CARL is now part of the university's strategic plan (University College Cork, 2013), and work has begun to translate CARL into a university-wide community-based research initiative. As CARL is a volunteer initiative, with only a very small number of paid coordination hours, it has a limited capacity to undertake projects. Since 2010, CARL has completed research studies with 19 community and voluntary groups and 28 students, with 12 more projects ongoing. While CARL began its life as a science shop with the aim of meeting the research needs of community and voluntary groups, principally through student research dissertation work, it is no longer called a science shop (see Chapter 6 on science shops). The term did not "translate" well in the university since the sciences queried the name, and the humanities and social sciences felt excluded. This misunderstanding arose due to the more restrictive English-language meaning of the word "science," encompassing the physical and life sciences, compared to the more liberal German meaning of "*wissenschaft*," which comprises all domains of knowledge and knowledge production.

CARL is an interesting case study for the establishment of a CBR initiative in a period of fiscal crisis and a concomitant retrenchment of government investment in higher education. It indicates that with a committed group of individuals—community partners, academics, and administrators—who believe in the principles of civic engagement, widening access to the resources of the university and promoting students' critical engagement with the wider community beyond the campus, it is possible to progress CBR, even in the initial absence of a formal university mandate. Moreover, the support of the wider European science shop community, their resources and counsel, along with the advice of senior university policy-makers, can offer opportunities for creativity in the design and running of a CBR initiative.

One example of the contribution students can make to the community is illustrated by a CBR project between a Master of Social Work student and a cancer support charity (see O'Connor, 2013). Cork ARC Cancer Support service sought to provide information and support through a blog. Initially, the master's student did a review of the research evidence to establish whether there was support for the efficacy of such a blog. Following this review, a blog was created on a pilot basis by the student in WordPress and evaluated. At the end of the pilot the blog had 1,000 users a month, it is still running, and feedback from users has been very positive. CARL is now working with this group to further develop their use of technology through the research and development of a mobile app for evidence-informed diet plans for cancer patients.

Community Knowledge Exchange (CKE) at Dublin City University (DCU)

CKE is the title of the CBR-facilitating unit or science shop at DCU, launched in 2012. It is cross-disciplinary and comprises a "Knowledge Broker", who facilitates exchanges between academics, community partners, and a management team of three DCU academics. CKE takes a theoretical and practical approach, influenced by thinking in contemporary science communication and Science and Technology Studies, to facilitate co-construction of knowledge within the local community. "DCU in the Community" was founded following the university Civic Engagement Strategy's stated aim "To share knowledge through a sustainable university-community dialogue based on the principle of exchange and mutual learning." DCU in the Community is the "public outreach" campus of DCU, based in the heart of Ballymun, which is one of Dublin's more socially disadvantaged areas. By "matchmaking" DCU researchers with local societal issues, CKE facilitates CBR activities and instills a culture of engagement within teaching and learning practice within DCU itself. CKE is now a vital part of the output of DCU in the Community.

There have been several community initiatives in recent years at DCU. However, the first that might be recognized as a science shop project was *New Communities and Mental Health in Ireland: An Analysis*, published by DCU in 2008 in partnership with Cairde, a group that challenges health inequalities among ethnic minorities. This project identified specific mental health issues and needs of Ireland's migrant and ethnic communities. Since CKE's official opening in 2012, two projects have been completed from the BA in Communication Studies—a study of volunteers from Volunteer Ireland and a report on mobility issues for the Dublin 12 Disability Mainstream Access Project. Further studies from the Faculty of Humanities and Social Science and the BSc in Health and Society at DCU are due in 2014. The target is to have 12 projects completed by the end of 2015.

DCU has also positioned itself as Ireland's "University of Enterprise." This creates its own tensions, as social enterprises interact constantly with schools and faculties. A science shop's participatory ethos fostering dialogue among equals runs up against success stories from the for-profit sector. However, this was an important aspect of the origins of CKE—to embed itself into the heart of university strategy and facilitate links between the enterprise and not-for-profit sectors. All CKE research, however, is carried out exclusively for the not-for-profit sector. CKE is at the heart of active civic engagement but crucially does not preclude mutual benefit to society *and* economy.

Engaging People in Communities (EPIC) at the National University of Ireland, Galway (NUI Galway)

EPIC is part of the Community Knowledge Initiative (CKI) at NUI Galway and it coordinates the community-based research aspect of the work of CKI. Created in 2012, it is a relatively new area of activity within CKI, and follows on from initiatives in student volunteering (ALIVE—A Learning Initiative and the Volunteering Experience) (program) and service learning, which were established at the inception of CKI in the early 2000s. Through the student volunteering activities and service learning programs, solid and sustainable collaboration between the university and the wider community has been established, and this has provided an ideal basis on which to build the work of EPIC. As well as coordinating community-based research, EPIC is involved in the related areas of knowledge exchange and advocacy. As part of CKI, EPIC is core-funded by the university, employs one full-time member of staff, and operates on a university-wide basis. It is an important point of contact for students and staff throughout the university, who want to be involved in CBR. In addition, because EPIC is based in a center for community engagement, it is "community facing" and functions as a vital first point of contact for community-based organizations that wish to engage in collaborative research with the university. EPIC strives to be an effective mediator of relationships within the university and between the wider community and the university.

EPIC is guided in its work by the principles of community-based research exemplified by Ochocka et al. (2010, p. 3), who define this approach to research as being community situated, collaborative, and action orientated. EPIC has been greatly influenced by the science shop model and puts elements of the science shop approach into practice through community-based research carried out by students, for dissertation and/or course-work purposes. It also supports community-based research activities of staff, and through its coordination of public knowledge exchange events, it provides a forum for sharing knowledge on community-based research and advocacy. In this context, EPIC has established strong links with individual staff members, teaching programs, and research centers within the university that are committed to advocacy, action, and community-based approaches to research. These relationships form the basis on which EPIC is building collaborative partnerships within the university, to support community-based research. EPIC has also been forging relationships with a number of CSOs, and with projects in the areas of the rights of migrants and asylum seekers, biodiversity and land use, design of space in urban environments, and socially engaged arts.

Policy Contexts—Ireland and Northern Ireland

In terms of institutional practice, the above vignettes give insight into the momentum being built at the individual HEI level, but we can also point to policy on higher education within Ireland and Northern Ireland that has the potential to buttress and support the development of engagement in its broadest sense. In January 2011 the Irish Minister for Education launched the *National Strategy for Higher Education to 2030* (DES, 2011), known within the sector as the Hunt Report. This policy vision report places "engagement," in its many guises, on a par with research and teaching and learning in higher education in Ireland. A central tenet of the Hunt Report is "a vision of an Irish higher education sector that can successfully meet the many social, economic and cultural challenges that face us over the coming decades, and meet its key roles of teaching and learning, research, scholarship, and engagement with wider society" (2011, p. 4). One of the high-level research objectives stemming from this vision concerns increasing research activity in niche areas that "are aligned with and are a significant support for Irish national economic social and cultural needs" (2011, p. 2). Additionally, "Higher education research will need to connect to enterprise and society in new and imaginative ways to harness its potential for economic and social well-being, including a more effective approach to knowledge transfer and commercialization" (2011, p. 12).

The Hunt Report positions engagement on a par with research and teaching, but there is much that remains to be done at the operational level, as currently there is no requirement on HEIs to implement an engagement mission. While the report does not directly name CBR, we would argue that CBR is a core element of engagement as it presents a new and extremely effective way to address the societal impact of research. The Hunt Report is further supported by the *Higher Education System Performance Framework 2014–2016*, published in December 2013, which seeks "To maintain an open and excellent public research system focused on the Government's priority areas and the achievement of other societal objectives and to maximize research collaborations and knowledge exchange between and among public and private sector research actors" (Higher Education Authority, 2013, p. 2). Institutions could be required to allocate funding for posts to support collaborative research or community engagement initiatives. Several of the initiatives outlined in the vignettes above have had funding threats or have lost funding and/or staffing allocation in recent years, despite the stated policy vision and support for this work. From a legislative perspective, the Universities Act 1997 states that the objectives of a university shall be not only to "advance knowledge, but to also promote the cultural and social life of society and to promote learning in society more generally," with dissemination referred to as the method of sharing research outcomes (part III, 1997). However, many within higher education see the public as the audience for research dissemination, rather than as potential partners in the research process. So while policy vision in Ireland broadly offers support for CBR, as yet there is no requirement for CBR practices to be implemented within every HEI, or for designated funding to support CBR coordinators within individual institutions.

In Northern Ireland, drivers for CBR are framed by UK policy, where there is a strong political emphasis on public engagement, particularly in terms of public engagement with research. In 2009, the Department for Business, Innovation and Skills (BIS) published a key report examining the future of universities in a knowledge economy. This report offered a blueprint of the way forward for higher education, and was written in the context of the "more constrained public spending environment" (BIS, 2009, p. 3) of that time. Between 1997 and 2009, the UK government doubled investment in the research base, resulting in "more publications and citations per researcher and per pound of public funding than any of our major competitors" (BIS, 2009, p. 55). One of the central tenets of the strategy was to "ensure that we better understand and exploit the ways in which research can make greater economic and social impact" (BIS, 2009, p. 3). It establishes that "the government will seek to remove barriers to this kind of interaction and . . . will provide incentives for wider engagement" (2009, p. 67) via Research Councils UK funding and via the Research Excellence Framework, which have sought to build "a vision for a research culture that values, recognizes and supports public engagement" (RCUK, 2012).

While the focus on public engagement with research does not necessarily directly correlate with CBR, it can create an environment where it has an opportunity to develop. In practice, many of the drivers of public engagement policy development have been economic rather than social, and, indeed, more recently, policy papers issued under the UK coalition government have focused on engagement with business. The February 2012 Wilson review on university interaction with business acknowledged the role of social enterprise and small to medium enterprises (SMEs) in student work-related learning, but makes no reference to community interaction:

> The review does not include any consideration of the role that universities play in meeting the needs of the public sector, although the role of social enterprise in supporting charitable organizations is included in the context of enterprise education.
>
> (Wilson, 2012, p. 15)

While science and research program funding continues to be ring-fenced at £4.6 bn, the current focus at a policy level is almost exclusively on university-business interaction and on the potential economic benefits that may flow from such interactions.

Within Northern Ireland itself, in 2012, DELNI produced *Graduating to Success: A Higher Education Strategy for Northern Ireland*. This strategy emphasizes the importance of research, teaching, and engagement and sets out 16 projects under four guiding principles of responsiveness, quality, accessibility, and flexibility. The strategy also recommends that a systematic approach toward community engagement on a local, national, and international basis is adopted and embedded within universities. Institutions are encouraged to review their social and community engagement strategies and to adopt a systematic approach to such engagement, based on best practice throughout the UK and overseas. In particular, they are encouraged to use their skills and expertise to benefit and engage effectively with local communities (DELNI, 2014, p. 42).

There is broad policy support for the development of community-based research in higher education at a European level. The European Commission, through its Framework 7 Science in Society funding strand, has facilitated research into and capacity building for science shops and community-based research since 2001. The Horizon 2020 research program includes a strand on "Science with and for Society," which will continue to support the engagement of civil society organizations with the research sector. EC-funded projects such as Training and Mentoring of Science Shops (TRAMS) have supported capacity building for this work in research institutions and in civil society (De Bok, 2008). The *Science, Technology and Civil Society* (STACS) report (Gall et al., 2009) recommended the creation of networks of research and higher education institutions engaged in participatory research with society.

In particular, the PERARES project has supported the development of science shops across Ireland. PERARES aims to increase capacity for mechanisms to support public engagement in research, such as science shops, and increase the public's role in setting agendas for research (PERARES, 2014). PERARES has supported networking across Ireland as well as internationally. One of its goals was to set up a cross-European mentoring network for new science shops. Through funding meetings, travel costs, and ongoing mentoring by partners across the EU for the participating Irish HEIs, as well as peer mentoring by new science shops, PERARES facilitated increased contact among Irish HEIs on both sides of the border. In addition, it helped to support the international Living Knowledge Network, of which many Irish HEI staff are members, and offered two international conferences on CBR, which have acted as essential learning and networking events for Irish and other HEI staff.

Building on the learning from these projects, which emphasize the importance of networks and mentoring to the development of CBR, several support networks have emerged across the island of Ireland.

Developing Practice and Building Networks

At regional and international levels a number of networks have been established in the last two decades to support the practice of CBR and other civic engagement activities within HEIs. Some of these enact existing policy or advocate for policy to be created, so as to develop a fertile environment for strategies and practices to emerge. Many of these networks have created their own policy visions or charters, which the leadership of HEIs can sign up to and embed, in the absence of a specific national policy (see Escrigas et al., 2014; Watson et al., 2011).

Over a decade ago in Ireland, those involved in developing CBRs identified a need to create similar platform or network from which to develop civic engagement, through both top-down and bottom-up processes. The seed-funded Service Learning Academy, initiated in 2005, "generated collaborative conversations on the implications for civic engagement within higher education between academics, policy-makers, senior administrators, students and community" (McIlrath and Lyons, 2009, p. 23), and it was facilitated by four HEIs, namely DIT, NUI Maynooth, DCU, and NUI Galway. Later, through a consultative process, seed funding awarded by the HEA allowed for the development of Campus Engage in 2007, under a project entitled "Civic Engagement, Student Volunteering and Active Citizenship." Campus Engage was a collaboration between another set of five Irish HEIs, namely DCU, NUI Galway (lead partner), NUI Maynooth, University of Limerick, and University College Dublin. The funds awarded by the HEA were matched by each of the five HEIs, and a key objective was to promote and support civic engagement in Irish higher education. Its activities included an international conference on civic engagement, a national conference on student volunteering, a survey of civic engagement activities in Irish higher education, the hosting of seminars and international scholars, and financing a seed-funding scheme to support civic engagement activities in Irish higher education. Having been awarded renewed HEA funding in 2012, Campus Engage is now located in the Irish Universities Association (IUA) at NUI Galway, which represents a neutral, national, and strategic home from which to mainstream civic engagement. The network is representative of all HEIs on the island of Ireland, with 17 HEIs having members on the steering committee. These members were nominated by HEI presidents, and represent a range of engagement activities, including CBR. For this second phase of Campus Engage, invitations were sent to a wide range of HEI staff, community partners, and student representatives, to meet to discuss how to build engagement nationally, and identify priority tasks that would be undertaken by working groups representing all stakeholders. The appointment of a full-time coordinator for Campus Engage in summer 2013 has proved to be a major support for this work.

Following discussion among Irish partners involved in the PERARES project at all-Ireland level, the Irish Network for Community-Engaged Research and Learning (INCERL) was established in 2011 by HEI coordinators of CBL (Community Based Learning)/CBR initiatives. Although this network has no funding, coordinators of CBL and CBR meet several times a year, primarily to support each other as practitioners of civic engagement. INCERL's main priorities are to address practice, policy, and research/scholarship in community-based research and learning, and members of the group have been involved in several collaborative presentations and publications. While there is considerable crossover in membership between INCERL and Campus Engage, this is seen as a positive factor in the networking process and the building of a critical mass. There are plans to replicate the mentoring model established within PERARES across Ireland through the

Campus Engage working groups. These mentoring and networking opportunities will help to foster the development of practice in CBR in both new and experienced Irish HEIs.

Within the UK, great strides have been made to cluster people and HEIs together to articulate and practice public engagement through collaborative activities and networks. Funders have made an explicit commitment to public engagement via the "Concordat for Public Engagement" (2012) and have encouraged HEIs to make a similar commitment by signing up to the "Manifesto for Public Engagement" (NCCPE, 2012). Funders have also put in place a range of resources to encourage and enable faculties to participate in research, which will have a social or economic impact. For example, Research Councils UK (RCUK), the strategic partnership of the seven research councils, has developed guidance for researchers to help them understand the routes to economic and societal impacts in the form of "Pathways to Impact" (RCUK, 2012). Alongside the Wellcome Trust and the national research funding councils, RCUK also co-funded the Beacons for Public Engagement (2012) and the National Co-Ordinating Centre for Public Engagement (NCCPE) (2012), both of which seek to support and embed culture change in UK HEIs. More recently, RCUK has funded eight Public Engagement with Research Catalysts across the UK (2012). In addition, the latest round of research assessment, the 2014 Research Assessment Framework, has research impact as one of its major strands (see Chapter 7 by Manners and Duncan for further detail on UK initiatives and networks).

Concluding Comments

Within this chapter we have explored the key principles of CBR, given examples of its practice on the island of Ireland through five HEI vignettes, outlined policy and vision at national and European levels, and discussed the availability of funding and the evolution of networks. We have presented CBR from the perspective of five HEIs located on the island of Ireland. There is room for further scholarship in this growing area of research practice, from a range of perspectives, including that of community partners as well as HEIs. We contend that we are now at a crossroads with regard to development and growth. The potential is there to turn solid and visionary national policy into implementation. However, we still face challenges in terms of resources for the enactment of policy at the local HEI level. There is a need to develop posts in each HEI to facilitate the work of CBR, delineate key performance indicators, and review progression criteria that recognize and reward staff for CBR activities. These requirements are set against a higher education system in Ireland that is moving through a time of flux and change and operating under deep financial constraints. However, if higher education cannot demonstrate its societal value, then what is the overall purpose of the academy? Higgins (2012, p. 1) presents us with a moral choice, "to be part of a passive consensus that accepts an insufficient and failed model of life and economy, for example, or to seek to recover the possibility of alternative futures." CBR is one way to respond to this challenge, because it is conducive to outward-facing HEIs and collaborative research activity that can lead to societal transformation.

CHAPTER 9

Community-Based Research in Australian Universities: Reflections on National Policy, Institutional Strategy, and Research Practice

Michael Cuthill

Context

There is no question, from both anecdotal and university reports, that Australian universities currently contribute much to industry, communities, and public policy through diverse interactions between science and society (Davis, 2013). However, this activity is not well articulated, and there are increasing references to missed opportunities for economic and social development. National policy direction is lacking, and rarely is there a clear strategic institutional framework within individual universities to guide such interactions (Cuthill, 2011). These policy and institutional deficits are evidenced downstream through capacity and motivational issues across the Australian higher education workforce (Advisory Council on Intellectual Property (ACIP), 2012). In this context, it is argued that the innovation potential of Australian universities is not being effectively utilized to support socioeconomic development (Table 9.1).

Community-based research (CBR), as one expression of the interactions between science and society, has much to offer within this national context (see Table 9.2 for description of other science and society interactions at one university).

However, it is difficult to explicitly identify where CBR activity is situated within Australian higher education policy and university strategy. There is very limited understanding of the extent, quality, or impact of it within Australian universities. As such, CBR is essentially invisible in Australian higher education except at the individual project level, where it is regularly reported, but thinly spread across various disciplinary journals.

This has led me to primarily base this review of CBR in Australian universities on my reflections, after more than 20 years of working in this area, while also drawing on a limited number of related reports.

Introduction

In order to appreciate why CBR is virtually invisible in Australian universities, it is first necessary to have some broad understanding of the national policy and institutional contexts within which CBR is situated. In essence, these are the two key components of a "system" that supports or constrains interactions between science and society (including CBR) in Australian universities. Ideally, national policy should direct institutional strategies and the diverse range of science and society interactions. In turn, in a self-reinforcing process, evaluation and reporting of such activities should feed back to inform institutional strategies and ongoing national policy development (Table 9.1).

However, in Australia, this system is fragmented due to disciplinary, sectoral, and political factors. The remainder of this chapter will explore in more detail each component within this system—national policy, institutional strategy, CBR practice—and in conclusion, present a misconception, a question and some possible actions.

National "Science and Society" Policy

In recent years, there has been greater government and industry attention on the interactive processes that serve to link science and society, with much emphasis on "engagement," "collaboration," and "partnership" between Australian universities, and public, private, and community sectors, both nationally and overseas (Coaldrake and Stedman, 2013; Commonwealth of Australia, 2012; ACIP, 2012; Bradley et al., 2008). This is not a new development. Such a move was foreshadowed by the Association of Commonwealth Universities (2001, p. i) well over a decade ago:

> Increasingly, academics will accept that they share their territory with other knowledge professionals. The search for formal understanding itself, long central to the academic life, is moving rapidly beyond the borders of disciplines and their locations inside universities. Knowledge is being keenly pursued in the context of its application and in a dialogue of practice with theory through

a network of policy-advisers, companies, consultants, think-tanks and brokers as well as academics and indeed the wider society.

However, recent Australian policy debate around such processes has been drawn thinly across five interrelated but distinct focus areas (Cuthill et al., 2014):

1. research commercialization,
2. university community engagement,
3. third stream funding,
4. knowledge transfer, and
5. widening participation and access.

None of these five focus areas has provided a solid policy foundation for the broad concept of how "science" collaborates, engages, and partners with "society."

A recent conceptual paper (Cuthill et al., 2014), focuses on *knowledge exchange*, an umbrella concept that encompasses the diversity of approach in those recent policy discussions. Such approaches are defined through four underlying principles (Davis, 2013; Cuthill, 2012; Australian Universities Community Engagement Alliance (AUCEA) 2006; Department of Education, Science and Training (DEST) 2006; Boyer, 1990).

Table 9.1 Four principles underpinning knowledge exchange processes

1. It is scholarly based.
2. It is genuinely collaborative.
3. It is mutually beneficial.
4. It contributes to the public good.

As Cuthill et al. (2014, p. 25) describe,

In practice, this concept [knowledge exchange] encompasses both scholarly interaction with industry focusing on the valorization of intellectual property; and more diverse forms of scholarly engagement involving public, private and community sector stakeholders, which contribute to economic and social development.

However, while dialogue relating to the broad concept of knowledge exchange has been on the national agenda for several decades now, Australian policy in this area is still not clearly articulated and remains fragmented and underdeveloped (Grattan Institute, 2013). As Intzesiloglou et al. (2011, p. 1) have argued (in a European context), while "... the benefits of knowledge exchange between universities and enterprises have been documented in various cases, there is still a long way to go considering the identification of the best-suited policy framework for the enhancement of this process, on national and regional levels."

The lack of clear policy direction as to how these knowledge exchange collaborations might be recognized, implemented, and resourced within higher education institutions has constrained the development of appropriate institutional responses within individual universities. Without an institutional strategy, the fragmentation continues in the practice environment, where a lack of project management and collaboration skills among Australian academics, and limited motivation to engage in collaborative knowledge exchange processes have been identified (Universities Australia, 2013; ACIP, 2012; Bexley et al., 2011).

Institutional Strategies and Capacity Issues

Ten years ago Gibbons et al. (1994, p. 11) observed that, "Universities are coming to recognize that they are now only one type of player, albeit still a major one, in a vastly expanded knowledge production process." To effectively respond to this changed environment, Australian universities need to clearly articulate and plan for the new emphasis on collaboration through science and society initiatives, which they still have not done.

Perhaps the most common title adopted within Australian higher education institutions, to cover the broad palette of science and society activity, has been *university community engagement*. However, this title has suffered through a lack of clear definition, with a recent paper identifying 48 terms that cover interrelated or overlapping "engagement" concepts (Cuthill, 2011, pp. 22–23). Attempts have been made to build some clarity around the university community engagement term. The Australian Universities Community Engagement Alliance (AUCEA, 2006, p. 1) took an early lead in their first position paper, arguing that

> Engaged universities are essential for Australia's economic and social future. While universities interact with their communities in a range of ways, university-community engagement specifically implies collaborative relationships leading to productive partnerships that yield mutually beneficial outcomes.

Around the same time, the business sector also took a stand in supporting stronger engagement with the university sector. The Business/Higher

Education Round Table (2006, p. 3) identified engagement as a core business for universities, "the *Third Mission* that complements the mission of teaching and the mission of research." This support provided momentum for an AUCEA-supported three-year project to develop a benchmarking tool for university community engagement (Langworthy, 2009). However, subsequent national take-up of the benchmarks has not happened. In a parallel project, 29 of Australia's 39 publically funded universities contributed to development of a University Engagement Quality Management framework (Cuthill, 2008, p. 31):

> This project sought to bring together the diverse perspectives of Australian academics and other university staff with an interest in engagement, to identify (a) common principles which underpin high quality university engagement, and (b) a quality framework which provides direction to Australian universities when developing institutional frameworks and processes for engagement.

An Australian University Quality Agency (AUQA, 2008, p. 3) report from this same period describes community engagement as

> ... encompassing all forms of interaction between universities and their various external communities, including engagement with regional partners, industry, government, alumni, Indigenous communities, community organisations, and other education sectors.

This broad description presented by AUQA suggests that university community engagement is a key approach for doing "business" in Australian universities.

As a result of this and other activity, it has been common over the past ten years to find that individual universities have appointed senior engagement managers and developed strategies relevant to their specific institutional mission, history, and strengths. However, these are generally contained in internal documents and not publicly accessible. What has been evidenced are institutional specific approaches to engagement, which have developed into diverse partnerships in terms of disciplinary and sectoral focus, depth of relationship, stakeholder motivation (e.g., commercial, public good, political, etc.), and duration, all based on varying interpretations of community, both conceptually and geographically. While there have been no formal assessments, it is possible to surmise that adherence to the four knowledge exchange principles (set out in Table 9.1) has been *ad hoc*.

Two case study publications directed at institutional-level engagement are of note. First, in 2005, Winter, Wiseman, and Muirhead published results from a university community engagement study involving nine universities in the state of Victoria. Their report found that all Victorian universities were directing attention toward university community engagement but they argued that there was a need to develop "... strategies that nurture such initiatives" (Winter et al., 2005, p. 7). While their benefits statement lacked an empirical basis, their findings offered perhaps the first suggestion that the educational, social, and economic benefits of an engaged university provide a strong rationale for government recognition and investment in strengthening this area. In addition, they found that engagement initiatives were seen to be at risk from increased competitiveness and commercialization within the higher education sector, coupled with ongoing threats of resource cuts from key funding agencies. The national policy and institutional strategy context has changed little over the subsequent nine years.

The second case study involved policy research I conducted for the vice-chancellor while at the University of Queensland (UQ), a research-intensive "sandstone" university. This two-year project focused on an audit and review of engagement, equity and outreach, and policy recommendations. Results subsequently informed development of the UQ Strategic Plan (2008–2013), where engagement was identified as one of three strategic priority areas, and ten of the 25 strategic objectives were under engagement. A comprehensive UQ engagement typology (Table 9.2) was developed, which responds to the previously quoted AUQA (2008, p. 3) requirement of describing "all forms of interaction between universities and their various external communities..."

Table 9.2 Priorities and constraints under which research users and producers work

Priorities and constraints	Research producers	Research users
Knowledge	Depth	Breadth
Documents	Long, prose	Short, multiple headings, dot points
Time frames	Medium–long	Short–medium
Outputs	Few and far between	Regular
Responsibility	Individuals and freedom	External parties and processes
Rigor vs. pragmatism	Rigor	Pragmatism
Authorship	Personal	Usually anonymous

The UQ engagement typology included "research," "equity and outreach," "community service," teaching and learning," and "fundraising, marketing & networking" (see Cuthill, 2011, p. 30, for more detail). Four of the key recommendations from this project that were subsequently implemented are as follows:

- identification of engagement as one of three priority areas in the UQ Strategic Plan;
- clarity of conceptualization and implementation through articulation of a university engagement operational plan;
- an executive-level leadership appointment and appropriate administrative structures; and
- quality assurance—monitoring and reporting systems for the operational plan.

However, two recommendations that are particularly relevant to CBR were not implemented. First, an *engaged research capacity-building* program, developed in response to staff requests recorded during the audit project, was not considered necessary. Second, profiling and recognition requirements identified by staff were not supported. These included relevant awards, marketing and communications strategies, and staff promotions and career pathways. Subsequent identification in a 2012 report (ACIP, 2012) of a lack of project management and collaboration skills, and the limited motivation of researchers to engage in collaborative knowledge exchange processes suggest ignoring these recommendations was an oversight that, according to the ACIP report, now appears to be applicable across all Australian universities.

In early 2013, the Regional University Network Engagement Working Group (RUN, 2013, p. 4) developed a conceptual framework that illustrates

> ... the process of leveraging university assets (students, staff and facilities) through operational activities (teaching and learning, research and service) centred on an engagement paradigm to produce economic, social, cultural, environmental, and individual "value" outcomes to the specific region and more broadly for Australia. These value outcomes, in a self-reinforcing, reciprocal and mutually beneficial process, provide feedback to support the university core mission.

This conceptual framework offers perhaps the most succinct and sophisticated overview of how science and society interact in Australian universities (Table 9.2).

While the university community engagement rhetoric has been clearly evident in all Australian universities over the past five to ten years, the move from rhetoric to reality varies tremendously, and there now appears to be a waning of enthusiasm for this term. Even the Australian Universities Community Engagement Alliance changed its name in 2013 to Engagement Australia (EA), perhaps as a move to encompass more broadly the diverse range of interactions between science and society. However, while EA has a strong focus on engagement within the humanities, arts, and social sciences, its level of engagement with the biophysical and natural sciences is unclear. It appears that the integration of concepts of community engagement into mainstream university activity in Australian universities still remains an elusive institutional aspiration. Insofar as it occurs, it still appears to be predominantly instigated at the individual or project level, around specific areas of interest. Little is understood or reported as regards either the quality or impact of the initiatives being implemented, and there are few empirical data on its impact in helping achieve an institution's mission, or in facilitating benefits to society.

Science and Society Interactions in Practice: A Case Study of CBR in Australia

The preceding two sections of this chapter have painted a rather gloomy picture of the national policy and institutional strategies that might be expected to direct and support the diversity of science and society interactions, and by association CBR initiatives. As noted previously, the combination of the policy and institutional strategy deficit has led to a practice within Australian universities that is characterized by a lack of collaborative skills and limited motivation of academics to effectively engage in the broad diversity of science and society interactions (Universities Australia, 2013; ACIP, 2012). Despite this situation I believe that there is considerable strength, diversity, and quality within CBR practice in Australia.

A review of recent editions of Australia's two key university engagement journals, *Gateways: International Journal of Community Research and Engagement* and *The Australasian Journal of University-Community Engagement*, suggests that there is a thriving CBR practice environment in Australia across various disciplinary and/or sectoral areas, for example, health, cultural studies, social justice, visioning/futures, development studies, education, and natural resource management. However, links between various project-level CBR initiatives seem tenuous at best, with Engagement Australia appearing as the most likely networking opportunity. To improve this situation, there is an immediate need for more systematic description of the CBR environment in Australia if support for, and quality of, CBR is to be enhanced.

If a better understanding of CBR can be established, stronger network development could support CBR in Australia through various advocacy, scholarship (of CBR), and "industry" guidelines in areas such as

- institutional structures and responses,
- quality standards,
- underlying principles/values,

- staff rewards and recognition,
- staff/student training,
- impact and reporting,
- curriculum development;
- CBR knowledge systems—conferences, websites, publications, workshops, online forums, and training.

These guidelines do not conflict with Australian higher education policy aspirations, which identify research collaborations and partnerships as a key focus for the broad scope of contemporary Australian university research. The challenge of raising the profile of CBR, from the individual or project level, to play a more prominent role within universities remains.

Arguably, the concept of "working together" in research occurs most effectively in either a research center or institute. Such structures provide the levels of support required to initiate and sustain broad, mid- to large-scale collaborative research. These structures do not exist in Australian universities in support of CBR. A Google search for "community research center Australia" identified only one university center and one (nationally funded) cooperative research center with the word "community" in their titles. There were no results for "community-based research." Obviously, some Australian research centers will incorporate a community research focus, perhaps somewhat hidden within their broader mission, but this poor profiling contributes to the overall lack of visibility of CBR in Australia.

During 2005–2012, I held the position of Director, University of Queensland (UQ) Boilerhouse, Community Engagement Centre. During this time, the center was the only broad-based (as opposed to sectoral-focused) community research center in Australia, with around 70 percent of work effort directly focusing on CBR. The center generally employed between 15 and 25 full-time equivalent (FTE) staff. We returned nearly $3 for every dollar of operational funding invested by UQ, plus substantial in-kind support from research partners. An impressive collection of academic, government, and public reports was produced.

The center's diverse range of programs all operated from a scholarly basis. For example, it hosted some 1,300 young people from low socioeconomic backgrounds over years, who participated in curricula based after school programs such as digital music and film-making, nutrition and cooking, women's leadership, financial literacy, sport and health, and graphic design. Families, teachers, and service agencies were also involved in these programs.

Examples of the breadth of CBR practice included projects relating to culturally and linguistically diverse communities, senior citizens, youth at risk, education pathways, community planning, lifelong learning, strategic regional planning for nongovernmental organizations, regional collaboration building, mental health, and integrated service delivery. The center also focused on the scholarship of engagement (Boyer, 1996) as part of an explicit center evaluation and reflective practice program (e.g., Cuthill et al., 2011; Cuthill and Brown, 2010; Cuthill, 2010; Scull and Cuthill, 2010; Cuthill and Schmidt, 2008). Broader description of the work of the UQ Boilerhouse is presented in various case study papers (e.g., Cuthill, 2010; Muirhead and Woolcock, 2008; Watson, 2007).

Relationship development with diverse communities was a core focus of all Boilerhouse center activity. For example, it entered into a co-location agreement with SeniorNet, an organization of 300 senior citizens, which provides training and social opportunities based around information and communications technology (ICT). SeniorNet took up (at no cost) 50 percent occupancy of the Boilerhouse computer room and use of the university IT infrastructure. Other agencies also co-located at the center at various times, including Red Cross, Sport and Recreation, and some local government workers. These arrangements continued to provide a solid basis for ongoing research partnerships, even after I left that university and the center was closed, further highlighting the longer-term value of relationship-based scholarship.

The success of Boilerhouse is further reflected through invitations to staff and me to make presentations on the work of the center in Great Britain and in various countries of continental Europe, North America, South Africa, and Southeast Asia. Both internal and external reviews of the Boilerhouse, over a seven-year period (2005–2012), unanimously reported the center a success from both university and community perspectives. In light of the positive scholarly, institutional, and community outcomes we achieved at the center, I am often asked what contributed to the success of the UQ Boilerhouse, particularly in light of the many challenges discussed previously (Cuthill, 2012, p. 93). Below, I posit some of the key factors in its success:

- influential, internal and external supporters and champions;
- good timing ("engagement" had been a topic of discussion, from 2005 when I took up my appointment, both in the Australian higher education sector and at UQ);
- a clearly articulated strategic plan and vision, agreed to by both internal and external stakeholders, which linked both the UQ mission and community needs;
- appropriate resources and institutional commitment to implement the center's mission;

- appropriate academic and public reporting of center outcomes;
- articulation of a value statement through evaluation reports that described project outputs and process outcomes for both the university and the community;
- hard work and dedication from a committed group of people who supported center projects over the past years, including a lively, dedicated, and diverse disciplinary mix of center staff.

As the Boilerhouse case study indicates, CBR can positively respond to traditional academic requirements (e.g., publication, funding success, and community service) even in a research-intensive university.

Conclusions: A Misconception, a Question, and Some Possible Actions

Misconception: Community-Based Research Is Easy!

In contradiction of what seems to be a relatively common perception, the requirements for collaborative CBR processes extend academics well past their conventional research training. Examples of priorities and constraints between academics and research participants involved in collaborative research are identified in a recently published paper (Cuthill et al., 2014). These have relevance in highlighting factors that may create tension within CBR collaborations.

The capacity of individual academics to facilitate a successful CBR collaboration in light of these factors relies on skill sets and knowledge not normally taught in "Research 101" classes. Negotiation, conflict resolution, priority setting, project planning and management, effective communications, and consensus building, all collectively add a whole new process dimension to the CBR practitioner's work. The best community-based researchers have a combination of skills, knowledge, and experience across research, project management, and facilitation.

A further challenge is that pathways for nurturing CBR scholars are difficult to locate at undergraduate, postgraduate, or research higher degree levels. This seems to be an area that academics stumble upon, rather than having clearly articulated steps through which they can progress. For early career academics, "... there is little opportunity or incentive to undertake knowledge exchange activity which incorporates time intensive relationship development and collaboration" (Cuthill et al., 2014). Indeed, at times there are direct contradictions between a university's requirements associated with traditional teaching and research activity, and the resource investments required for genuine CBR, built on mutual trust and shared understandings. As a result of increased teaching loads, lack of mentors, skill and knowledge deficits, and no defined professional pathways, academics struggle to find the time or resources to build a successful CBR career.

A Question: Are Academics Ready to Work Collaboratively and Share Power?

CBR directly addresses power-laden considerations of "whose knowledge counts," through its explicit intent to acknowledge and integrate different forms of "knowing" into the knowledge production process. These different "knowledge systems" are based in diverse, but overlapping contexts, for example,

- individual local knowledge, drawing on the lived experiences of an individual in a place;
- collective cultural knowledge (e.g., Indigenous Australians have an understanding of natural resource management approaches built on tens of thousands of years' application);
- political knowledge, encompassing a broad concept of those in positions of power who are able to influence decision-making processes, thereby sidestepping formalized knowledge production;
- scientific or expert knowledge, being the peer-reviewed knowledge produced through scientific research.

Involving diverse knowledge systems in the knowledge production process is challenging. Here we are directly involved in the messiness of the real world, experiencing firsthand the oftentimes contradictory agendas, politics, personalities, and time frames of different stakeholders. Individuals and organizations within a problem domain will likely have different perspectives, based on their different histories, cultures, or goals. However, each source contributes something different whereby the whole is much greater than the sum of the parts.

Such an approach looks to address epistemological questions as to how different perspectives and different "types" of knowledge are brought together, cross-referenced, and validated (Cuthill, 2012; Gibbons et al, 1994). Sharing power in the research process can be challenging for scholars, who are brought up in a system that has long positioned them as the expert producers of knowledge. In contrast, involving people from diverse knowledge systems in the knowledge creation process identifies scholars as just one stakeholder among many knowledge producers in a new, more fluid and interdependent approach.

Actions to Strengthen CBR Policy and Practice in Australia

Describing the current context for CBR in Australia provides a starting point for both dialogue and action. If community-based research is to achieve its full potential, then a clear strategy is required, something more substantial and interactive than the individual reflections presented here. To start the discussion, I have identified seven steps that I believe will help progress CBR in Australia.

First, identify the stakeholders involved within the broad concepts of science and society, and CBR in Australia, and start a dialogue. There is a need to better understand the scope of scholarship that has moved toward collaborative research approaches, including across the natural and biophysical sciences, and the arts, humanities, and social sciences.

Second, identify and describe the strength, diversity, and value of CBR in Australia. Community-based research is now conducted by diverse disciplines working in public policy development, industry research and development (R&D), environmental management, health, social justice, and many more applied research processes. The potential in bringing together learning around science and society initiatives, from across disciplines and sectors, remains as yet relatively unexplored.

Third, articulate and argue the socioeconomic benefits of investing in CBR (Universities Australia, 2013). The RUN framework provides a conceptual framework for such activity. While discussion around economic benefits from linking science and industry is relatively common (Australian Academy of Technology Sciences and Engineering, 2013), the total contribution across economic, social, cultural, and environmental value areas still needs to be better understood, and, importantly, better communicated.

Fourth, work together (a community of practice?) toward a national "science and society" policy, and development of appropriate institutional responses that support CBR. There are numerous networks, research groups, and projects that adopt a science and society approach. As noted, these are spread rather thinly across diverse disciplines and sectors. Much of this effort might already comply with the four principles underpinning knowledge exchange processes (Table 9.1). If so, there is sense in exploring how we might develop more effective and smarter networking across these groups, to build a critical mass of support for clearly articulated national policy.

Fifth, develop the capacity and motivation of scholars to conduct CBR. There is a need to identify and develop appropriate training opportunities and pathways for undergraduate, postgraduate, and research higher degree students. The next generation of CBR scholars will require appropriate skills, knowledge, time, and resources to conduct high-quality, high-impact CBR. Academic career and promotion pathways for CBR scholars must also be addressed to keep these students motivated once they have completed their studies. Articulation of a broad set of staff attributes, required for undertaking science and society initiatives including CBR, should be developed for use in staff position descriptions, and translated to promotions and/or tenure criteria.

Sixth, raise the profile of CBR through increased reporting of high-quality, high-impact community-based research. CBR moves away from traditional approaches to scholarship. As such, it continues to be viewed with some degree of suspicion in the academy. However, better profiling of the diverse initiatives occurring within the academy, and the associated socioeconomic benefits, will help raise understanding of such research as legitimate and valuable scholarship. Arguably, issues relating to CBR theory development, methodology, quality, and impact still need to be better articulated and more broadly debated.

Seventh, change national funding guidelines to recognize the interdisciplinary and multi-sectoral nature of science and society initiatives. Scholarship that is based on collaboration must be looked at differently from more traditional disciplinary-based approaches. Currently, national funding categories are identified under a discipline or sectoral focus (despite increasing emphasis on collaborations and cross-disciplinary research proposals). This leaves little opportunity for arguing the value of the interdisciplinary, process-orientated approaches that most CBR adopts. While Australian funding assessments remain focused on disciplines, there is little incentive for academics to make funding submissions based on multidisciplinary, collaborative approaches.

There is a serious contradiction here, when, as noted, major higher education reports over the past number of years have emphasized the need for academics to come out from their ivory towers and engage with their diverse communities. This call for greater collaboration needs to be actioned through the creation of appropriate opportunities to access national competitive funds.

In conclusion, the international literature on knowledge exchange and related concepts has blossomed, all with an explicit focus on partnership, collaboration, and engagement with external partners, where universities are identified as one stakeholder among many knowledge producers in a new, more fluid and interdependent approach to scholarship. As a result, calls for "new" kinds of universities that are responsive to the needs of society, and adopt collaborative approaches to their scholarship, are increasing. Community-based research is one of the tools for implementing these calls. International experience suggests that developing national knowledge exchange policies and institutional strategies are challenging tasks, but achievable. If implemented, they will provide a policy and practice framework that enables CBR to provide added "value" to the university mission, while supporting sustainable community development.

However, in Australia, the broad concept of knowledge exchange, encompassing those initiatives that effectively connect science and society, remains on the periphery of mainstream academia, despite the rhetoric that positions it as integral to a university mission (Bradley et al., 2008). Without national policy direction and appropriate support, the current university business model, already under pressure from government cutbacks, is unlikely to be able to respond constructively and consistently to either the collaborative knowledge exchange agenda, or the implementation of community-based research in Australia.

CHAPTER 10

Organizing Culture Change through Community-Based Research

Scott J. Peters and Maria Avila

Community-based research (CBR) has instrumental potential as a method for solving social and technical problems, facilitating learning, and advancing knowledge and theory in a variety of disciplines and fields. When it is not just based in communities but also authentically participatory, it has an additional political potential as a means for enacting and pursuing key democratic values and ideals, and for developing leadership and power. The challenge for CBR practitioners and theorists is to work out ways to realize CBR's *full* potential. In this chapter, we will explore our conviction that CBR's full instrumental and political potential can only be realized and sustained through the difficult work of institutionalizing democratic organizing principles and practices. This requires us to do more than simply practice CBR methods in public engagement projects. It requires us to pursue *culture change* within and beyond our colleges and universities. Paradoxically, the kind of culture change it requires can only be achieved and sustained through organizing.

In what follows, we begin by naming three main aspects of culture within (and beyond) higher education that we seek to change. We follow this by noting an impressive but also sobering historical example of organizing culture change through CBR that Scott has discovered in his research of the "extension" work of land-grant colleges and universities (the word extension is, of course, deeply problematic; see Freire (1974)). We then turn to an account of Maria's organizing work during the years she served as director of the Center for Community Based Learning at Occidental College in Los Angeles, California. We conclude by offering a few key lessons and questions we carry with us as we continue our efforts to organize culture change through CBR.

Culture Change

Culture is a complex and deeply contested concept. For the purposes of this chapter, we use the word to refer to widely shared patterns of beliefs, values, attitudes, behaviors, and practices. Our emphasis on culture *change* is linked to and flows from our critique of the dominant culture of academic institutions. Our critique is centered on problems that hinder the realization of ideals and values that we associate with a view of democracy as both a way of life and a kind of work. As we see it, the work of democracy engages people from all walks of life in meaningful opportunities to come together across lines of difference to name, consider, and address public issues and problems in ways that enable them to advance their self-interests and common interests, as well as larger public interests (see Boyte, 2004).

As we have experienced it, we find three main problems with the dominant culture of academic institutions that need to be changed if these institutions are to make positive contributions to the work of democracy:

First, teaching and research tend to be pursued by academics in ways that are disconnected from ecologies of place, and out of relationship with external publics and other academics. Or, alternatively, they are pursued in ways that involve only thin, transactional, and short-term relationships with selected external groups that are treated as clients and customers of academic expertise and services. This pattern of behavior is in part based on patterns of beliefs, values, and attitudes about the position scholars and scientists should take in the work of democracy: namely, one that is detached, disinterested, irresponsible, and unaccountable, above or alongside civic life (with the exception of technical assistance and service provision). The defense of this position has both epistemological and political dimensions (see Peters et al., 2010).

Second, people's schedules tend to be packed with an endless stream of activities that are not intentionally and strategically connected, or are only strategic in an individual résumé or career-building way (e.g., students positioning themselves to get jobs, faculty positioning themselves for tenure and promotion). Relatedly, there is little encouragement and support for public reflection and evaluation of the purposes and significance of the activities in which people engage.

Third, dominant forms of politics and leadership in academic institutions do not encourage and support an ethic and practice of full participation (Sturm et al., 2011) Shared governance is talked about a lot, but rarely practiced. Further, politics tends to be viewed as an evil to avoid at all costs, or as something that can and should be replaced by science (see Crick, 1992; Fischer, 1990).

Changing the culture of academic institutions in ways that address these problems cannot be achieved through moral exhortations, wishful thinking, or protests. It requires the strategic and patient development of public relationships, and of leadership committed to cocreating new knowledge and power with others through positive, productive, and deliberative forms of politics. This is the main work of organizing, as we understand it. This is also where CBR and organizing can be fruitfully interwoven. Culture change requires organizing, and organizing requires CBR. And it is only when organizing and CBR are pursued for both instrumental problem-solving and cultural and political transformation purposes that their full potential can be realized. To sustain this kind of work over time requires more than the development of and training in "best practices." It requires efforts to legitimize and institutionalize democratic organizing principles and practices.

We want to acknowledge that a different type of culture change is already well under way in academic institutions, and that it underpins and reinforces the existing culture that we are interested in changing. This different type of culture change is not always or only the product of intentional organizing (see Newfield, 2008). It is also a result of complex global forces such as neoliberalism that are restructuring many systems and institutions. We want to acknowledge that the latter two of the three problems with academic culture that we named above are present in the dominant culture of American society as well. What we face, therefore, is not a struggle between a "bad" academic culture and a "good" community culture. Each has problems, just as each also has strengths.

We mention these realities and are mindful of them in order to avoid being overly romantic and naïve about what is involved in successfully organizing positive, democratic culture change, and legitimizing and institutionalizing democratic organizing principles and practices in colleges and universities. Those who pursue this work face many serious challenges. They are up against strong countercurrents and trends, both on campuses and in communities. Yet, there are many historical and contemporary examples of organizing for culture change through CBR that have made and are making a difference. We need to consider and learn from them. To that end, we turn now to two such examples. We begin with a little-known historical example that is both impressive and sobering.

Peters—A Historical Example

Discussions of CBR, contextualized science, and higher education's civic mission and public engagement work are often approached and discussed—wrongly, in our view—as ideas that are completely new and without precedent. They often include a discursive move that draws a stark line of difference between the present and the past—a move that effectively erases from the historical record the democratic aspirations and work of women and men who came before us. I found such a move in the following passage from a draft of the prospectus the editors wrote for the book you are now reading:

> Science does not just travel one way from the university to society as in the past, simply disseminating knowledge. Rather, it is now much more likely to be a two-way process where social needs influences scientific research and where we are beginning to value socially robust knowledge even in the most traditional contexts.

When I read this passage it caught my attention and gave me a sense of *déjà vu*. It sounded strikingly familiar, like I'd read it somewhere before. And in essence, I had. I'd read the same general idea in the following paragraph from *The People's Colleges*, a history of Cornell University's extension work in New York State by Ruby Green Smith that was originally published in 1949:

> There is vigorous reciprocity in the Extension Service because it is *with* the people, as well as "of the people, by the people, and for the people." It not only carries knowledge from the State Colleges to the people, but it also works in reverse: it carries from the people to their State Colleges practical knowledge whose workability has been tested on farms, in industry, in homes, and in communities. In ideal extension work, science and art meet life and practice. Mutual benefits result for the people and for the educational institutions they support. Thus the Extension Service develops not only better agriculture, industries, homes, and communities, but better colleges.
>
> (see Smith, 2013)

The "Extension Service" Smith is talking about here is the Cooperative Extension Service (CES) that was established through the Smith-Lever Act of 1914. CES is a permanent, cooperative partnership between the United States Department of Agriculture (USDA), land-grant colleges and universities, and state and county governments. Through CES, land-grant institutions eventually placed a new kind of academic professional called an "extension agent" in nearly every county in the nation. By the end of the 1930s, there were about 6,000 such agents on the payroll, complemented by about 1,500 campus-based specialists in areas related to agriculture, home economics, and youth development. With an overall budget of about $30 million, extension agents and specialists worked with more than half a million local leaders and over a million youth who were enrolled in the youth development, 4-H clubs (see Lord, 1939).

CES still exists today, a century after the Smith-Lever Act was passed. And it has grown. Its budget in 2013 was almost $2 billion. It has a staff of over 2,000 campus-based academic professionals and more than 8,000 community-based educators, who work at approximately 2,900 county and regional offices with hundreds of thousands of community partners. And there are more than 6 million youth enrolled in 4-H clubs (see Zublena, 2013).

The Extension Service and the larger land-grant system, that it is part of, is a national system that includes 109 colleges and universities spread out across all 50 states and several US territories. They have long been depicted in the history of higher education literature as having only an instrumental "service" mission consisting of one-way information dissemination, technology transfer, "applied" research, and the provision of academic expertise and technical assistance. They are also depicted that way in the contemporary public engagement literature. For example, the authors of a book published in 2012, *The Road Half-Traveled: University Engagement at a Crossroads*, wrote the following:

> Cooperative extension, from its founding, has been a program that supports a university-linked system of information transmission from state "land-grant" colleges and universities to the populace through a network of professional "extension agents" who provide public and outreach services.
>
> (Hodges and Dubb, 2012, p. 3)

Positioning land-grant universities as being similar to settlement houses, they also wrote:

> Although university-community partnership work has deep historical roots, there are important differences between today's movement and the land-grant and settlement house movements of a century ago. In particular, today's movement puts less emphasis on provision of university expertise for communities and places greater emphasis on building mutually beneficial and reciprocal partnerships.
>
> (2012, p. 194)

While there is some truth in these depictions of Extension and land-grant institutions, they are also misleading. In my research I've discovered that during the early decades of the Extension Service's 100-year history, some (but of course not all) women and men who administered or conducted extension work, including Ruby Green Smith at Cornell University, which is New York State's land-grant university, did so in ways that were deeply relational and reciprocal, involving much more than one-way transmissions of information or provisions of university expertise. At times it included CBR, in ways that were intentionally and explicitly aimed at realizing its full instrumental and cultural potential. We catch a glimpse of this in a passage from an article written by R. J. Baldwin, who was Director of Extension in Michigan for over 30 years, which was published in 1934 in Extension's national journal, the *Extension Service Review*:

> The program of extension work in agriculture and home economics for 20 years has been based on the policy of personal participation on the part of farm people in the analysis of economic, social, and other problems, and in the carrying out of the solutions of them. Through these experiences they have discovered and developed their own capacities for learning and leadership. Studying, thinking and acting together has stimulated growth, nourished initiative and inspired self-dependence. Out of their achievements in farm, home, community, State, and national programs have come much confidence, courage, and understanding... This development of people themselves, through their own efforts, I believe is the Extension Service's most valuable contribution to society.
>
> (Baldwin, 1934)

What Baldwin describes here is in essence a participatory variety of CBR. It reveals an important historical example and precedent in American higher education of the institutionalization and practice of a variety of CBR with both instrumental and cultural potential. The women and men who engaged in it did so, to use the phrase from the passage quoted earlier from this book's prospectus, "even in the most traditional contexts," contexts that included the farms and homes and neighborhoods of common, working people. In such contexts, extension agents, working as organizers, found and developed local leaders who designed opportunities and processes for engaging and involving, in Baldwin's words, "farm people in the analysis of economic, social, and other problems, and in the carrying out of the solutions of them." Such problems were often technical, relating, for example, to diseases and pests in farming. But, as Baldwin noted, they were also often economic and social, relating to such things as poverty, unemployment, crime, lack of recreation and entertainment, and community or neighborhood decline. The analysis and solution for these kinds of problems involved difficult political work that required people to learn how to deal with differences in power and interests, and differences in people's views and judgments about not only what should be done to "solve" problems, but also how to name and frame them. Some of the women and men who conducted this work attempted to institutionalize democratic organizing principles and practices in ways that simultaneously built on and advanced deep culture change in, and beyond, higher education. They made efforts to build and sustain "mutually beneficial and reciprocal partnerships," as argued in Hodges and Dubb (2012) above. And they had some real success.

However, to borrow from the title of the book I quoted from above, this chapter in land-grant and Extension history amounted to a road only half traveled, if that. In part, the work of these women and men was compromised by their own limitations and failings. Like all people, they had flaws and contradictions. They didn't always practice what they preached. And their organizing practices weren't as effective as they could have been in conducting the critical work of analyzing, building, and exercising power. Additionally, they were marginalized by powerful interests and forces, many of which were well beyond their control or even influence. Their work was also countered by others in Extension and the land-grant system who were walking a different road, one that favored and advanced particular self-, and common, interests (e.g., those of corporate agriculture) rather than larger public interests, and that neither included nor welcomed much attention to democratic cultural ideals and values (see Peters, 2013). The forces that propelled and legitimized this other road achieved a great victory: they won the battle of the story of what extension work is and what it's for (see Canning and Reinsborough, 2010). Reproduced in literature even today, the winning story is that Extension is "a program that supports a university-linked system of information transmission" for instrumental economic and material ends.

Despite all of this, I've found reason for hope in what I've discovered and heard in narrative interviews and research I've conducted during the past decade with contemporary land-grant faculty, staff, and students. I've discovered expressions of the same set of values that Ruby Green Smith communicated and embraced in her 1949 book. And I've heard stories of work and experience that include the practice of the same kind of CBR that R. J. Baldwin spoke of back in 1934 (see Peters 2008; 2010; Peters et al., 2005; 2006). What I have not heard enough of, however, are stories of success in reinstitutionalizing and relegitimizing CBR and the democratic organizing principles and practices it takes to pursue and realize its full potential. In fact, many stories I have been hearing in recent years are about the resurgence of a technocratic view of Extension's work. This view is centered on the development of "evidence-based programs" to address complex social issues and problems such as childhood obesity. Such programs are, in their ideal form, supposed to be constructed from the findings of randomized controlled trials (ironically, such research is often labeled as CBR). And they are supposed to be implemented *to the letter* using fixed, predetermined scripts. Despite the fact that little that is effective in the real world is ever achieved by implementing anything "to the letter," people appear to be taking this view seriously—thanks in part to demands by funders and government agencies for quantitative "proof" of a program's effectiveness, and the incentive of hundreds of millions of dollars of National Institutes of Health (NIH) funding for "translational research" (see Scriven, 2008; Wethington and Dunifon, 2012).

I believe that historical and narrative research and writings can contribute to the project of strengthening and legitimizing democratic values and practices that aim to realize the full potential of CBR. But up against the power of those who are changing the culture of land-grant institutions in technocratic rather than democratic directions, fueled by hundreds of millions of dollars of NIH funding, I know that what is really needed is action research, organizing, and CBR, intentionally interwoven in ways that are powerful and effective enough to achieve and sustain democratic culture change. This is what Maria Avila sought to do with her colleagues in Los Angeles. Her work offers an important contemporary example of what it looks like and takes to organize for culture change through CBR.

Avila—Organizing in Los Angeles

I'm a community organizer, which also makes me a community-based researcher. I believe both CBR and community organizing aim at increasing justice in society through the use of democratic practices, to involve local people in researching issues affecting their communities, and at taking collective action to create societal and culture change. My introduction to community organizing started in northern Mexico in the 1970s. After my arrival in the United States in 1981, I was involved in several short-term organizing-related projects, but it was my work with the Industrial Areas Foundation (IAF) from 1990 to 2000 in New Mexico and California that solidified my organizing practice.

It is important to elaborate on what is meant here by community organizing. Most people usually have an image of community organizing as relating to mobilizing, protest, confrontation, and civil disobedience, usually regarding a specific issue such as securing a union contract or stopping an environmentally damaging project like the Keystone XL oil pipeline that is currently being proposed in the United States. While this type of organizing can be very effective, its goals are often short term, and not part of a strategy to create long-lasting culture change in institutions, communities, and society. Due in part to the issue-focused and short-term nature of it, the bulk of the work is often done by paid, professional staff. Therefore, its purpose may not necessarily be the development of local community and institutional leadership.

In contrast, the IAF model of organizing aims to build leadership within member institutions, who are then taught public skills that enable them to transform their institutions and their communities. These leaders, in turn, learn how to find other leaders that can join them in their long-term organizing efforts (see Gecan, 2002; Ledwith, 2005). This intentional and strategic ongoing process of growing a collective of leadership is often missing in mobilizing and protest-based organizing approaches, in CBR, and in public engagement in general. Building a collective of leaders and knowledge, however, can significantly strengthen current CBR practices. Building long-term sustainable leadership is what underpinned my work at Occidental College.

When the Center for Community Based Learning at Occidental (Center/CCBL) was created in 2001, I was encouraged to apply for the job of director by an Occidental faculty member with whom I had partnered through my IAF organizing in Los Angeles in the 1990s. At first I was reluctant to apply. My impression was that faculty and administrators at Occidental viewed community-based learning only as a vehicle to engage students in doing community service or outreach, and that they did not believe it would be in academia's interest to engage in creating long-lasting institutional and community change. My attitude began to change during the interview, in which several faculty members, two administrators, one community partner, and one student participated. In this interview I asked each of them about their vision for the Center, and why they were interested in interviewing a former community organizer. A number of their responses showed that they were interested in engaging faculty and students with community leaders in solving issues that affected their communities, and to integrate this in courses across the disciplines. I was subsequently offered the job, and I accepted. As the founding director of the newly created CCBL, I then proceeded to start organizing the community within the College. I was director of CCBL from 2001 to 2011.

To help inform my organizing work at Occidental, I did an overall assessment of the field of community engagement at the national level. This was how I learned that many pioneers of this movement, which started in the 1980s, were at that point (early 2000s) engaged in a discourse regarding three concerns (see Stanton et al., 1999). First, they felt that the original goals of transforming faculty and students into democratically and politically engaged citizens had, for the most part, failed. This point was included in the "Presidents' Declaration on the Civic Responsibility of Higher

Education," which was signed by a number of presidents from higher education institutions in 1999. Signatories of the declaration lamented the fact that community service had not led to the development of students' civic participation:

> We are encouraged that more and more students are volunteering and participating in public and community service, and we have all encouraged them to do so through curricular and co-curricular activity. However, this service is not leading students to embrace the duties of active citizenship and civic participation. We do not blame these college students for their attitudes toward democracy; rather, we take responsibility for helping them realize the values and skills of our democratic society and their need to claim ownership of it.
>
> (Campus Compact, 1999)

Second, these pioneering scholars were concerned that academic institutions were not engaging with their surrounding communities in ways that involved reciprocity of interests, resources, and knowledge (see Ehrlich, 2000; Maurrasse, 2001). Third, faculty interested in connecting their teaching and research to community projects discovered, not only that their institutions did not reward this type of scholarship, but also that they often penalized faculty for pursuing it. While organizations like Campus Compact were gaining traction by successfully rallying a number of higher education campuses to integrate civic engagement-related language in their mission statements, these moves were not always coupled with changes in institutional decisions and policies on tenure and promotion, nor with the adequate allocation of resources for public engagement work. These three concerns were at the heart of the culture that required transformation in the early 2000s. The aim of changing these aspects of academic culture is what underpinned my community organizing work at Occidental.

My first step in organizing was undertaking an analysis of the culture and history of the college's past community engagement through hundreds of one-on-one meetings, at first primarily with faculty and later with community leaders. These meetings also helped me find the leaders who would cocreate with me the vision, mission, and programmatic activities for CCBL. A team of faculty emerged, which later became the Center's faculty committee, and which was connected to faculty governance. This was followed by a process through which faculty leaders and I would engage in learning together about the college and surrounding communities, including an analysis of power dynamics on and off campus that could block or support the work of the Center. The process included critical reflection through which we would evaluate the progress of our work, the interest of those in the leadership team, and overall political dynamics.

Four specific community organizing practices evolved as the basis for the civic engagement model we developed for CCBL:

1. *Doing one-on-one meetings* to assess the terrain, understand the history and culture of the college, understand people's interests and ideas for action, and identify leaders.
2. *Building a leadership team* to create collective knowledge, collective vision, and collective action.
3. *Analyzing power dynamics* to have an understanding of power structures inside and outside the campus, and to create strategies based on the realities of power dynamics and available/accessible resources.
4. *Engaging in critical reflection* to assess progress, identify areas needing attention, and re-center the work on the self-interests of the individuals involved in the leadership team.

These same practices were also used in the development of community and student leadership teams. In reference to the three concerns discussed above, they resulted in the following:

- The institutionalization of community-based learning and community-based research in various departments and disciplines, with an understanding of, and a commitment to, reciprocal engagement involving students, faculty, and community partnerships.
- The creation of a program, Education in Action (EIA), through which students were trained and hired to assist faculty with community-based learning and research to develop their civic engagement skills.
- The creation of a regional network of educators and community leaders whose main goal was the long-term transformation of their organizations and communities into a relational, college-going culture called the Northeast Education Strategy Group (NESG).
- An increased awareness among faculty and administrators of, and skill development related to, the integration of community-based learning and community-based research in the reward system.

These achievements have become part of the culture of how the college engages with its surrounding communities. Through an intentional overlap of leadership between the faculty committee, EIA, and NESG, courses and research related to the educational success of children and youth attending schools surrounding the college still exist, three years after I left Occidental. And NESG community leaders express even today that their professional and leadership skills, as well as the culture of their schools/organizations, were transformed through the organizing practices of our engagement model. Most importantly, however, the understanding and the practice of building leadership on an ongoing basis continue to be central to the current CCBL director, the faculty committee, EIA students, and NESG leaders.

That the CCBL continues to exist without me as the organizer is due to the fact that I spent a significant amount of my time building the leadership that would continue beyond my tenure, with a major emphasis on ensuring that there were faculty members who felt ownership for the work of the CCBL. This primary focus on faculty ownership was the result of analyzing the power dynamics of the institution from the beginning. Through this power analysis we learned that compared to administrators and students, faculty tend to stay the longest at the college, and their tenured status gives them job protection. Investing in developing long-term sustainable leadership paid off with community leaders and students as well. The current CCBL director, for instance, is someone whom I guided in her development as a leader first as a community member of NESG and later as a staff member of CCBL. Furthermore, several students who were part of EIA and of NESG continued their engagement with the CCBL after they graduated.

The culture change that took place at Occidental and its community partners happened through the relationships and leadership built, the discoveries made through reflection, and the political actions taken as a collective. These are all elements of CBR. It was through this process that during the last couple of years of my work at Occidental, faculty and community leaders together with the Center's staff realized that we had been combining CBL and CBR throughout the process of creating the work of the Center as a new democratic space in the college, with implications for the community. That is, CBR's participatory and action research elements were complemented by community organizing's leadership building, understanding of power, and learning through reflection.

Given all of this, the argument can be made that through community organizing we transformed the culture of the college and of the surrounding communities. A more accurate statement, however, would be that through community organizing we transformed *parts* of the culture of the college and of the community. It also needs to be said that while telling a story of something that happened in the past can often give the illusion that it all happened smoothly, the truth is that we hit numerous bumps along the road. I want to briefly name some of the most challenging ones.

While faculty committee and EIA student leaders were clear about what we were trying to do, and they all embraced the community organizing model that emerged, we were often questioned about my largely *behind-the-scenes* organizer role, with implications that I was having others do my job as director of the Center for me. In my view, a community organizer's main job is to find and develop leaders. This requires organizers to function more as strategists and coaches than as staff following a specific job description and set of rules. Being strategic and dynamic, and focused on developing leadership is foreign to the way our academic institutions function. As we noted in the introduction of this chapter, in the dominant academic culture, staff and even faculty members are expected to (and rewarded for) fill(ing) a significant amount of their time with activities, and by attending meetings that often do not lead to specific strategic action or result. And most of these meetings are not run democratically. There seems to be a cult of being present for the sake of being present. The argument that I was not doing my job as director was used several times to attack me and the Center, especially during transitions of senior leadership.

All this made the Center and our work vulnerable. It required us to renew our organizing strategies. And it often affected the morale of the staff and the student and faculty leadership, and our work with NESG. Therefore, our culture transformation goals were often diverted by the need to defend our approach, the staff, and the Center. Despite the setbacks, bumps, and barriers we encountered, however, I believe that what we accomplished speaks of the potential of interweaving community organizing and CBR to create long-term culture change in our academic institutions and our communities.

Conclusion

Here in our concluding section; we share three key lessons we jointly draw from our two respective experiences outlined above, along with two of the questions we are now asking as we continue our work.

Lessons

First, the historical example from land-grant extension work reveals an impressive legacy of organizing culture change through CBR that can be drawn on as a source of authority and inspiration. But in the end the main lesson it offers is deeply sobering. The example helps us see the limitations of culture change efforts, even those that manage to permanently institutionalize impressive structures and funding streams. These things can be, and in this example actually were, captured by people who were not walking a participatory CBR road. The road of organizing for culture change through a kind of CBR that aimed to realize both instrumental and political aims ended up being only half-traveled, if that. The lesson here, then, is not just about limitations and co-optation, but also about the permanent nature of the work of organizing culture change through CBR. It is never over and finished, even after big institutionalization victories are won. That's because the work ultimately isn't about structures or funding, but people.

Second, the example from Maria's work through CCBL at Occidental College in Los Angeles offers a positive lesson about the potential of organizing practices combined with CBR. It shows that they can lead to changes in key parts of the culture of academic institutions and communities. We need to emphasize here that the goal in the Occidental example was not the complete transformation of the college and the community. Rather, it was to achieve specific strategic transformations that would legitimize and get lasting support for a way of doing the work of teaching and research that aligns with and uses organizing principles and values. Importantly, the cocreation aspect of the CCBL's model of engagement offers a lesson about the possibility of changing a specific aspect of academic culture: namely the commonly held division between academics as researchers and community members as practitioners. In the CCBL example, this division was blurred and to some extent even overcome. Academics and community members were all researching and discovering, and they were all acting as change agents and practitioners of public work.

Third, the challenges and setbacks we see in both examples offer a lesson about where democratic culture change fits in the priorities, goals, and interests of both academics and their nonacademic partners. The lesson is that it doesn't always fit, or rank highly as a priority. Perhaps it is better to put it this way: shared governance, CBR, and community organizing are not widely recognized as part of the current norms and traditions of public engagement efforts. This lesson must be constantly kept in mind when we approach the work of building public relationships across lines of difference.

Questions

Related to our lessons, there are two questions we carry with us as we reflect on our respective work and experience.

First, we question not only the ability, willingness, and availability of required resources (time and money) but also the *wisdom* of academics and community partners operating in ways that blur the divisions between their expected roles and work. The key concern behind the wisdom aspect of this question has to do with the danger of blurring the line between research and propaganda. How to pursue our commitments and interests without being blind to unwelcome truths and without engaging in wishful thinking is a big challenge for academics and nonacademics alike. This challenge offers an important reason why a blurring of roles and work needs to be approached cautiously and carefully.

Second, we question whether our view of organizing culture change through CBR in strategically modest and partial rather than comprehensive and complete ways will be widely accepted and supported, both by activists who tend to demonize and attack academic institutions instead of working relationally and strategically to transform them, and by administrators who can't seem to break out of an either-or, zero-sum mentality, and who tend to see even modest attempts at culture change in democratic and participatory directions as a threat to academic rankings and measures of "excellence."

Despite our questions, we know that there are people inside and outside academic institutions who not only have ideas that resonate with ours, but also already practice them. We also are convinced that the blurring of roles and work between academics and community practitioners is an ideal worth pursuing, despite its risks. It is key to the aim of realizing CBR's full instrumental and political potential. But we are not so naïve as to think that the complete blurring of roles, goals, and practices is possible for all of academia, or for all of society. Nor would it be desirable. Our concern is that in our present culture, spaces where CBR can be practiced in ways that attend to its full potential are rare. And spaces that support participatory democracy in academia and in society are rapidly shrinking. Therefore, our interest is in reclaiming existing spaces (such as those in land-grant universities) and creating and sustaining new ones (such as those that CCBL created on the Occidental College campus and in the community) where the work of democracy can be pursued. We hope to find others to learn from and work with as we take our work to the next level, organizing and cocreating through CBR the culture change we believe is badly needed in academia and our larger society.

CHAPTER 11

Community Engagement as Fabric in Which to Weave in Teaching/Learning and Research

Ahmed C. Bawa

Introduction

Higher education around the world struggles in the cauldron of socioeconomic and political upheavals and with the impact of the neoliberal imaginations of governments across the world; the growing influence of technology in the core activities of universities; and the impact of vast changes in the modes of industrial production globally. Thus, its purposes and roles are in transition. At one end of the spectrum, Bill Readings' *The University in Ruins* (1996) invokes a rather bleak, pessimistic view about the future of the social institution of higher education. This is counterbalanced by a range of policy-provoking writings that implore national governments to invest more heavily in higher education as a necessary condition for the construction of democratic, egalitarian societies (World Bank, 2002; UNESCO, 2009). As these transitions in the purpose and roles of higher education emerge, so does that of community engagement (CE) that is currently going through a rethinking of its purpose.

As demand for higher education continues to grow at unprecedented levels, partly as a response to the needs of the knowledge economy, partly because of the democratization of the education systems, the shift from elite to mass-based systems becomes apparent (Sharma, 2012). These global shifts provide us with new opportunities to reimagine CE even when there is a broad global consensus on its importance. For instance, as massification takes hold, the idea of CE as a mechanism for the young of privileged elites to spend time and to work in "poor" communities changes. We must now create the opportunity for students to engage in the theory-praxis complex in the kinds of communities in which they have grown up and developed—communities that they know well. These are very different projects. In some ways, this chapter addresses the transitions in CE as it continues to struggle to take hold in the core of higher education.

South Africa has a rich history of university-community engagement, and its theory and practice have been studied in great detail. Several national conferences have been convened and the South African Higher Education Community Engagement Forum (SAHECEF) maintains an ongoing intellectual and practical investment in the growth of CE. The Council on Higher Education, at one such conference, asked Martin Hall to present an analysis, and this has been very effective in providing the basis for the emergence of a robust debate (Hall, 2010). It is current and it captures the key points. The Higher Education White Paper of 1997, which preceded the Higher Education Act of the same year (Ministry of Education, 1997), has, as its tagline, an agenda for the transformation of higher education. It identified teaching, research, and CE as the three pillars of the system. CE is described in the white paper in a political form: as a way in which universities are called upon to "demonstrate social responsibility... and their commitment to the common good by making available expertise and infrastructure for community service programmes"—a way to build legitimacy, something South African higher education struggles with in powerful places. An underlying theme of the white paper referred to above is the role of higher education in generating a civic consciousness among graduates and academics and to "promote and develop social responsibility and awareness amongst students of the role of higher education in social and economic development through community service programmes" (1997, p. 10). That white paper emerged from a large, all-embracing, consultative process, and so we can be sure that the expectation that universities would embark on CE as a core activity is well established in policy. In fact, higher education in South Africa has engaged for more than five decades in a very rich, contested, challenging, diverse set of activities and intellectual engagement that span the whole spectrum of CE—with some success and some failure.

It is, however, a good time for a process of rethinking, reimagining of CE—to revisit it in all its imaginations, to understand why it is that it has yet to capture the commitment and imagination of faculty and administrators at institutions of higher learning. Are there new approaches to be explored? Why has this rich history failed to secure a place for CE at the center of higher education?

A Historical Snapshot

The history of the practice of CE in South African universities is deeply intertwined with the nature of South African society in the period between the 1960s and the 1990s. To understand its new trajectories, it is important to understand the roots of CE and the challenges that it has faced. In the mainly rural-based historically black universities, CE was driven primarily as an outreach model that sought to bring relief to communities under stress.

The nature of CE was somewhat more complex in the urban-based historically black universities and the liberal historically white universities that intersected in direct, though sometimes ambiguous, ways with the waves of urban political, social, and labor struggles against the apartheid regime. Let us explore this a little. There were forms of traditional outreach from these institutions to communities with which they formed bonds of various kinds, such as student engagement in health clinics located in communities or in tuition classes at secondary schools, drama performances doing the community circuit, and so on. The dominant outreach model hinged on the university reaching out to stressed communities—as a way to build institutional legitimacy, helping communities to manage under stressful conditions and providing the opportunity for students, who were primarily from privileged backgrounds, to work in communities, which would help them to understand their responsibilities as engaged citizens.

The decisive, quintessentially South African, engagement enterprise emerged at the intersection between university-based activist scholars and students and the struggles against apartheid in communities, in the labor movement, and in the political terrain. Just for the purpose of developing a flavor of this kind of engagement, two examples are drawn upon from what was at the time the University of Natal. Similar activities also occurred at other institutions.

The Law Faculty, under the leadership of the flamboyant David McQuoid-Mason, assembled the Street Law Project, which became a prototype for expansion in other societies around the world. He described this in an interview as follows:

> The overall mission of the Centre for Socio-Legal Studies' Street Law and Democracy Education Program at the University of Natal is to enable high school students, school teachers, prisoners and community groups to understand the importance of human rights, democracy and the law, to demystify the law, and to show them how the law can be used to advance and protect human rights. The advantages of the methodology used are that they are interactive and based on experiential learning.
>
> (McQuoid-Mason, 2002)

Both university students and scholars went into communities and schools, and the project produced a generation of activist lawyers. This occurred at the height of apartheid, when the very possibility of addressing human rights issues at the community level carried dangers of repression. This, together with a number of other initiatives such as the Community Law Project, which ran paralegal courses for community activists, provided the ideal opportunity for students of law to engage with a radical approach within the framework of gross human rights violations and a violently repressive state.

The second example is the Trade Union Research Project (TURP), a natural outcome of what became known as the Durban Moment, capturing the emergence of a new phase of unprecedented levels of working-class organization, consciousness, and mobilization, starting with worker activism in the textile industry and then spreading to other sectors. At the heart of these events was a group of activist scholars both within and without the academy. Among them was Ari Sitas, a professor of sociology at the University of Natal, who identified an opportunity to establish a center that would intersect directly with these working-class struggles by providing constant flows of research and producing reports and research papers for direct use by the nascent union structures. TURP, as in the case of the Street Law Project, achieved its aim of providing an intellectual home to activist students, who were driven by the desire to link their academic pursuits and their scholarship with working-class struggles against apartheid. It also became home to unionists who wished to reflect on their struggles. Based in the Department of Sociology, it became a vital link between the trade union movement and higher education—to the extent that University of Natal became integrally involved in the education of worker leadership within the trade union movement in collaboration with the Workers' College in Durban. The university senate took the unprecedented step of recognizing certificates offered by the Workers' College as being suitable for admission to degree programs at the university.

To provide a sense of scale, by 1994 there were 87 such structures at the University of Natal alone, each with its own *dynamic interface*—a term coined by Richard Bawden (1993)—with external constituencies of various kinds, each unique and dynamic in its own fashion. The leadership of the university embraced this kind of engagement. This was a liberal university with a fractured, uneven, but existing commitment to the broad battles against the apartheid system. Much of the institution's vibrancy rested in these CE structures, all of which were under threat from the apartheid regime. The university provided them with some level of protection from its raw repression. Having said this, several activists were brutally assassinated by the apartheid regime. As pointed out above, community engagement provided an opportunity for the university to develop dynamic interfaces with communities, the labor movement, and civil society more generally. This helped to open the way for the institution to be linked—albeit with tenuous bonds—to the struggle for democracy and helped it therefore to develop levels of legitimacy with the broad liberation movement.

While all of this was happening, the white university ran, in the spirit of apartheid, a separate, segregated medical school for students of color and fell into line with the admission restrictions laid out by the regime. This may in fact have been part of the impetus for these activist scholars to deliberately broaden the base of the university—to extend the deployment of its resources to broader, progressive, antiestablishment agencies and communities—to ensure, paraphrasing the Freedom Charter, *that the doors of learning shall be opened.*

Post the 1994 Transition

After the 1994 democratic transition, a new dynamic set in. Funders such as the Ford Foundation created funding programs that attempted to grow CE and especially programs of service learning. While this injection of resources was very substantial and important, it failed to capture the enormous potential of the existing models. It fostered models that had developed in the United States and elsewhere, and while there was much to learn, the conditions were very different. The Ford Foundation's Community Higher Education Service Partnerships (CHESP) program epitomized the new adventures in CE: their dependence on external soft money, their anxious formalization in terms of their place in universities, their rigidity with prescriptions about the nature of the programs and the roles of the various players, and so on. In retrospect, they had little chance of success. Naledi Pandor, Minister of Education at the time, speaking about the CHESP program, announced:

> Community engagement is no longer on the margins of academic life in our universities. It is located in the DVCs' office in some of the institutions. It is to be found in the introduction of short course in service learning for new academics and student leaders. And it is also included in some of the postgraduate modules in higher education and orientation programs.
> (Pandor, 2008)

This approach dampened the innovation, the spontaneity, the volunteerism among academics and students. Passion was replaced by compliance.

The Purposes of Community Engagement

It is not surprising that every university in South Africa has statements about CE in its vision and mission statements and in their strategic plans. All of them have projects of one kind or the other that answer this mandate. And yet, there are regular debates and discussions about this. Academics complain bitterly that CE continues to be treated as something outside of the core activities of the university—as an activity that is nice to have but not essential.

Going back to the white paper of 1997, one is made aware of the national understanding of the importance of CE as an educational and social instrument as it extols universities:

> To promote and develop social responsibility and awareness amongst students of the role of higher education in social and economic development through community service programmes.
>
> (Ministry of Education, 1997)

And later on, the white paper lays out as one of its goals at the level of institutions the need for universities:

> To demonstrate social responsibility of institutions and their commitment to the common good by making available expertise and infrastructure for community service programmes.

It is clear that the purpose for CE laid out in the white paper is conceptualized as a social good, as a means to allow students to build good citizenship and social responsibility, and to allow universities to demonstrate their commitment to social development.

Martin Hall, in a seminal article on CE for the Council on Higher Education, begins an interesting debate about why it is that CE finds such difficulty at hooking itself into the core of the institutions even though there is such a clear, unambiguous policy framework. He asks the question (and answers it),

> Why, then, is the imperative of community engagement regarded as radical, risqué and anything other than taken-for-granted? That community engagement is so regarded suggests an epistemological ambiguity in the knowledge project of our universities—an ambiguity, the literature suggests, common with other higher education systems.
>
> (Hall, 2010, p. 2)

This is a deeply provocative question and it opens up the intellectual space for us to understand why it is that CE is still so much on the edge of the university rather than at the center. Hall lays out the challenge:

The conceptual work required for community engagement must start with an exploration of the ways in which knowledge is constructed within what, for convenience, can be called the traditional university... A more likely explanation is an epistemological disjuncture in the way knowledge is structured and organised in South African universities.

(2010, p. 7)

Hall goes on to critique the concerns of Young and Muller that relate to the relativism of "knowledge" constructed through the processes of CE, what they refer to as social constructivism (Young, 2008). He identifies the two key issues that underlie their concerns: "how forms of knowledge are structured" and "the role and location of the authority that serves to validate the structure and content of knowledge and the location of authority" (Hall, 2010, p. 10).

Adjusted Epistemologies? New Epistemologies?

A challenge facing higher education systems of the world is the vast intensification in their engagement (or their search for engagement) with external constituencies—driven by the key location of universities in knowledge economies. The ivory tower is no more. It is fair to assume, therefore, that the questions posed by Muller and Young (Young, 2008) pertain to knowledge construction in a more general sense. The debate in South Africa that ensued in the mid-1990s around the ideas tabled by Michael Gibbons and others about the evolution of new modes of knowledge production in university-industry collaborations (as witnessed in Europe) was precisely about these issues (Cloete et al., 1997). This is symptomatic of the vast changes that have occurred in the global production of knowledge and the systematic infusion of knowledge into production processes. Much has transpired since then.

Peer review mechanisms have been at the very center of knowledge production processes—the way in which "science" has maintained its legitimate hold on validation processes relating to publishing, grant-making, evaluation and assessments of examinations, and so on. It remains a sort of gold standard though there have been some very high-profile lapses in its efficacy in recent times. Most to blame appears to be the existing publish-or-perish culture that is so pervasive. But perhaps more seriously is the desire to generate industry-friendly results—often attached to grants, payments, job security, and so on. In short, there are growing concerns about the role of peer review as a validating facility. This is increasingly exposed in the basic sciences, where, both in the biological and physical sciences, there have been many challenges to peer review in its role in the established traditional hierarchies of knowledge dissemination. This is reflected too in the growing influence of the open access movement, under the aegis of which it is likely that new forms of validation of knowledge will emerge, depending perhaps on more organic and devolved systems.

This is one representation of very fundamental transitions appearing in the purposes of higher education—the shift toward higher education that is more engaged and more devolved in terms of some of the basic tenets of quality evaluation, accreditation, and validation of knowledge processes. The deep pessimism about the future of universities that some commentators, such as Readings, have developed is based on the idea that the core purposes of these institutions are being eroded, being subverted through pressures of instrumentalism of various kinds: massification, industrial engagement, governmental steering and funding for specific projects, demands of the knowledge economy, and so on. It is increasingly clear that there are changes afoot. There has never been greater demand for higher education. With the advent of the knowledge economy, the challenge facing universities was to be either sidelined (while industry established in-house research and development facilities and teaching operations) or change and work toward new understandings of the relationships between universities and the world outside through interesting innovations of Bawden's *dynamic interfaces*—seeing them grow increasingly larger and more complex.

With regard to South Africa, I argue that CE should become a formal site for the production of new knowledge so that it is firmly located within the core functions of the South African university. This is a fundamentally different project compared to that put forward in the Higher Education White Paper of 1997. The key questions then would be those related to the validation processes for the knowledge produced in such engagements.

Community Engagement as a Site of Knowledge Production

Like others, South African society is complex in many ways. One representation of this is the fact that there are multiple knowledge systems coexisting, interacting, and clashing with each other. This may be contested in terms of the definitions of the word "knowledge." There are *kinds of knowledge* such as knowledge by acquaintance, knowledge that (snakes hiss, for example), knowledge how (to do something, for example), knowledge why (it is raining today, for example), and so on. In the South African context one may argue that there are also *different knowledges* that are accessible to, used by, understood by, and defended by people that may fall outside of the dominant knowledge agendas of universities and the science system. Adam Ashforth's book entitled *Witchcraft, Violence, and Democracy in South Africa* (2005) points toward a very prevalent knowledge system in a modern, urban context that is interwoven into the fabric of people's lives—people who live simultaneously in a scientific, modern world and in a world dominated by witchcraft as a belief system.

A simple example will demonstrate the importance of this context of multiple knowledge systems. As is well known, South Africa is the global epicenter of HIV/AIDS. It has made excellent medical progress in addressing the pandemic after a terribly sad start with the confusion and devastation caused by the Mbeki government's earlier rejection of science in the treatment of HIV/AIDS. It has also attempted a very substantial program of HIV/AIDS prevention, which depended on understanding the deeply sociocultural basis of the pandemic. The key element here was the building of understanding of young people about the centrality of the sexual transmission of the retrovirus. However, as Ashforth points out, there are interwoven understandings of the transmission of the disease at the popular level. Without knowledge of the *knowledges* within which the (mis)understandings are based, there is no possibility of developing a relevant set of prevention policies. He describes the scene at a funeral of an HIV/AIDS victim:

> In a scene replayed tens of thousands of times in recent years in South Africa, a relative appeared at the Khanyile family's door in the informal settlement of Snake Park on the outskirts of Soweto to inform them of a funeral. A cousin in a town not far off had passed away. A young man in his late twenties or early thirties, the deceased had been sick for some time. In their message announcing the funeral, the dead cousin's parents specified nothing about the illness, other than to say he had died after a long illness. The relative visiting the Khanyiles, however, whispered the cause: Isidliso.
>
> Khanyile and his family took note. They know about this isidliso, otherwise called "Black poison," an evil work of the people they call witches. Along with whatever treatments the deceased relative would have secured from medical practitioners in his town, they knew without being told that he had been taken to traditional healers to combat the witchcraft manifest in the form of isidliso. All the Khanyile family members concurred with this diagnosis except one. A daughter, Moleboheng, twenty-seven and skeptical, thought the cousin's story was "nonsense."
>
> "He died of AIDS, obviously," Moleboheng told her mother after the cousin left. She was far too polite and sensible to say this in front of the relative, for then the relative would report to others that her family were starting vicious rumours.
>
> (Ashforth, 2002, p. 121)

Hence the importance of encountering, integrating, and differentiating these system intersections. It is vital to the well-being of a complex democracy to understand the multilayered relationships between these coexisting, cohabiting, co-temporal knowledge systems. Without understanding this, the idea of building efficacious evidence-based interventions and policy determinations would be impossible. The key question is how understandings (and knowledge) are to be garnered about these alternative knowledges—except through engagement. Ashforth spent two to three months every year with a family (in a community in the township of Soweto, Johannesburg) for seven years before he gained enough confidence among his adopted family to be able to learn about a paradigm that is so different from the one with which he had spent his life engaging.

The National Research Foundation (NRF), South Africa's key research funding agency, invested substantially in an area designated as indigenous knowledge systems (IKS)—an undertaking somewhat forced on the NRF through dedicated funding from the Department of Science and Technology—a direct, instrumentalist attempt to drive research in areas such as traditional health systems, African philosophical systems, ethnomusicology, ethnobotany, and so on. As it turns out, the bulk of this funding went toward staid "usual science" research such as chemical and botanical studies of plants used by traditional healers in the treatments that they prescribe. There has been little, if any, scientific exploration of the nature of practice of traditional healers, and apart from an interesting attempt at the University of KwaZulu-Natal, very little, if any, attempt has been made to investigate intersections between traditional health systems and "Western" medicine (Gqaleni et al., 2010). The failure of the South African research system to, of its own accord, address the issue of IKS raised the ire of high-level government officials about what they perceived to be the alienation of the science system from "African science"—current complex realities of post-1994 South Africa. It was seen by some officials as a deliberate attempt to undermine alternative knowledge systems, those that lay outside of the scientific paradigm. Ashforth reports that

> The South African discussion of IKS has been stimulated by the Portfolio Committee on Arts, Culture, Science, and Technology chaired by ANC poet and novelist Mongane Wally Serote. Serote is an enthusiast of the idea of IKS. In a paper presented in 1998 to a roundtable on intellectual property and indigenous people organised by WIPO, Serote argued: "Indigenous knowledge and technologies that were denied, destroyed and suppressed in the past will form the basis of our rebirth.... Indigenous knowledge, folklore and technologies have the potential to assist in the rebirth of our nation."
>
> (2005, p. 151)

The perceived undermining of this kind of knowledge by South African science represents to many its alienation from the challenges of nation building and development. One may imagine the posing of the rhetorical question: At what stage will the 25 public universities in South Africa become South African universities? Do universities in South Africa understand their role in generating knowledge about the local context—the signature of a South African university? Or when will South Africans see their lives and their belief systems represented in the formal enterprises of their universities? There is much knowledge embedded in peoples' practiced lives, in their consciousness, and, perhaps most significantly, in oral histories, in the stream of generational memories. This knowledge is not codified. There are scientific ways of getting at this knowledge but there are deep and growing concerns about the power relations between the bearers of the knowledge and its seekers. One way of addressing these power relations is through the development of CE protocols that allow the bearers of the knowledge to be active participants in the research enterprise.

This chapter is an attempt to understand how to locate CE (in all its manifestations) within the purposes of the South African university so that it is a defining element of the knowledge project of these institutions. This is one way of ensuring that CE is a part of the intellectual vibrancy of South African higher education instead of something that is good for them to do.

Returning to the Mode 2 Debate

Gibbons et al., in their monograph *The New Production of Knowledge* (1994), explore new approaches to research and knowledge generation that emerged in European university-industry collaborations to which they offer the name Mode 2 as opposed to more traditional forms of knowledge production, epitomized perhaps by theoretical physics, say.

Michael Gibbons did indeed consider ways in which the conceptual framework designed in their monograph addressed the matter of knowledge production through CE and the challenges of validation in what he refers to as a Mode 2 society. In a paper presented in South Africa, he addressed this as follows:

> It is but a small step to grasp that, in a Mode 2 society, engagement will be determined to the extent that universities encourage reverse communication and actually help society to learn to speak back effectively. Further, engagement as a core value will be determined by the extent to which universities invest resources in the facilitation and management of transaction spaces and support the appropriate boundary work that is necessary to generate the cooperation that is required to formulate and pursue complex problems through research. In other words, engagement as a core value will be evident in the extent to which universities do actually develop the skills, create the organizational forms and manage the tensions between Mode 1 and Mode 2

research. It is by commitment to resolving these tensions—by shifting from the production of merely reliable knowledge to socially robust knowledge—that universities will be able to demonstrate that they have embraced engagement as a core value. It is, in my view, a challenge that all universities need to embrace, but I think it far more likely to be taken up by the new generation universities, because they are relatively speaking unencumbered by massive research investments in discipline-based science.

(Gibbons, 2005, p. 24)

This provides a sort of framework within which to think about knowledge production in CE as a Mode 2 knowledge activity. Is it an epistemological basis for considering new forms of knowledge production? This will depend on the extent to which this "experimentation" proceeds. Gibbons' exploration of CE as one form of Mode 2 knowledge production is problematized by Muller in his response to Hall (Muller, 2010). His major concern is the challenge of the validation of knowledge produced through engagement. Cuthill responds to this by first acknowledging that

. . . scholarship that departs from the traditional Mode 1 approach has been viewed with some degree of suspicion. However, engaged scholarship takes this perceived weakness to task; responds to the call for increased engagement, partnerships, and collaboration within the higher education sector; and emphasizes both the need for academic rigor and quality, and social accountability.

(2012, p. 86)

In the light of this, it may be appropriate to investigate an area in which this methodology could be important. Indigenous knowledge is embedded in communities, in their cultural traditions, and in their practices. It is local knowledge, developed locally, evolving continuously through practice and reflection and in its encounters with other forms of knowledge, including that of modernity. There are vast quantities of knowledge resident and evolving in these contexts—knowledge about agriculture, medicinal plants and their use, midwifery, astronomy, and so on. How does this knowledge feature in the knowledge project of universities in South Africa?

An interesting though difficult challenge that arises in the codification of this kind of knowledge is the complexity of the power relations involved—a reflection of power imbalances in the postapartheid condition. This is often couched in terms of the sociopolitical (and perhaps economic) ownership of the knowledge and intellectual property. (See, for example, Blakeney (2009) for a description of the exploitation of the cultural knowledge of local communities in the Kalahari Desert of the *Hoodia* tuber as an appetite suppressant.)

Addressing power relations in engagements between universities and communities is therefore important. The key feature of Mode 2 knowledge production that (at least partially) addresses this is the multidimensional construction of research teams—their transient nature, their construction from inside and outside the academy, their multiple expectations. Members of related communities are often included in these teams. The research is done both in university-based laboratories and at community-based sites. The outcomes of the research are published in multiple forms and voices: some peer-reviewed in scientific journals, others not; verbal reports in the vernacular; reports of various kinds; etc. CE emerges then, not just as a site for knowledge production, but as a methodology for the production of knowledge, for the codification of knowledge embedded in communities. Let us address this in more detail through two contrasting examples.

Project 1

Paul Mduduzi Mokoena, at the time in the Department of Biotechnology and Food Technology at the Durban University of Technology (DUT), chose to study ways in which the processes of fermentation in the preparation of food had evolved in the amaQadi community in Inanda, just outside Durban. Bawa, Gqaleni, and Mokoena referred to this project at a symposium, trying to draw out some of its salient features:

> According to Chelule et al. (2010) traditional fermentation is a form of food processing, where microbes, for example the lactic acid bacteria (LAB) and yeasts are utilized. The microbes use food as a substrate for their propagation. This is a form of food preservation technology, used from ancient times. Over the years, it became part of the cultural and traditional norm among the indigenous communities in most developing countries, especially in Africa. The rural folk have come to prefer fermented over the unfermented foods because of their pleasant taste, texture and color. This popularity has made fermented foods one of the main dietary components of the developing world... These indigenous foods are locally prepared in small scale in the homes of people; and their quality depends on the inherited skills of the household occupants.
>
> (Bawa et al., 2014)

This could not be a purely lab-based project. Being sensitive to the challenges of the ownership of this knowledge, Mokoena, with a group of students, chose to develop a CE-based methodology that would bring three generations of the women of the community into the process of knowledge assembly and codification. To get the project under way, the leader of the community, Chief Nkosi Ngcobo, who asked for a meeting with the university before the start of the project, was invited onto the campus but he instead insisted that the meeting take place in the community itself. This engagement turned out to be a meeting between the vice-chancellor of DUT together with the research team led by Mokoena and about 40 members of the community including teachers, members of staff of the local further education college, the local librarian, and lay members. Chief Ngcobo led the delegation. It was a 4-hour engagement with Dr. Mokoena and his team describing in detail what they hoped to achieve and how they were going to gather information, samples, and data and what was going to happen to the outcome of the work. The vice-chancellor was asked to express his views about the idea of a longer-term engagement between the university and the community—with several expectations aired by the chief and members of the community. At the end of the process, a memorandum of understanding was signed in the presence of the community members.

Even at this early stage of the project, it became clear that the issue of language would be important as the chief chided student researchers who defaulted to English as a means of communication. He asked how they would gather the information they required if they were not able to speak with the women of the community in the language they were comfortable with.

Three forms of publication of the results ensued. The first was a formal report to the community in the form of a verbal report. The second was publication in a scientific journal. And the third appeared as a report of collaboration between the DUT group and a Chinese group working on a similar project in rural China.

Project 2

The second project involved faculty and students of a number of departments at DUT working with counterparts at University of KwaZulu-Natal (UKZN) on a community engagement project in an urban complex in Durban called Kenneth Gardens, a complex of about 250 households that was originally created for working-class "white" families in 1948. It is now home to a racially mixed low-income community. It was identified as a CE site in consultation with the community. DUT students entered the partnership after the CE project had already been initiated by Monique Marks, at that time professor of sociology at UKZN. Students at DUT have work-integrated learning (WIL) built into their curriculum, and so this was an opportunity for these students to actively engage in that learning. Students from Virginia Commonwealth University (VCU) joined UKZN students in a project highlighted as Building Global Bridges (BGB). Marks, Erwin, and Mosavel in a paper on service learning reflect on the experiences of the UKZN and VCU students in the Kenneth Gardens community.

> The discussion sessions which both UKZN and VCU students and staff participate in became an important vehicle to work through the praxis of the research process. For many of the students, although not all, this was their first experience with carrying out *sustained* research in the field, as opposed to having fleeting encounters with research participants. Discussions, often lively, ranged from intersectionality of researcher and participants' social identities; the process of informed consent within different social and community contexts; the complexities of thinking through methodologies and research ethics; the challenges of working on an international cross-university research project, researcher and participant expectations; and how language and translation shapes interviews and people's narratives. More particularly students felt that there was an opportunity to engage with tensions, challenges and benefits that are not usually raised in methodology text books, such as how power relationships between researcher and participants, as well as between community members, impact on which questions are answered and which are not. Importantly, there was an understanding of how analysis and critical reflection are part of the process of data collection rather than compartmentalized as the next step in the research cycle. During these sessions students got to critically reflect on what it means to *do research* within a community setting.
>
> (Marks et al., 2014)

It is quite clear that this was a knowledge-based project—one that prepares undergraduate students for research "within a community setting." For the DUT students in the broad project, this becomes an opportunity for them to reflect on the application of the knowledge they garnered and engaged with during their classes—to work through the theory-praxis mesh even at the undergraduate level.

Marks, Erwin, and Mosavel go on to paint a vivid picture of what it takes to create such spaces of engagement. Mokoena does the same. There are many reasons for this but primary among them is the intensity of the gap in the power relations between institutions of higher learning and the community, between researchers and the community, and between individuals and interests within complex communities. There is also the issue of the ownership of any intellectual property that is produced in engagement projects.

What Do We Learn?

There are a number of lessons to be learned. None of these are new and others have addressed them previously. Even when internal and external policy choices are made that support its integration of CE, when vice presidents and deputy vice-chancellors are appointed to lead the initiative, when there are active centers of research and practice to maintain a vibrant intellectual enterprise, CE remains at the edge in most universities.

What is clear from the two project examples is that there is a requirement for significant investment. The capacity to organize and to prepare the prior engagement with communities, and so on, has to be catered for. The one way to achieve this—and perhaps the only way for financially stressed universities—is by integrating the enterprises of engagement into the core activities of the university—teaching/learning and research. Most university vision and mission statements and strategic plans represent engagement as one of the three core pillars of higher education in resonance with the Higher Education Act of 1997. But some have chosen to reflect their core pillars as teaching/learning and research, with engagement being the construction of Bawden's dynamic interfaces through which the university connects through those two core activities with its "external constituencies," its social partners, as a way to fulfill aspects of its knowledge-building, knowledge-disseminating mandates. In addition to providing a basis for addressing affordability and sustainability issues, this opens the way for the development of a response to Muller's critique of Hall's paper. The epistemological foundations of the knowledge processes of CE (and other forms of engagement) must be created in the same way as those of any other knowledge process in the science system. Engagement is an important mechanism for knowledge production and dissemination at the intersection of theory and praxis. Much has been written about this. CE provides one site where this kind of engagement can occur.

Related to this, but from a slightly different perspective, is the considerable work that indicates how CE acts as a formidable construction to support citizenship development, the building of agency, the development of critical skills, and so on. The work of Ira Harkavy and others in this area is well established and provides a very powerful basis on which to develop this thinking. It remains a quintessential role of universities. There is a real challenge in understanding what form of engagement will be optimal in the future as higher education systems massify. For one, students will engage increasingly in the communities from which they derive. It is clear that CE can be a powerful agency for individual and institutional transformation.

In contexts such as South Africa's, where there are strong and deep-seated cultures of orality and where there are a number of knowledge systems coexisting with each other, CE will play an increasing role in the construction of research exercises, which take into account the complexities in the power relations involved. It lends itself to the unearthing of knowledge embedded in the communities—through processes that will be sensitive to the postcolonial relations between different parties in the engagement. This places CE firmly and squarely in the core business of the South African university. In fact, this knowledge production defines the South African university—the generation and codification of knowledge deeply embedded in its communities.

The Street Law Project, the Trade Union Research Project, and hundreds of other CE activities generated scholarship and activism of the highest order and contributed to social and political change. Today's CE projects will have aims and objectives that are also transformative, that reach more strongly into the knowledge-building project, generating knowledge about the local context—bearing this as a responsibility, and seeing this as signature of what a South African university is. It will contribute to the continuing transformation of institutions, communities, and individuals.

CHAPTER 12

The Community-Based Research Tradition in Latin America

Jutta Gutberlet, Crystal Tremblay, and Carmen Moraes

Introduction

This chapter captures insights from the long tradition Latin American intellectuals and practitioners have had with participatory and action-oriented research. Rosa María Torres in Peru, Carlos Núñez Hurtado in Mexico, Orlando Fals Borda in Colombia, and Paulo Freire, Carlos Rodrigues Brandão, and Michel Thiollent in Brazil are important names, among many others, who have contributed to the creation of a postcolonial, critical epistemology and methodology in Latin America over the past 50 years. This engagement, rooted in the region, has also influenced research and community outreach in other parts of the world. The particular historical and political context in Latin America has profoundly influenced the emergence of this theoretical movement and its praxis in popular education. In the chapter, we analyze in detail the work of the scholar and educator Paulo Freire, who has strongly shaped popular education. We situate the community-based research tradition in theory and with concrete practical examples from different Latin American countries and we highlight current persistent challenges this research tradition is facing.

The Latin American Historical Context

Over the past six decades, Latin American scholars and practitioners in the field of popular education, community education, and participatory action research have had a profound impact on the debate around social transformation and the wider human development, not only within Latin

America, but also in other parts of the world. However, in Latin America, the particular colonial past has resulted in political oppression, social and economic inequities, large socially and economically excluded segments of society, illiteracy, and widespread and systemic poverty. As a response to these social and political circumstances and more recently in opposition to the devastating military dictatorships, followed by an insecure political transition phase, Marxist and critical social theorists such as Antonio Gramsci have significantly influenced scholars on the continent, turning popular education into a key political project for social transformation.

The major contribution of popular education that has evolved since the 1960s has not been in the type of praxis, but in the intent and quality of pedagogic praxis. This transformed perception of popular education meant working with the people and their daily lived experiences, with a strong belief in the liberating power emerging from actions through popular culture and popular wisdom. Recognizing human beings as subjects able to transform their own history now meant recognizing the individual and collective process of dialectic humanization. It is out of the urgency of countries such as Brazil, where at the beginning of the last century over half of the population was still considered illiterate, lived in extraordinary misery, and suffered from oppression, that the intellectual and praxis-oriented Brazilian educator Paulo Freire began his work on popular education, which was to transform pedagogy, contribute to our understanding of how knowledge is created, and challenge education worldwide. As stated by Celso Beisiegel:

> Paulo Freire is an exponential figure. We had popular education before Paulo Freire and after Paulo Freire. He is a milestone. But, paradoxically, is one of the fruits of a time of great ferment and political radicalism and cultural creativity.
> (1989, p. 132)

The climate of political exacerbation occurred not only in Brazil, but also in other Latin American countries. Soon after World War II, there were important historical events such as the Cold War, the conflict of Berlin, and the Korean War. In 1959, the Cuban Revolution brought visibility to socialist alternatives, made a huge impact on political life in Latin America, and intensified the radicalization movements. The dominant economic and political sectors feared the extension of this influence. Northeastern Brazil was seen, both internally and externally, as a possible second Cuba. As a response, the Kennedy government developed US Agency for International Development (USAID) programs, aiming to finance "sectors committed to democracy," particularly in the Northeast of Brazil. Paradoxically, much of these USAID resources were used for literacy programs, conducted in Rio Grande do Norte, based on the Paulo Freire method. In time, USAID assessed this work as being a subversive education process and discontinued funding for it.

The Brazilian political platform to reestablish the centrality of the presidency by the government of João Goulart, the so-called fight for basic reforms—including university reform, banking reform, and land reform—exacerbated the political tensions in the country at that time. In the field of education there was the creation of popular culture centers (Centro Popular De Cultura [CPCs]) and the national student union, the movement for basic education (MEB), and the National Conference of Bishops. The movement of popular culture in Recife for example was started by Miguel Arraes in Rio Grande do Norte, with Djalma Maranhão, ex-communist, developing important programs such as the campaign "De Pé no Chão também se Aprende a Ler." It is within this context that Paulo Freire's influence on pedagogy emerged, specifically his adult literacy teaching method, which was to spread to many of the other movements in Brazil and eventually to many other parts of the world.

Another important date in the historical development of popular education in Brazil was the year 1961, when Cuba announced a national literacy plan. As stated by Beisiegel, "Cuba virtually provided literacy to all its population in one year's time" (1989, p. 135). The main purpose was to transform a population that had been excluded due to their poverty and living conditions into participants of the revolutionary process.

Popular Education and Social Transformation with Paulo Freire

Born in Recife in the Northeast of Brazil, Paulo Freire (1921–1997) learned early on from the dispossessed that ignorance and lethargy were produced by what he called a "culture of silence," created as a result of paternalism as well as economic, social, and political domination. He believed that the whole education system was one of the major instruments to maintain the status quo, that "culture of silence" (Freire, 2011). Committed to changing the situation of oppression and domination, Freire developed a unique methodology addressing social change through education, and generating a political awareness and sense of understanding of the specific historical context of society and the importance of becoming agents of change for oneself. His work built on that of many other thinkers and philosophers, such as Lucien Goldmann, Jean-Paul Sartre, Erich Fromm, Louis Althusser, and Ortega y Gasset, as well as revolutionaries such as Martin Luther King and Che Guevara. Particularly in his early work, Paulo Freire was influenced by Jacques Maritain, some existentialist philosophers, the *isebianos* (researchers from the Instituto Superior de Estudos Brasileiros (ISEB) of the Ministry of Education, who advocated national development strategies), and a Romanian scholar named Zevedei Barbu. His book *Pedagogy of the Oppressed*, finished by the end of the 1960s, included additional Marxist authors such as Mao Tse-tung and Lenin, a result arguably of his conversations with the Chilean Left.

The theory and praxis developed by Freire were widely used in literacy campaigns in the Northeast, the poorest region of Brazil. They were so successful that he was considered a subversive and thus a major threat to the ruling order. He was jailed after the military coup in 1964, and subsequently left the country to seek political refuge in Chile. His pedagogy was one of the main objects of the repression unleashed by the *Military Civil Revolution* in 1964. Throughout his exile in Latin America as well as in Europe, Freire developed and disseminated reflections and theory on social transformation through education. His writings became extremely influential, transforming education and particularly adult education in the developing world and beyond.

> People educate each other through the mediation of the world. Each individual wins back the right to say his or her own word, to name the world... The awakening of critical consciousness leads the way to the expression of social discontents precisely because these discontents are real components of an oppressive situation.
>
> (Freire, 1970, pp. 15, 18)

In *Pedagogy of the Oppressed*, Paulo Freire outlines a method for the teaching of critical awareness, which he terms "*conscientização*." He explains why the oppressed, instead of striving for liberation in the first instance, often tend to become "sub-oppressors" themselves, in an attitude of what he calls "adhesion" to the oppressor. The very structure of their thoughts has been conditioned by their subaltern reality by which they were shaped. These dialectical reflections on the process of *conscientização* are important insights for practitioners in participatory research, aiming to generate awareness and liberation from disadvantage through participation in the research and, ultimately, to build better communities.

Pedagogy of the oppressed is pedagogy of humankind, a methodology for people engaged in the fight for their own liberation; as Freire states, the oppressed must be their own example in the struggle for their redemption. *Conscientização* means the deepening of awareness—historical awareness—as a result of the emerging social transformation. In this process, meaningful communication is crucial:

> When a word is deprived of its dimension of action, reflection automatically suffers as well, and the word is changed into idle chatter, into verbalism, into an

alienated and alienating "blah." It becomes an empty word, for denunciation is impossible without a commitment to transform, and there is no transformation without action.

(Freire, 1970, p. 68)

Influences on Research and Community Outreach

Theoretical and empirical reflections informing participatory research approaches, from rapid rural appraisal to social action-oriented research, have all benefited from the work of Latin American scholars. Participatory research, originating in the global South, developed out of Marxist and critical social theory, and is committed to social transformation and sustainability. This work finds important methodological support from Latin American consciousness-raising practices and the liberation theory developed between the 1950s and 1960s. The work of Freire and Fals Borda were particularly well known internationally. João Francisco de Souza, a Marxist scholar influenced deeply by Freire and also from Northeastern Brazil, brought important contributions to the field of popular education and participatory research. De Souza worked during the last years of his life in the Centro Paulo Freire—Estudos e Pesquisas, in Recife, building on the work and scholarship of his great mentor.

With his works *State and Popular Education*, and *Politics and Popular Education*, the Brazilian scholar Celso Beisiegel also builds on the work of Paulo Freire and is an important voice defending free public education and criticizing the policy trends of further commodification of public education. He is one of the few theorists whose work has focused on urban populations as subjects in the process of a historical construction of Brazilian education.

Carlos Rodrigues Brandão was one of the first Brazilian scholars to write on research within a participatory framework, with its demand for participant commitment. This demand for commitment means that scientific research is also a political project of the group whose situation of class, culture, or history needs to be changed. The intervention aims to create liberating social change through awareness from the new knowledge generated collectively. Thiollent (1988), who brings the early work of Kurt Lewin on action research together with the Brazilian influences, reminds us that the goal of action research is to produce knowledge, gain experience, contribute to the discussion, and advance the debate about the issues addressed in a cooperative or participatory mode (p. 14).

In addition to the Freirean legacy in Brazil, the spirit of participatory research and popular education has influenced other forms of social action including theater. In the 1960s, Augusto Boal developed a performance style whereby members of the audience could intervene in a performance and suggest different actions for the character experiencing oppression. Theater became a vehicle for grassroots activism, the thinking being that audience participation would empower the people, not only to imagine change but also to practice that change. The performances thus reflected the role of collective power to generate social action. Boal's work, expressed first in his book *Theatre of the Oppressed* (1979), could be considered as one of the most revolutionary cultural and artistic practices of the last century.

The Colombian Orlando Fals Borda brought together action research and participatory research. And through the organization of an international conference in Cartagena in 1977 on action research, he enlarged its international visibility and intellectual credibility. According to Budd Hall (2005), who participated in the 1977 event, it was Fals Borda who first coined the concept of participatory (action) research or PAR. As Fals Borda affirms:

> [t]he participatory discourse or counter discourse, on the other hand, initiated in the Third World... postulates an organization and structure of knowledge in such a way that the dominated, underdeveloped societies articulate their own socio-political position on the basis of their own values and capacities and act accordingly to achieve their liberation from the oppressive and exploitative forms of domination imposed by opulent (capitalist) foreign powers and local elites and thus create a more satisfactory life for everyone. In this way a more human Weltanschauung, or world outlook, could be fashioned.
> (Fals-Borda, 1987, p. 331)
>
> PAR can make an important contribution is this field in which knowledge and action are combined for social progress.
> (Fals-Borda, 1987, p. 332)

With a profound vision of a science of the "common people," Orlando Fals Borda and other practitioners and theorists in Colombia and other Latin American countries committed to strengthen the political movements associated with revolution and democracy at the time. In Nicaragua, for example, the active support from Orlando Fals Borda persuaded the Sandinista government to undertake popular education as an official government program. Hall (2005) recalls the impact of the democracy movements of Chile, Argentina, Colombia, Brazil, and other Latin American countries in the development of participatory research methods as part of the organic nature of those movements.

Field studies and projects conducted in Nicaragua, Colombia, and Mexico demonstrate how PAR methodology, using various techniques, has helped further the interests of exploited groups and classes (Fals-Borda, 1987). The coordination commission of El Regadío in Nicaragua is a successful example of PAR contributing to social transformation. Fals Borda illustrates how strategic research methods were used to challenge the peasants of El Regadío to analyze their patterns of dependency, paternalism, and authoritarianism "inherited from the traditional exploitation systems of the past which continued to flourish there despite the revolution of 19 July 1979" (p. 333). Another example of demystifying research through participatory methodology, involving training community members and interviewers in collecting, organizing, and analyzing data, is detailed by Fals Borda in a case study examining housing conditions of the poor in Puerto Tejada, Colombia (Fals-Borda, 1987).

Networking Popular Education and Community-Based Research

Paulo Freire's teaching has been central to the lives of most Latin American popular educators. Carlos Núñez Hurtado, born in Guadalajara, Mexico, in 1942, writes that when he encountered Paulo Freire in Costa Rica for the first time, he was the most human being he had ever known in his life, and beyond Freire's science and knowledge it was his profound humanity, in the full sense of commitment, that had mostly impacted on him. Núñez Hurtado became active as an educator in the 1960s. In his career in the sociopolitical arena, he was active in many areas, including housing, rural and urban grassroots initiatives, popular communication, citizens' movements, and national and international politics. He also contributed to the building of Alforja Study and Publication Centre in Central America (CEP Alforja) and to the Latin American Council for Adult Education (CEAAL). These two networks produced many important publications on popular education, participatory research, and social transformation in Latin America (CEP Alforja and CEAAL, 2012). Other authors working on participatory and collective social science approaches referenced by CEP Alforja and CEAAL (2012) are Anton de Schutter, Paul Oquist, Guy Le Boterf, Gerrit Huizer, João Bosco Pinto, Marc Lammerink, Carlos Rodrigues Brandão, and João Francisco de Souza, all of whom may be considered as foundational scholar-activists in the field called community-based research today.

The Role of the Social and Solidarity Economy in Community-Based Research

The solidarity economy is a democratic space that is both influenced by and in turn influences the contemporary community-based research movement. It has a vibrant history throughout Latin America and has contributed to driving social change through bottom-up community-based approaches to development. It has become an important economic model in the response to poverty reduction and the creation of employment opportunities. It is based on the principles of solidarity, partnership, reciprocity, gender equity, sovereignty, and mutual support. Marcos Arruda (2008), socioeconomist at the Institute of Alternative Policies for the Southern Cone of Latin America (PACS:Instituto Políticas Alternativas para o Cone Sul) in Rio de Janeiro, and member of the Facilitation and Coordination Committee of the Alliance for a Responsible, Plural and Solidarity-Based Economy (ALOE), defines solidarity economy as

> a system of socio-economic relations centered on human being, its need to evolve, develop and fulfil its potential, its work, knowledge and creativity; planned and managed democratically; and aimed at generating satisfaction of its material and non-material needs, rights and aspirations, including the right to a dignified life, a healthy environment and enabling conditions for the fulfilment of one's potentials and qualities, well-being and happiness.
> (Arruda, 2008, p. 16)

Arruda (2008) describes the growth of solidarity economy as a response to profound social crisis, unemployment, and social exclusion—primarily caused by the opening of internal markets and recessions. Resistance to corporate globalization and neoliberal policies has led to social movements searching for viable alternatives. Gutberlet (2009) also highlights the strengthening of solidarity economy in Latin America as a response to inequality and exclusion, and demonstrates how instruments such as micro-credit, for example, can significantly contribute to livelihood enhancement, particularly for the informal sector.

Laurell (2000) points out that governments supporting these alternative approaches were voted into power in Venezuela, Brazil, Argentina, Chile, Peru, and Bolivia. Some examples of national commitment to solidarity economy can be seen in Venezuela's Ministry of the Popular Economy, Brazil's National Secretariat for Economic Solidarity in 2003, and Argentina's "Manos a la Obra" program initiated in response to their devastating economic crisis in 2001. Initially conceived as a solution to the economic crisis, solidarity economy in Latin America has proved to be a dynamic and sustainable economic approach supported by governments across the continent, contributing to real social change.

In Brazil, solidarity economy, and supportive legislation, is particularly strong. The development of a national organization called the Brazilian Forum on Solidarity Economy in 2003, representing a number of social enterprises, was indicative of its growing strength (Puntasen et al., 2008). Further to that, a review of solidarity economy by the government in 2005 revealed that 15,000 democratic enterprises collectively employ 1,250,000 men and women.

In Venezuela, grassroots and community initiatives, as well as aggressive government legislation, established a variety of innovative practices and approaches that aimed for a more democratic and participatory economy. The government oriented its economic policies around the principles of "endogenous development," as an alternative to the neoliberal development model, and has passed laws to strengthen the socialist transformation of the country. Through the "popular economy law," established on the principles of a solidarity-based economy, local governments and public institutions supported the growth and development of this economy through procurement practices that favored cooperatives and small enterprises. As a result, the total number of cooperatives in 2004 was 945,517, up from 215,000 in 1998 (Harnecker, 2005).

In Peru, the Grupo Red de Economía Solidaria del Perú (GRESP) is an association composed of civil union associations, nongovernmental organizations (NGOs), religious organizations, Peru-based international cooperation agencies, and people who promote economic relationships of solidarity in the economy. Nedda Angulo, vice president of GRESP, writing in 2007, points to the success of GRESP in building solidarity economy in Peru through the organization and networking of groups including the National Council of Coffee in Peru, a group of 35,000 coffee producers, and the Central Artisan Organization, with 1,600 artisans.

Argentina also recognized solidarity economy as a model that can provide crucial employment and the reduction of economic inequality in society. The "Manos a la Obra" program, initiated in 2001, finances the development of labor cooperatives in many sectors, and is a particularly significant policy initiative supporting socioeconomic development. Viviana Alonso (2005), of the Inter Press Service News Agency, wrote of the many examples of organizations involved in economic activities in Argentina that have horizontal structures, are run in a democratic, participatory manner, and are not solely profit driven. These include regional cooperatives of small farmers, bankrupt factories that were abandoned or closed by their owners and reopened by the employees, self-managed companies, communities that have come together to find solutions to meet basic needs like health care, housing, or food, and barter networks whose members trade goods and services.

Progressive governments in Latin America are also pursuing regional integration, such as the creation of the Union of South American Nations (UNASUR), the Bolivarian Alliance for the Americas, and the Community of Latin American and Caribbean States (CELAC *Comunidad de Estados Latinoamericanos y Caribeños*) (Riggirozzi and Tussie, 2012). These regional networks are adopting solidarity economy as part of region-building efforts, and integrating the discourse into their agendas.

The flourishing of a solidarity economy and the culture of social movements have helped to secure the foundations and strengthen the nature of bottom-up community based research (CBR) approaches to research in Latin America. Early practitioners and intellectuals such as Paulo Freire, Fals Borda, and others have, through their emphasis on the role of people's own knowledge as a key element in strengthening community, contributed toward the formation and expansion of social and solidarity economy in Latin America. The particular interdisciplinary methods these thinkers have brought to the table have supported the progress of a radically different economic development approach, which is community centered and participation oriented.

Regional and Local Community-Based Research Initiatives

Since 2005 the Participatory Sustainable Waste Management (PSWM) project, a collaboration between the University of São Paulo and the University of Victoria, in partnership with recycling cooperatives, local governments, and some NGOs, has been working toward strengthening and improving the activities of selective waste collection, separation, and recycling in the metropolitan region of São Paulo in Brazil. The empirical outcomes from this project are the fruits of collaborative, action-oriented, and participatory research. Using Paulo Freire's methodology of thematic investigation and *conscientização*, participants collectively generated new interdisciplinary and inter-sectorial knowledge in meetings, workshops, field visits, and dialogues carried out by the project, using community-based methodologies.

The project assisted in the structuring, organization, and strengthening of cooperatives, associations, and community groups involved in the recovery of resources from the solid waste stream through supporting cooperatives, micro-credit, and the practice of solidarity economy. Activities such as participatory video documentation, digital inclusion workshops, gender equity and comanagement initiatives, and collective commercialization have all helped to develop the capacity of the leaders of recycling cooperatives. Through these and other activities, the program contributed to the increase of income and empowerment, so that the recyclers could contribute more effectively to public policy-making and thus diminish urban poverty and improve environmental quality. Establishing participatory project management structures was a priority from the outset, in order to ensure the long-term success of all project activities. Collective and adaptive management helps the project to respond to opportunities and challenges that arise, and has ensured that project activities are relevant to the needs and interests of recycling groups (see Gutberlet, 2008; 2012; Gutberlet et al., 2013; King and Gutberlet,

2013; Nunn and Gutberlet, 2013; Tremblay and Gutberlet, 2011; Yates and Gutberlet, 2011). Ultimately, this collaborative research process, conducted over six years, highlighted the complementary nature of academic knowledge to the local knowledge present among the recyclers. Cogeneration of knowledge and collective learning provided effective and feasible strategies and resolutions that help to tackle acute social and environmental problems, as discussed in the described research project. Finally, the collaborative research contributed to the identification of challenges, conflicts, deficiencies, and strengths, which helped to identify constructive interventions to tackle the issues within the informal and organized recycling sector, ultimately improving the quality of life of the recyclers.

Another strong example of CBR is the Brazilian social solidarity network Comitê de Entidades no Combate à Fome e pela Vida (Committee of Entities in the Struggle against Hunger and for a Full Life, COEP). It was established in 1993 by the sociologist Herbert de Souza, and led to a development of citizen interventions across the country. COEP is now a thriving network of networks, active federally in all of Brazil's 27 states, and also at the municipal level. Its strategies include encouraging members to support and participate in development projects to combat poverty, organizing campaigns to mobilize public and institutional resources to end poverty, and promoting cooperation among its affiliates in their development work and campaigns. Its members include government agencies, and organizations from both the private sector and civil society (Saxby, 2004).

In 2004, a People/Mobilizer Network was launched, in which the participants, via the Internet, gained access to information and knowledge about various social themes. By 2008, COEP's members had contributed resources to more than a thousand projects, for both community relief and long-term development. Many of these projects are small-scale localized projects, but some, such as the electrical utility Furnas, made significant contributions to COEP projects (e.g., $5.8 million in 2003). While COEP has not generally played an operational role in individual projects, the network has significantly improved them by promoting learning, communication, and coordination among its members through discussion forums, seminars, conferences, and annual meetings. Today, there are more than 1,000 organizations in 110 involved communities.

COEP has been instrumental in scaling up and replicating successful community-based projects. An example of this is the cooperative of self-employed workers (COOTRAM) Cooperativas de Serviços in the Manguinhos Complex, a poor favela in Rio de Janeiro. Fiocruz, a public health institution, mobilized a number of organizations (including universities, banks, and private sector bodies) to develop a pilot project to support the creation of a popular cooperative. The project was subsequently replicated through another six universities throughout the country, resulting in the creation of the National Program of Popular Cooperative Incubators (PRONINC – Programa Nacional de Incubadoras de Cooperativas Populares), This program has been one of COEP's most visible achievements, being taken up as government policy through the Programa Comunidade Solidária and resulting in 38 "cooperative incubators" around the country focused on supporting informal and organized recyclers throughout Brazil (Schnell and Saxby, 2010). Some of these initiatives included fostering the creation of regional networks of associations of collectors, including those from the informal sector; strengthening selective collection of materials in public buildings; promoting awareness and dialogue, and environmental education; supporting the demands of the National Recyclers Movement (MNCR Movimento Nacional dos Catadores de Materiais Recicláveis) to strengthen capacity through thematic workshops, training courses, campaigns, and the production of educational materials; stimulating dialogue and better negotiation between recycling cooperatives and industry; and contributing to the production of information, and campaigns to inform public policy-makers in developing programs for the inclusion of *catadore/as* or gatherers (INSEA, 2013). Each year COEP will focus on a specific theme for social development and well-being at a national level, with a view to impacting at community level.

The Bolivian Centre for Multidisciplinary Studies (El Centro Boliviano de Estudios Multidisciplinarios, CEBEM) embraces bottom-up community knowledge production and collaboration in areas such as democracy, regional and urban development, and environmental management. It is a leading organization in the country for the promotion of new communication technologies for education and information and knowledge exchange. CEBEM, which was established in the 1980s, concentrates its efforts on the study of the scope and impact of state policies that transform relations within society, altering traditional ways of functioning in the economy, and impacts on the composition of the popular sectors and practice of social and indigenous movements. In pursuit of its mission, CEBEM has developed strong relationships with academic institutions and cooperates with the governments of Bolivia and other Latin American countries and beyond. One of its key objectives is to establish relationships for ongoing dialogue with different stakeholders in the country with the aim of understanding the collective guidance and alternatives for social change.

Argentina's Latin American Centre for Service-Learning (Centro Latinoamericano de Aprendizaje y Servicios Solidario, CLAYSS) is a service learning network that includes more than 90 civil society organizations, public administration bodies, and universities from Latin America and the Caribbean, the United States, and Spain. CLAYSS was born out of the economic crisis of 2002 in order to find ways for universities and colleges to "help fight poverty and create social justice in social relationships" (Hoyt, 2014, p. 1). Professor María Nieves Tapia, the founder of CLAYSS, points to the current economic situation in much of Europe and the United States as an opportunity to demonstrate "how much universities can do to address specific problems." Further, she suggests that the North is finally starting to listen to the South where the "quality of civic engagement practice and the theory is older and deeper than what exists in the North...we have been dealing with poverty for centuries and have been working *with* communities, and not *for* them" (Hoyt, 2014, p. 2).

Conclusion

The field of what is called community-based research in some parts of the world owes much to the sophistication, the political commitment, and the social imagination of Latin American scholar-activists. In Latin America, one finds the roots of praxis in the theory and practice of popular education, participatory research, theater of the oppressed, participatory video, feminist research, indigenous-centered research, and solidarity learning. While Freire and Fals Borda are perhaps the best known of the Latin Americans working in this field, they were part of an entire generation of activist intellectuals who not only responded to the dictatorships of the 1960s and 1970s but contributed to the democracy movements that brought the dictators down in country after country.

The learning from their work and experiences is being applied in today's Latin America in the movements of recyclers, in the rise of indigenous people's demands for recognition, in the resistance to neoliberal globalization, in the participatory budget movements, and in more. What remains a challenge for us as a global movement is that the richness of the Latin American activist intellectual experience is largely invisible to a world that operates mostly in English. But it is clear that thousands of thoughtful women and men dedicated to another possible world are continuing to make a difference in the development of community-based, participatory, and action-oriented research and urging for a stronger engagement and commitment from universities to help address the needs and demands of local communities. These "knowledge innovators," as Hall et al. (2013) describes them, have "facilitated various means of creating, sharing and accessing knowledge that is not part of what is often called the western canon" (p. 4). The history and culture of population education and civic engagement in the South is rich and extensive and is embedded in the structure of their universities. Service learning and community engagement, for example, are necessary components of student learning, bridging theory and practice in very real and impactful ways. Latin America brings a wealth of knowledge and experience in the global movement toward building a knowledge democracy and a more equitable world.

Although there have been significant achievements in the cooperative and solidarity economy movement in Latin America, there are still many challenges. In a report for the United Nations Research Institute for Social Development, Saguier and Brent (2013) highlight that solidarity economy policy implementation is almost exclusively limited to the realm of poverty eradication and does not really lead to restructuring the dominant economy. Such alternative policy frameworks do not appear to be challenging the dominant modes of production, which ultimately leaves their future vulnerable to competition or displacement. In making this point, Aranda (2011) points to the example of Argentina's large-scale soy production, 99 percent of which is exported to large corporate actors.

Thus, the community sector is still vulnerable and has the potential to be marginalized by the still dominant capitalist model of economy. Ultimately, the mechanisms of oppression, described by Paulo Freire, still persist and require close attention and radical action by bottom-up, grassroots-oriented community-based and action-oriented research. Global networks, such as GACER (Global Alliance on Community-Engaged Research), GUNi (Global University Network for Innovation), APUCEN (Asia-Pacific University-Community Engagement Network), CEBEM, and CLAYSS, can play an important role in promoting change and transforming higher education and knowledge production. These networks can act as disseminators of new ideas, debating innovations in community-based research and popular education. As we move toward a future with the increasing challenges of population growth, food and water security, economic inequality, and political conflict, to mention a few, participatory approaches to deliberation, cooperation, and education are needed, and insights from Latin America can inspire collaborative solutions.

SECTION III

Perspectives

CHAPTER 13

Community-Based Research: Searching for Its Foundations

Ronald Barnett

Introduction

"Community-based research" implies research that has a base in the community, but what base might this be? The term base is ambiguous. It might be pointing to foundations of research having their place in the community such that there could be some kind of fixity of research *in* the community. For those who think in diagrammatic form, the image of the pyramid might appeal: here, the weight and larger portion of the shaping of research would lie in the community, the research itself being significantly influenced if not determined by the community. The suspicion could arise here that in community-based research, the community-as-base forms the real engine of research and the research itself is an epiphenomenon—a cognitive or even a mere cultural adornment of, and for, the community.

On the other hand, the base here might be more akin to the base of medieval cathedrals, which is to say rather shallow. Under the edifice, there lies little by way of base or foundation. The academic community would here remain on show and in command; the wider community would have a negligible part to play. Or, finally, by way of opening images, perhaps the base is more like that of a high-rise building, in which the upper floors (the research) offer interesting views, and quite a bit of flexibility (they even move in the wind), while the lower floors and the foundations (the base) are largely hidden from view and are largely uninteresting.

So what, then, is this "base," in community-based research? And what is the relationship between that base and the research that sits on it? What is the influence of the base? And what autonomy might be retained in the actual conduct of the research? Where lies the power in community-based research? And in which processes of validation lies the legitimacy of research? Several, if not most, of the contributions to this volume have at least implicitly hinted at this set of issues, but it is be worth engaging more directly with them. *En route*, some matters only dimly present may emerge more fully.

After exploring matters of knowledge production and validation in a complex and unstable world, I shall turn to a consideration as to how those observations might play out both in relation to universities and to "community." In the process, I want to draw attention to some limitations in the idea of "community-based research" but also, via the idea of the ecological university, to some of its possibilities. Rather than "community-based" research, an alternative term—such as "community-oriented" research—may be more apposite and may help to generate practical principles that are appropriate to the presence of multiple and diverse communities in a complex and global world.

Opening Sallies

Arising from the opening questions are matters of power, validation, authority, academic freedom, institutional autonomy, knowledge production, knowledge management, and knowledge distribution. The terms community and research are, of course, themselves hostages to fortune and would warrant examination (and perhaps "community" has been disinterred more in this volume than "research"). Not far behind are matters of knowledge ethics—as we may term it—and knowledge responsibilities. But here I wish to probe at the matter of "the legitimation of knowledge" specifically, to adapt a book title of Ernest Gellner (1974), and then to come at the relationship of knowledge to "community."

That book of Ernest Gellner's was entitled *Legitimation of Belief* (1974). In it, he explored the ways in which belief systems come to derive their authority. For Gellner, a fundamental shift had occurred (around the time of the Enlightenment) in that legitimacy had changed from a concern with what was known (Gods, mysteries, miracles (not Gellner's examples)) to a concern with the ways in which knowledge was won. Essentially, that shift heralded the coming of the scientific revolution. After all, nothing was sacred about any scientific proposition for it could be overturned tomorrow; what was important was the process by which knowledge was now to be secured. And Gellner traces ways in which philosophy, sociology, and anthropology all shed light on this shift in legitimizing belief and ways in which those disciplines were themselves influenced by it. (Much of modern Western Anglo-Saxon philosophy has been about attempting to give formal accounts of the processes of turning belief into knowledge, favoring successively accounts that hinged on ideas of "verification" and "falsification.")

That story—of turning belief into knowledge and establishing secure processes by which knowledge could be produced—clearly cannot be fully told without paying some attention to the rise and development of universities (and here, especially, the European universities that were established in the Middle Ages, with their successors both in Europe and beyond). The broad story seems to be that characteristically forms of knowledge had to prove their worth outside the academy—through amateur-based study by passionate individuals and groups—before they were admitted. This was the case for physics, chemistry, and geology in the nineteenth century (Finnegan, 2005), and then through the twentieth century, as apparently esoteric fields such as engineering and sociology were granted entry into the academy. Subsequently, the university has been closely associated with the systematization of knowledge, and the formal process that has come to be known as research. This is a continually unfolding story, involving some huge processes, many of them now cross-national, large research teams and infrastructures and fast-changing processes of knowledge production and dissemination (not least with the digital revolution).

In what way is all this relevant to the community-based research? Both matters—the legitimation of belief systems and the systematization of knowledge in and by the university—have direct bearing on the theme. For the very idea of community-based research poses in sharp form the following questions: Wherein lies the legitimacy of knowledge? How significant is the role of the university in this legitimation process? Does community-based research represent a fundamental shift in this legitimation process?

There is yet a further matter to which we must be alert at the outset. Broadly speaking, until the middle of the twenty-first century (roughly up to and including World War II), knowledge inquiry was conducted by the universities but in a loose set of alliances and interchanges with the wider society. In the nineteenth century, many universities were founded on the basis of newly emerging industrial needs. In Victorian England, scientists and scholars who made their living primarily in the universities would give public lectures in local community settings and recognized it as their responsibility to do so (Gordon and White, 1979, chapter 7). The post-World War II period saw a quickening of interchanges between the academic—particularly the scientific—community and politicians. It was largely after that war, with the rapid expansion of the university system, that universities were granted institutional autonomy, and indeed it was then that the concept of "the ivory tower" was born.

In other words, the sharp separation of universities from the wider society is a relatively recent phenomenon—and, it seems, rather a brief one at that. The past two to three decades have seen moves on the part of the state to establish a more interactive *modus vivendi* with—if not downright *dirigiste* stance in relation to—the universities. Arguably, therefore, insofar as there are moves afoot to connect the university with the wider society, this is but a return to an earlier state of play. After all, several of the medieval universities grew out of practical concerns and needs in relation to—and separately to—the law, administration, and medicine.

The idea of community-based research, accordingly, has to be understood against this complex background of knowledge legitimation, the role of universities, and the changing relationships between universities, the wider society, *and* the state. At one level, there is nothing new in the idea of community-based research for it is at least a hundred and fifty years old. (The universities in continental Europe have long been creatures of the state, rather than independent of it, notwithstanding the interest there in (Lernfreiheit a concern that the state should not directly interfere in processes of knowledge production.) In the sections to follow, this chapter will examine the contemporary idea of community-based research against this philosophical, historical, sociological, and indeed political background.

The universities have (recently at least) been too adrift from the wider society and insufficiently accountable in their quest for knowledge and in their dissemination of it. The challenge on them to demonstrate their credentials for public engagement has been too long a coming. Indeed, the university has responsibilities to extend societal understandings of issues and situations and so assist the growth of public reasoning and public action based on reason. I argue for a kind of university that I term the ecological university, one that is directly attuned to its environment and playing its part not just in sustaining that environment, but also in improving it.

On the other hand, it is necessary to be cautious over the very term community-based research, for it leaves on the table, as intimated, matters of knowledge legitimation. Part of the idea of "the ecological university" is that it opens itself to the wider community and, indeed, ensures that knowledge processes are participatory, but then a question arises over such wider participation. Wherein, amid community-based research and its implications for wider participation in knowledge processes, is such legitimation (of those knowledge processes) to be derived? There is a risk of confusing legitimation and participation. Care needs to be taken in embracing the idea of (community) participation such that the legitimation (and so the very legitimacy) of what counts as knowledge is not impaired.

Fluid Times

We live, so we are told, in fluid times. Famously, Zygmunt Bauman has—in a series of books—made much of the metaphor of a liquid world (see Bauman, 2000). This liquidity moves on different levels—in social institutions and systems certainly but also in less tangible dimensions of identities, beliefs, values, and concepts (through which the world might be understood). The university is implicated in what we might call the hard-wiring of institutions and systems, for example, new policies, new laws, and new articles of association, but also in the "softer" and more elusive development of beliefs, values, and cognitive frameworks.

In the distinction between the systems level and the conceptual level of the liquid world, we see two different kinds of complexity. The first is that of complexity of systems, often caught in photographs of intertwined seaweed and so forth. These are unstable, unpredictable, and chaotic, even if some semblance of order can sometimes be detected within them. The second order of complexity, that of belief systems, may conveniently be termed super-complexity (Barnett, 2000). "Belief systems" is actually a generous phrase since it harbors a greater sense of order and, indeed, system than is usually warranted, for again here lie complex and ill-related and amorphous beliefs, concepts, ideas, and values that are devoid of system. This order of complexity is characterized by three features: the cognitions to be found here are proliferating; often conflicting; and moving in a diffuse space of persons and communities, being held in the mind and in collaborative processes.

The fundamental difference between these two orders of complexity can be captured in the following way. Complexity (of systems) is real and gives rise to systems overload and personal anxiety (e.g., in the health system and in the doctor attempting professionally to cope with increasing numbers, and demands, of patients more drugs and more audit requirements). Nevertheless, in principle, the demands of this kind of complexity could be satisfied (with more resources, more sophisticated management systems, and so forth). The questions posed by the second order of complexity—super-complexity—however can never be fully resolved. In answer to the apparently simple question "What is a doctor in the twenty-first century?," there can only be competing and expanding responses that offer no definite resolution.

As stated, the university is implicated in both of these orders of complexity. It is both a complex and even chaotic set of systems. It is also a space for competing and proliferating accounts both as to what it is to know the world and even as to what a university is, or might be. The university is a super-complex institution—as well as being a complex one—in a super-complex world.

How do these reflections on complexity relate to the dominant theme of community-based research? The connections are twofold, to do with our two forms of complexity.

On the one hand, knowledge—considered as sets of cognitive systems—has become more fluid, spilling out across each other and out into the wider society. Partly, this development has been given momentum by the encirclement of the academy and, indeed, by interchanges with the wider society. Partly, it has been fueled by the coming of the age of the Internet, and partly, it has been propelled by the emergence of a global world, a phenomenon of which universities—as global institutions—have been able to take advantage. *Sociologically*, the university moves in a liquid space; and it is a space that spreads in the direction of "community"—that amorphous set of spaces beyond the university that speaks of collective interests and a public sphere—and also promises much more in that direction than hitherto realized.

On the other hand, what counts as knowledge becomes especially problematic in these liquid circumstances. And this is where the connection with "super-complexity" comes in: attempting to give an account of the very concept of "knowledge," which lies at the heart of the university as a social institution, is now fraught with difficulty. Community-based research is but one space involved in this problematic. Just what bearing does, could, or might "community-based research" have on our very understanding as to what it is to know the world? To what extent does the idea of the community-based *truth* claims carry water? Community-based research—and the role of the university in such research—has *epistemological* import, therefore.

Taking Stock and Cashing In

I have asserted that, for a relatively brief period of its history, broadly the second half of the twentieth century, the university became unduly separate from society and that the recent past has seen moves, both intended and unintended, to bring the university back into a closer relationship with wider society. In a sense, therefore, the idea of community-based research is not new. For much of its history, and particularly in many Western countries, the university emerged in response to practical concerns in the wider society and was deliberately intended to address those concerns.

If, however, those statements were all that might plausibly be said, that might be the end of the matter insofar as "community-based research" was concerned. The university has long been connected with its wider society, and today—after a sojourn of being concerned primarily with itself—it is even more inserted into society. There are, though, two flies in this particular ointment.

First, the recent greater level of interconnectedness between the university and the wider world has a specific general interest propelling it forward. Crudely speaking, this may be described as an interest in economic reason. With the emergence of the global knowledge economy, universities have come to be prized—around the world—for the economic capital that they can help to generate (through both teaching and research, and more recently through "knowledge transfer" and the marketization of "intellectual capital"). As a result, we have witnessed the formation of what has variously come to be termed academic capitalism (Slaughter and Leslie, 1997) or cognitive capitalism (Boutang, 2011).

This raises, in acute form, an issue on which we have been touching throughout these reflections, that of the legitimation of knowledge. Perhaps the most vivid and most powerful specification of this new order was that so perspicaciously provided by Lyotard now 30 years ago, when he introduced the principle of performativity (1984). Truth was now to be understood, not as a function of what is known abstractly, but as a function of the power of systems that it releases and drives (whether in the technological, social, personal, or institutional spheres). This principle was tendered by Lyotard as part of his description of "postmodernism." If modernity had characteristically been a world of formal reasoning and critical and consensual dialogue over truth claims, now—in the postmodern world—that order was shattered, there being no rational principles on which one could rely. Legitimacy was merely a matter of power, efficiency, and pragmatism. In a sense, "truth" as such had evaporated.

Now, we are told, we are in a post-post-modern world (Peters, 2011)! There is (somewhat surprisingly for some) a real world, with power structures, and huge interests in the economy and in maximizing the economic return that universities seem to offer. Accordingly, the idea of community-based research poses in sharp form the matter of "community, what community?" And what form does its knowledge interests take? Are they those of economic reason or do they characteristically have some other orientation?

The second fly in the contemporary "universities-in-society" ointment is this. The idea of "community-based research" derives its force in part from tacit connections with notions of the public sphere and of the university having a public role to play. In other words, there are—in its syntactical hinterland—intimations of answers to the questions just posed. "Community-based research" is intended, not to be a vehicle for economic reason, but one for a community-enhancing form of reasoning. But what form of reasoning might this be?

Perhaps it is through the very concept of "community-based research" that knowledge claims (and emerging forms of understanding) can be legitimized, neither through an academicism that is now defunct nor in terms of performative or economic reason. The *challenge* lies in spelling out just what such a legitimation might look like, if indeed it is available. Without such a legitimation, all talk of "community-based research" is spurious, completely lacking foundations.

The Very Idea of Community-Based Research

As implied, the idea of community-based research is clearer as to what it is not, rather than as to what it is. Some positive purchase can be had, however. Community-based research is hinged on the notion of community, and community points to social ties that are both communal and reciprocal. There is also the presence of a public sphere, in which there are forums for communication and the growth of understanding that have an element of collective recognition even while the space allows for, and encourages, disagreements. A challenge, however, to be met here is that the very notion of a public sphere is in difficulty, for today we are surely faced with multiple publics. Nevertheless, at the heart of such ideas are sentiments of otherness, hospitality, and fraternity.

Such elements of social solidarity come into play where transactions are guided by a sense of a collective social good. In turn, it follows that "community-based research" cannot be research that is guided by economic return, hierarchy, or rankings, or be such as to treat people as a means to knowledge. But further, community-based research too cannot be research that merely advances academic interests or even just results in epistemological gains. Plainly, community-based research is research that is founded on an interest in the well-being of the community. But, as intimated, what more it is—or might be—is still an open matter.

In his early work, Jürgen Habermas (1978) drew attention to the way in which knowing efforts derive from certain kinds of social interests, termed by him "knowledge-constitutive interests," and he distinguished cognitive, instrumental, and critical interests. A question that the idea of community-based research poses, therefore, is this: Does community-based research derive from a different kind—a fourth kind—of "knowledge-constitutive interest" or is it some amalgam of the three interests that Habermas distinguished?

Let us say that community-based research does indeed represent a new kind of knowledge interest, reflected neither in any of those three other interests—cognitive, instrumental, or critical—nor even in any amalgam of them. The idea of knowledge deriving from an interest in community has sentiments of reciprocity, civil society, sociality, dialogue, equity, and the public sphere that mark it out as a distinctive interest. And here we look to Habermas' later work on communicative reason (Habermas, 1984; 1987), with its focus on consensual dialogue as a means of justifying truth claims. Perhaps, too, not far away are additional sentiments of social ownership and even social transformation and even yet of universality.

But if it is the case that community-based research represents a new kind of knowledge interest, then we have a large challenge facing us. On the one hand lies the epistemological challenge of establishing a way—or ways—in which "community" can come into play in filling out a new conception of knowledge and truth claims. On the other hand there is the practical challenge of working out the societal, institutional, political, and policy implications of any such (new) conception of "community-based" knowledge. For this latter task, the social theorist surely has the responsibility of attempting to identify a set of practical principles to which community-based research should adhere. Only through fulfilling this dual epistemological and social-theoretical task might the idea of community-based research find any kind of secure legitimation. (After all, "legitimation" is precisely such a hybrid concept, containing both a conceptual element in (pure) reason and a social-theoretical element in practical reason.)

Most of the contributions to this volume can surely be said to be addressed to the second of these tasks, that of exploring the social and practical conditions and circumstances in which community-based research can successfully thrive. In the remaining part of this chapter, I shall delve further into the epistemological dimension of the idea of community-based research and offer some practical principles by which it might be pursued, situating it against the background of what I term the ecological university.

The Idea of the Ecological University

The idea of the ecological university would be realized in universities that took seriously their interconnections with the world and sought not merely to sustain the world (through those interconnections), but actively and deliberately sought to improve the world. More than that, an "ecological" university would be sensitive to the several ecologies through which it engaged—or potentially engaged—with the world. Those ecologies include ecologies of knowledge, social institutions, the economy, culture, and persons. In each case, the ecological university would be oriented toward the well-being of each ecological system, whether that of individual persons, institutions, or the wider society.

The *fundamental* orientation of the ecological university, accordingly, would be neither toward economic return or efficiency on the one hand (an instrumental orientation) nor toward a warranting of formal truth claims and embedding them in intellectual fields (a cognitive orientation) on the other hand, but would be one of enhancing societal and personal well-being. Its activities—in research, teaching, and wider societal engagement—would all be tackled with such an orientation in mind. Further, this would be a university, not merely intent on orchestrating its knowledge resources and its human resources in the service of the well-being of the ecologies with which it was interconnected, but it would actively intervene in those ecologies so as to yield benefits within them.

The standard performance indicators of university performance that speak to cognitive agendas (indicators of academic output and citation impact) and instrumental agendas (indicators of turnover, throughput, and economic impact) would be otiose for such a university. Instead, it would seek quite different indicators, indicators that illuminate the ways in which, and the extent to which, it was engaging with its wider hinterland, especially with the social and civil ecologies with which it was intimately connected (both in its home country and globally) *and* having an impact on their development.

For such a university, the idea of community-based research would be of interest, as a guiding or even steering principle for its self-understanding. Some critical questions and observations would surely be prompted, however, right at the outset. An immediate first observation would be that, in its community-based interactions, the ecological university would have a major interest in *teaching*. Indeed, the ecological university would take a special interest in teaching and would be exploring ways in which—for example, in social action projects, and in promulgating its research to different publics— it might extend its pedagogical functioning in novel ways. The ecological university, after all, would have a particular interest, not only in widening social understanding of its research efforts and outcomes, but also in enabling groups in the wider society to be empowered to take action themselves, on the basis of their wider understandings of themselves and their possibilities, in society and in the world.

To turn to the matter of community-based *research* and the ecological university, we see an immediate difficulty. The ecological university would be sensitive to the various ecologies in which it moves and thence to the manifold communities that are caught in their webs, and thus the very concept of "community" would be troublesome. In its practical engagements with the wider society in any venture of any size and complexity—say, in the area of health and medicine—the university will be intimately involved with a large number of (at once intermeshing and possibly conflicting) communities, plural. There will be dimensions in its engagements with those multiple communities of both the (systems) complexity and the (conceptual) super-complexity of which we spoke earlier. (Different communities will have quite different perspectives on and interpretations of what "health" and proper health policies might look like in an advanced society *and* globally.)

But now the very idea of "community" presents a further problematic. There can be no romanticizing of "community," so as to imply an organic and self-contained grouping, with a relatively orderly set of unified horizons accepted by all. Now, in an Internet age, a global age, a literate age of multiple perspectives and horizons, "community"—if it is to retain traction as a concept—has to be sensitive to the ephemerality, the diffuseness, and the varied scope of the term.

Many are urging that we should see a development of "universities without walls" (Finnegan, 2005), a development that becomes all the more possible and challenging in an Internet age. Indeed, many universities are taking up this challenge and placing both their teaching and their research wares into the "community." Not only are course units and research findings being shared with wider publics, but universities are enlisting the active engagement of their various publics in the design of research and even inviting public engagement with massive research databases in fields as diverse as astronomy and archeology, and the diverse fields will generate their own *cognitive communities* (plural) *in the wider society*. "Community-based research" is, therefore, in a sense, already with us, but the phrase is perhaps becoming inadequate and misleading. Rather, a much more complex set of interactions is opening up in the forms of community-sensitive research, community-participatory research, community-engaged research, and so forth. The "base" here is far too static.

Furthermore, while "community" speaks of dialogue, reciprocity, recognition, and respect for persons, the *lifeworld* (Habermas, 1984; 1987), nowadays there are questions as to whether "community" can or should be confined in this way. Can it not be entertained that some communities are structured around interests in systems building, in surveillance, in economic growth, in corporateness, and so on, precisely in ways that treat persons as means rather than ends (if indeed persons as such are recognized at all)? Does, for example, the idea of "the financial community" not carry weight today? Are communities now also much more diffuse, distributed—often via the Internet—across countries, social class, and ethnicities?

These reflections are important here. How, for example, is the idea of community to play out in relation to biomedical research? This is a world in which there are massive forces, interests, and players, involving global pharmaceutical companies, politics, and national and regional regulatory regimes, as well as academic interests across the natural and social sciences, humanities, and professional fields, in addition to patients, citizens and parents, and local and national consumer groups. Perhaps, for such a socio-practical field, a useful distinction might be made as between *lifeworld* communities and *corporate* communities. Manifestly, in such a socio-practical field, "community" becomes a concept fraught with difficulty.

Nor can there be a case for the university arbitrarily limiting its notion of "community" (to local or even national groupings more representative of the lifeworld) and focusing its research efforts there. For such research efforts will only be doomed to limit themselves, if indeed they could ever find any practical way of being realized. For example, suppose an "ecological university" wished to develop a research program in pharmaceutical research that was oriented toward "the community" in seeking to develop generic drugs to counter the research programs of multinational drug companies. Such a research program only makes practical, financial, and political sense if the university concerned adopts the widest sense of community and negotiates a position amid conflicting interests of the many communities involved in the terrain.

Legitimating community-based research has, therefore, to take on complex practical considerations and matters of knowledge-in-action, political epistemology, and corporate capitalism as well as acting out concerns for the lifeworld of peoples and individuals, all of whom are distributed across multiple communities (with single individuals playing out roles both in corporate communities as well as in lifeworld communities).

Finding a Base for Community-Based Research

If in "community-based" research the term community is fraught with difficulty, no less is the term based. For what is this "base"? Let us heretically pick up the example with which we have just been engaging. It could be said that pharmaceutical research in Western universities has been *far too much* "based" in the community, namely in the pharmaceutical community. In this research, Big Pharma—as it is often termed—has notoriously so orchestrated biochemical and pharmaceutical research that it has played to corporate concerns of the large international pharmaceutical companies. Tactics such as pharma company staff members writing papers for the academic (peer-reviewed) literature but having academics presented as the authors, manipulating patents where universities have played a major part in the research, and keeping confidential the results of drug trials research undertaken by universities have been employed so as to reduce universities' control over company-funded research.

It may be said that this has little or nothing to do with community-based research, but, as implied, this begs the question as to what is to count as "community." The point here is less to call attention to a particular set of practices based in the community and more to put into question the very notion of community-*based* research. Part of the force of the term, we may take it, derives from a sense that the research should be less based in the interests of the academic community and more in the interests of the wider community. Let us overlook the question begged here as to whether or not we can, any longer, speak of an *academic* community and turn to the epistemological matters that the notion of community-based research raises.

Over the 900-year history of the modern university, knowledge has come to be systematized in a disciplinary structure and in a collective endeavor that has come to be known as "research." Through entities and practices such as peer-reviewed journals, specialist seminars and conferences, and intangible rules and procedures connected both with methodologies and communication structures, what counts as knowledge is a matter of this collective set of dynamic conventions, conducted in an orientation of neutrality and disinterestedness.

Here, we consider the concept of *epistemic communities*, and its associated sentiments of claims to knowledge being secured and sedimented through collective efforts on the part of the members of those communities, its members having been judged collectively to have the *legitimate* right to a voice. (By and large, sociologists are not judged to have this right in engineering communities and physicists are not often judged to have this right in anthropological communities.) It is the hard-won nature of the research of such specific epistemic communities, with its largely value-neutral orientation, that has made it valuable not only to governments (with the role of academic adviser growing in importance) but also to wider societal communities themselves.

Against this background, the idea of community-based research raises awkward problems. Are the epistemic communities of the academy to yield their control over aspects of the research enterprise to wider societal communities? And if so, just which aspects are they to be? To what extent can such control be yielded without jeopardizing the integrity and validity of "research"? The matter here is essentially epistemological: What is to count as "knowledge"? "Knowledge," after all, is more than mere belief; it is even more than true belief. It is true belief that has come up to some kind of standard. It is "warranted" true belief. So the issue arises as to what is to count as a warrant, bearing in mind that just what counts as a warrant has varied not only across intellectual and professional fields but has also varied through time.

Admittedly, the dimension of power enters here. As Foucault (1980) observed, systems of knowledge can be said to constitute "discursive regimes" backed by sources of power. And recently, Michael Young (2008) has distinguished between "knowledge of the powerful" and "powerful knowledge": knowledge may have powerful backers but it may also provide powerful resources for negotiating one's way—or a community's way—in and through the world. This distinction carries weight, particularly in the idea of powerful knowledge. Knowledge is not only to be described as a set of social processes (by the sociologists) but it also raises criteria of warrant or—if not truth then—truthfulness (Williams, 2002). Truth claims are precisely those claims that may be examined and granted support or dissent by those who have authority to pronounce on the matter—by epistemic communities, indeed. The very notion of "peer review" contains the idea of persons who have authority to pronounce on truth claims and of their rightful membership of the relevant epistemic communities. And here, we should note, the most junior lecturer has the formal right to question the most senior professor and even, on occasions, pass judgment on his or her truth claims.

Imagining the Ecological University

These reflections raise profound issues for the whole idea of community-based research and thence for ideas of the university that are sensitive to such an idea. Some proclaim that what is in question here is the epistemological character of research and that community-based research points to a new epistemology, but what exactly is that to mean? What is to be the epistemological status of community-based research? Is the community to be permitted to have some measure of authority to pronounce on the veracity of truth claims? Are the communities in the wider society to be granted membership of the relevant epistemic communities? If so, to what extent and in what ways are such communities in the wider society to be granted such a status?

There lies here an issue to do with the social relations of knowledge *management* rather than the social relations of knowledge *production*. It is to such a distinction that an idea such as that of the ecological university has to be alert, if it is to do serious practical as well as serious theoretical work. The idea of the ecological university speaks to beliefs that the university has a responsibility, not merely to have regard to its interconnections with the wider society, but also to its well-being. More especially, this university is alert to the manifold ecologies through which it forms those interconnections—ecologies of knowledge, persons, social institutions, the public sphere, and even the economy—and seeks to enhance their well-being. For such a university, accordingly, engagement is not an option but a necessity of its functioning. But, as implied, what is to count as a proper engagement is moot.

Research, and the knowledge thereby gained, is of potential value to the community on account of its being robust and hard-won. Its knowledge is reliable. Moves in the direction of community in the framing of research have a responsibility not to jeopardize the integrity of the knowledge so won. Critical realism distinguishes within an ontological realm, the realm of the "real" world, in which lie generative mechanisms that in turn generate the "actual" world, out of which emerges the "experienced" world (Bhaskar, 2002). It is in this third realm—the experienced world—that epistemology comes into play, namely our efforts to know the world. The ecological university would be a university in which those efforts to come to know the world would seek understandings both of the ways in which generative mechanisms—such as power structures, ideologies, and inequalities—are afoot in the social world and of ways in which communities can be legitimately involved in the shaping of the research process and in the implementation of knowledge and understandings that flow from that research. Such an ecological university would be sensitive, therefore, to the manifold ways in which communities can be implicated both in the ontological structures underlying knowledge and in the forming of imaginative frameworks for understanding the world and for enhancing its well-being in putting such knowledge into action.

Conclusion

The notion of community-based research is an awkward term. It both promises too much and, in the process, falls short of its potential. Deployed without due care, it could herald the corruption—and thereby the lessening—of the very knowledge whose power it is seeking to enlist (in the service of the community). The university—in particular, the ecological university—does have a responsibility to reach out to the community, to have a care or concern for the community, and to play its part in enhancing the well-being of the community. The university can and should, where practicable, enlist the community in its research activities, as indeed many universities do (e.g., placing massive research-generated databases in the public sphere). But rather than speaking of community-based research, other terms such as community-*sensitive*, community-*transacted*, community-*involved*, community-*engaged*, community-*oriented*, and even community-*participatory* research may be more helpful.

In other words, lurking within the idea of community-based research are crucial distinctions that should be made and—if brought out—may help the university and its communities together glimpse possibilities not hitherto recognized. Unless the idea of community-based research is critiqued and dissected and reconstructed—in a positive and practical vein, sensitive to the complexities in which the university (in the liquid global world of the twenty-first century) finds itself—"community-based" research may be overloaded with epistemic expectations that it cannot reasonably meet.

Some practical principles beckon for the ecological university in meeting its responsibilities toward its various wider communities. So far as practicable, in undertaking any research venture:

1. An inventory should be drawn up of the manifold communities (plural) implicated in the intended research, not only at the epistemological level of understanding, perception, and utilization, but also at the ontological level of causal structures.
2. Efforts should be made to reach out to those communities in shaping the research, in its conceptualization and its methods. (This would hold for research in the hard sciences as well as research in the social sciences, humanities, and professional fields.)
3. Consideration should be given to ways in which the public sphere might be enhanced, through making results of the research available through open access databases and through opening dialogue with the publics involved.
4. The researchers involved should seek to become public intellectuals in speaking out and transmitting the research to the widest set of audiences (which would in turn pose communication challenges, so that such messages would be comprehensible to multiple audiences) involving, again, understandings of (the communities of) the powerful and the relatively powerless.
5. Where appropriate, the researchers concerned should involve themselves in action in, and with, the relevant community (or communities) so as to maximize the enhanced well-being that the research might in principle offer.

A set of practical principles such as these would admittedly circumscribe so-called community-based research but they would also help to realize the potential of the community-*oriented* university—and the ecological university—in the complex and global world of the twenty-first century.

CHAPTER 14

Higher Education and the Public Good: Precarious Potential?

Mala Singh

Introduction

Concerns about and critiques of neoliberal policy regimes in higher education have heightened the search for alternative normative and organizational models, many of which have coalesced around the necessity to reimagine and defend the public missions of higher education. This has given the notion of the public good greater resonance as an alternative or supplementary frame of reference in debates about higher education and social change. This chapter identifies some frequently raised issues in the analytical literature on the public good in order to indicate the range of conceptual and operational challenges at stake. It argues that the ideological constraints and practical difficulties in moving toward a public good regime make the potential and prospects of the notion uncertain and almost precarious in constituting a new foundational basis for thinking about the social value of higher education. Nevertheless, resisting or mediating public "bads" and increasing or joining up a variety of public good interventions remain as necessary and valuable tasks in the face of contending social purposes of higher education.

The Purpose of the University

Writing in 1963 in his book *The Uses of the University*, Clark Kerr pointed to the fact that the university in its contemporary form as a multiversity has a variety of purposes ascribed to it, which may well be in contention with one another. He characterized the contest among the purposes in the following way:

> These several competing visions of true purpose, each relating to a different layer of history, a different web of forces, cause much of the malaise in the university communities of today. The university is so many things to so many different people that it must, of necessity, be partially at war with itself.
>
> (2001, p. 7)

The clamor of contending purposes is no less insistent today. In many higher education systems, the notions of the knowledge society and knowledge economy, despite differences in the social presumptions and change agendas underpinning these two notions, are central to the current framing of internally and externally defined goals and purposes of higher education. As a result, higher education institutions are attempting to respond simultaneously to the entrepreneurial demands of the knowledge economy and the broader "social good" aspirations of the knowledge society (Sorlin and Vessuri, 2007). The debate about higher education and the public good is one reflection of competing expectations from contemporary higher education, re-posing questions about the ideological and practical implications of the changing "social compact" between higher education and society.

Concerns and conceptions about the public purposes and social uses of the university are neither a contemporary preoccupation, nor a phenomenon specific to societies in the global North or global South. The professional training responsibility of medieval universities (in medicine, law, and theology), the democratizing rationale of land-grant universities in the United States (Morrill Act, 1862), the notion of the "developmental university" in postindependence African countries (Coleman, 1984), and expectations that universities in the Middle East will contribute to democratizing the state and society as part of a strong civil society movement (Mojab, 2000) are examples, in different ages and societies, of proposals and projects to forge a connection between higher education and social purposes. Such examples presume some underpinning notion of societal good. However, in an era of globalization and internationalization, thinking about the social purposes and public value of higher education has been shaped by the impact of some recurring trends: externally driven regulatory formulas for efficiency and accountability as the public purse shrinks even further; stakeholder pressures for changes in traditional modes of governance, knowledge production, and skills development; demands for partnerships that are more responsive to knowledge economy and innovation discourses; and the growing global power of the competitive reputational economy (Hazelkorn, 2011) as research assessment and ranking systems become more compelling. The meanings and possibilities of the public good in higher education are bound to reflect the pushes and pulls of these prevailing trends. The dominance of knowledge economy notions is evident in many higher education policy frameworks and debates (Shattock, 2009; Wilson Review, 2012). At the same time, numerous critiques of overly economistic framings of higher education have yielded counterproposals for revalorizing public good objectives in the ethos and work of higher education institutions (Hind, 2010; Bailey and Freedman, 2011). The public good discourse in higher education is now enjoying greater visibility and attention in both analytical literatures and the policy domain. The analytical literature on the subject is on the increase, with a growing number of books and articles elaborating on the conceptual, normative, and policy dimensions of the issue.[1] Expressing a commitment to the public good in higher education is now common in the policy world in a variety of national, regional, and international settings.[2] There are also several instances of structured policy, advocacy, and research initiatives intended to increase understandings of and information about higher education and the public good.[3] The current economic and social crises in neoliberal policy regimes in higher education have heightened the search for alternative normative and organizational models, many of which have coalesced around the necessity to reimagine, strengthen, and defend the public missions of higher education as part of a larger restoration of public values and public interest in institutional life. This has given the notion of the public good greater resonance as an alternative or supplementary frame of reference in debates about necessary transformations within higher education as well as the role of higher education in social change.

Many analyses of the public good take as their starting point critiques of "public bads" in higher education (Kaul, 2001, p. 268; Marginson, 2007, p. 324). Currently, these are often presumed to be the negative consequences of neoliberal imperatives in the form of corporatization, privatization, commercialization, individual consumer choice arguments, and economic reductionism (Kezar et al., 2005). The public good literature has moved somewhat beyond rhetorical declarations and normative defenses to important conceptual clarifications and elaborations of "publicness," "publics," and "public goods" and, to a lesser extent, to identification of areas, targets, and projects for public good transformations, reflections on what publicness in the disciplines means,[4] and attempts to document public good initiatives and approaches in higher education. There is also clear recognition that the pursuit of public good possibilities in higher education should not be confined to community engagement but also seen as an integral part of the teaching and research functions of higher education (Jonathan, 2001; Chambers and Gopaul, 2008).

The growing analytical literature is valuable in providing much-needed clarifications of the conceptual and theoretical foundations of public good approaches, marking out key constitutive elements of the notion of the public good, capturing explorations of public good possibilities in teaching,[5] research, and third-function activities, and providing examples of contextualization and localization of public good notions (Sall et al., 2003; Leibowitz, 2012). However, a critic like Dill is dismissive of much recent analysis of the public good in higher education[6] as being "largely rhetorical and qualitative rather than being empirical" (2011). Dill's critique is not entirely unwarranted. Sustained attention to concrete practices aimed at institutionalizing the public good, especially at the level of system and institutional design, and engagement with the public good as a field of "strategic planning"[7] or of empirical research has been less substantial than expected. This raises quite pragmatic questions about the range of institutional and behavioral changes that are needed in order to concretize the public good.

In the remainder of this chapter, I identify some frequently raised issues in the analytical literature on the public good in order to indicate the range of conceptual and operational challenges that are at stake in pursuing the public good. I then examine questions about the possible coexistence or non-commensurability of public good goals and neoliberal imperatives in the current contest of purposes. I argue that the ideological constraints and translational difficulties in moving toward an overarching public good regime make the potential and prospects of the notion uncertain, ambiguous, and almost precarious in constituting a new foundational basis for thinking about the value of higher education to the needs of social change. Nevertheless, resisting or mediating public "bads" and increasing or joining up a variety of public good interventions remain as necessary and valuable tasks in negotiating a path across the contending purposes of higher education.

On Conceptions and Dimensions of the Public Good

Concerns about the public good can be understood within the context of two opposing discourses about the purposes and value(s) of contemporary higher education. Despite many well-founded critiques of it, the still dominant discourse, especially in the policy world, is associated with what is familiarly described as a neoliberal paradigm of higher education—the idea of higher education as an essential part of the "knowledge economy," a producer of knowledge and skills for economic competitiveness, and a facilitator of private interests. The association of higher education and the public good, despite a growing presence in research and policy, is still part of a secondary debate. This latter discourse presumes that higher education is a contributor to achieving broader public purposes that encompass, but are not reducible to, narrowly framed economic goals and private interests. A strong version of this position is that contemporary higher education is to be viewed not only in its entrepreneurial role in a knowledge economy but in its civic role as a facilitator of a "knowledge democracy"—a contributor to " the quality of democratic life and democratic processes" (Biesta, 2007, p. 468). Despite their differing ideological nuances, both these discourses presume that higher education can and ought to contribute to "societal good." They are both grounded in the view that higher education institutions are socially accountable institutions and therefore have to deliver social benefits through their core functions.[8] The two discourses have, however, quite different associated assumptions and expectations about the roles of states and markets in higher education, the purposes and accountabilities of higher education, the weight of public and private goals and interests in producing social benefits, and the responsibilities of citizenship in addressing individual and societal obligations.

A look at the analytical literature shows that the connection between higher education and the public good is being articulated largely along two main motifs—higher education itself *as* a public good and higher education *for* the public good. Included in the debates are reassertions of the importance of public missions and public responsibilities of higher education, concerns about the imbalances in the weight given to public and private interests in policy and practice, the democratic and civic roles of public higher education, and higher education as a constituent part of the public sphere. There are also associated debates about social justice and the need for structural transformations in higher education. It appears that, analytically, the frontiers of the theme are still being marked out and the jurisdictions and possibilities of the notion are being articulated more fully and concretely. In such debates though, the idea of higher education institutions (and of academe) as social critic is a far less emphasized theme.

From the point of view of defining or conceptualizing the public good, persuasive arguments remind us that there is no single or fixed formula for stipulating the content of the public good, especially in abstraction from specific sociopolitical struggles. The notion is seen to require ongoing contextualization, negotiation, and trade-offs. For Calhoun, the public good is not a given, self-evident notion. He argues that there is a "continuous reshaping of the identity of any public (and of communities within it) as well as of the goods which different actors pursue" (1998, p. 20). His much-quoted phrase "which public? and Whose good?" (1998, p. 20) is now almost part of the "common sense" about the public good. It reminds us that both "public" and "good" are fuzzy and shifting notions, neither unitary nor homogeneous, and contextually shaped and contested even within the same contexts. Analysts have argued that there are many publics rather than *a* public, that publics are not simply "out there" but are constituted, enacted, summoned, called into existence, and that they could be overlapping in interest, time bound, and contingent (Mahony et al., 2010; Benington and Moore, 2011). To this increasing layering of complexity in the notion of "public," one can add analyses that make the point that publics are not self-evidently progressive and cannot be presumed automatically to have emancipatory interests in contradistinction to private constituencies. There are publics, for instance, that value a consumer approach to higher education (Rhoades, 1987). Arguments have also cautioned against understanding the public good as no more than an aggregation of private goods (Marginson, 2007; Calhoun, 2009).

The kinds of conceptual ambiguities indicated above extend to how higher education is understood in its public good dimensions. Debate about higher education itself *as* a public good often focuses on the responsibility of the state for the resourcing of higher education and also on the state's regulatory and oversight role, even where state funding is not substantial. In this regard, analysts have pointed to incongruities in the notion of the public university as a state-funded and nonprofit institution since, increasingly, higher education resourcing tends to come from both public and private sources, and entrepreneurialism characterizes the approach of both public and private institutions (Dill, 2005).[9] Given the difficulties in distinguishing cleanly between public and private higher education, analysts like Dill and also Calhoun (2011) argue that it is better to focus on the public accountability of all higher education institutions, irrespective of public or private funding.

Another crucial debate in this outline of public good complexity focuses on the difficulties of viewing higher education as a pure public good in light of the fact that higher education avails of a mix of both private and public benefits. Individuals benefit through acquiring credentials, increased employment and income possibilities, and social mobility. However, society too benefits from a more educated workforce and citizenry, a larger tax base, and less dependency on government welfare support (IHEP, 1998). Analysts have also reminded us that higher education has the potential to reproduce inequalities as much as to undercut them, through simultaneously operating exclusionary and inclusionary mechanisms (Jonathan, 2001; Marginson, 2007). In relation to the latter, the literature points to trends toward massification and impressive growth in student participation rates, which have resulted in increasing both private and public benefits (Altbach, 1999) but not without a dark side—increasing differentiation and stratification in higher education according to student socioeconomic profile and quality (Shavit et al., 2007; Brennan and Naidoo, 2007).

Attempts to elaborate on the key dimensions of the public good have often encompassed normative concerns about shifts in what is valued in and about higher education in the current conjuncture. The regulatory emphasis on efficiency and effectiveness in the face of large-scale public expenditure cuts is argued to have downgraded the intrinsic or nonmonetary value of education in favor of the economically instrumental and the commodifiable. This normative shift is viewed as a threat to higher education as a general source of public benefits. Hence the many critiques of the absolutization of the economic purposes of higher education (labor market and employability imperatives in teaching, industry imperatives in research). In response, a range of counterproposals seek to valorize the noneconomic purposes of higher education, which are seen to hold greater possibilities for public good outcomes. Such proposals argue that higher education should afford transformatory intellectual and cultural experiences for students as well as opportunities for personal development (Barnett, 1994); ensure that there are spaces for the pursuit of knowledge that is not narrowly instrumental (Burawoy, 2011); promote public discourse (Calhoun, 2011); contribute to the building of critical and civic capabilities for democratic citizenship (Bergan, 2005; Chambers and Gopaul, 2008); and provide a far-seeing intellectually imaginative leadership role not only in being responsive to what citizens aspire to presently but also in providing "resources for deepening and modifying those aspirations as circumstances change" (Jonathan, 2001, p. 79).

The above-mentioned concern about changing values in higher education draws attention both to normative orientations that undermine or constrain the public good as well as to the normative principles and values that are thought to be constitutive of the public good. The values focus raises two sets of questions that are important for the purposes of both analysis and practice. One question pertains to the necessity to translate normative public good commitments into structural and operational changes—What kinds of ethical practices, both institutional and individual, follow from normative commitments to the public good in higher education? What in fact constitutes a public good praxis? The second question relates to whether the notion of the public good simply functions as a meta-level umbrella term for a variety of associated values such as social justice, inclusivity, and fairness, or whether it adds a distinctive "public" dimension to the kinds of values indicated above.

Finally, some analysts have highlighted the role and importance of the dialogic, the deliberative, and the interactive in processes of identifying and working toward the public good as opposed to market coercion or statist fiat. This dialogic dimension in reaching consensus on and operationalizing the public good is part of larger debates about deliberative democracy and the role of rational-critical debate among citizens in negotiating agreements on social choices and actions (Habermas, 2006; Bohman, 2000). Central to this debate are claims about the university (more often in aspiration than historically realized) as a discursive platform par excellence, a place for "reasoned discourse" (Calhoun, 1998, pp. 2–3), and a crucial component of and guardian of the public sphere (Delanty, 2001; Burawoy, 2011; Docherty, 2011). Critical questions posed to Habermas' notion of the bourgeois public sphere (Calhoun, 1993) are also pertinent in assessing claims about the university as a bulwark of the public sphere—Who can participate and who is still excluded from participating in a "rational-critical debate" in this public sphere space? Despite the growth and diversity in student and staff numbers, and many more instances of higher education-external partner collaborations, the extent of rational-critical debate on public good questions within higher education institutions themselves and between institutions and external communities (beyond contractual considerations) appears to be patchy and uneven.

The issues surveyed briefly above straddle conceptual expositions and clarifications of the public good, normative bottom-line principles, structural and behavioral conditionalities, modalities and strategies for action (including identification of sites of potential transformation), and cautionary insights about the public good and its limits as much as imaginative possibilities for its realization. What this intends to convey is a sense of the emerging contours of the public good analytical landscape and signal the range and complexity of the dimensions that have to be considered in invoking and acting on the public good in higher education. However, while acknowledging cautionary insights about the contextual and contested nature of the public good, there are risks of paralysis or continuing inertia in overstating considerations of public good contingency and complexity. What the insights above do point to is the need for close political and empirical analyses of "publics" and "goods," especially the particular kind of good that higher education is or facilitates. The debates above are valuable in providing a quite concrete set of reference points for undertaking focused contextual analyses of public bad impacts and public good possibilities. On the basis of such analyses, an appropriate set of approaches and tasks could be fashioned in seeking to move beyond normative proclamations and symbolic commitments to the public good in higher education.

The Public Good: Alternative or Supplement?

Changes to make higher education more responsive to the knowledge economy have necessitated the introduction of new policies, institutional structures, resourcing strategies, achievement indicators, staff expertise profiles, and external partnerships. The attempt to institutionalize the public good in higher education would equally require concomitant changes to policies, structures, funding models, evaluative systems, etc., which could then serve as concrete platforms for the effective realization of public good aspirations and goals. One would have to consider what national and institutional systems would look like if designed, steered, and evaluated from the perspective of advancing the public good.

The move from the idea of the public good as normative ideal to policy platform and concrete change mechanism in higher education requires attention to the strategic and operational dimensions of the public good. In making this move, it is difficult to avoid the question about whether the public good postulate is to be viewed as an ideological alternative to current economically overdetermined conceptions of higher education or as a supplementary internal policy strand and strategic pathway that is under-addressed in the current knowledge society framing. What, for instance, is the role and status of a notion like the public good within a network of organizing concepts that are currently hegemonic, such as knowledge economy, innovation, entrepreneurialism, and world-class excellence? As indicated earlier, the diversity of social expectations of higher education and the contradictory pulls of multiple social demands has increased in the context of current knowledge society discourses. Is the public good one goal and policy plank among others within the higher education system, in a "marketplace of ideas" and narratives about change, alongside economic competitiveness, educating for employability, advancing individual interests, and increasing consumer choice? Or does the public good trump all other values and approaches and, in fact, constitute the foundational narrative and platform from which the "structural transformation" (Calhoun, 2006b) of higher education could be launched?

Different sides of this question have been argued. Crouch (2011) proceeds from the view that the public values conflict is not a simple one only between state and market and maintains that all three realms of state, market, and values attempt to relate and balance public and private interests. "Public and private should be used as end points on a continuum, not as alternatives" (2011, p. 73). Calhoun reminds us that "Public and private purposes are not always divided by a neat line" (2011, p. 3). Kezar speaks of the need "to create a new vision for higher education that respects a balance between market forces and the public good" (2005, p. 26). Newman and Couturier argue that the market should be steered to "benefit society and serve the greater public good" (2002, p. 2). In some higher education systems, it is evident that there are policy initiatives that seek to juggle economic competitiveness priorities and public good commitments within a knowledge economy framework.[10]

Given the proliferation of socially oriented goals for and demands on higher education and the resulting struggle to hold together a mix of often contending social, intellectual, and economic development agendas, it is unsurprising that the management of "complexity" (Barnett, 2000) becomes a compelling contemporary imperative rather than framing the issue of higher education transformation as a matter of stark choices between public and private goods. Hence the attractiveness of the argument that the public good in relation to higher education may be better viewed as a notion that requires thinking beyond the distinctions of states and markets, public and private, individual and societal, and transformation and reproduction, toward a position that seeks a greater balance between and among these elements.

There are, however, analysts who are skeptical about the possibilities of achieving public good objectives in a sustained and widespread way within the current knowledge economy regime, seeing neoliberalism in higher education as the "antithesis of public good" (Chambers and Gopaul, 2008, p. 61). Docherty, for instance, sees the university as being central to "ideas of freedom and justice" and the extending of democracy (2011, p. 11) and opposes the idea that the public sphere (of which the university is a key institution) is a marketplace of ideas of all kinds. Part of the concern about the coexistence of the public good strand within the dominant neoliberal organizational model of higher education is the danger that it might be reduced to a bounded pacificatory discourse, with limited potential to challenge the status quo or form the basis for real alternative practices.

Views about the irreconcilability of public and private good logics in structuring change in higher education are also premised on the way that the contemporary state is characterized in neoliberal regimes. Sivanandan argues, for instance, that the "market state is antithetical to the good society" (2013, p. 1). This implies that public good transformations of higher education is a corollary of a larger project of state and societal transformation. A variant of this view can be seen in the position that there are distinct limits and conditionalities to the contribution of higher education to the public good if higher education transformation is viewed as a political project separate from or unrelated to social reform of policy, structural arrangements, and practices in other social sectors. Jonathan (2001) puts it well:

> Just what higher education can contribute to the public good depends on how we order that practice: whether it will deliver what it might depends on how we order supporting social practices.
>
> (p. 86)

The absence in many countries of feasible alternative political projects to radically transform the neoliberal "market state" into a "public good state" begs the question as to whether public good initiatives in higher education must, by and large, await larger state and global economic regime transformations as a condition for their sustained success. What are the possibilities for such initiatives to be inserted (bottom-up and appropriately contextualized and negotiated) into the current conjuncture in order to begin to shift the balances from the privatizing missions of higher education to more publicly oriented ones? The tactical reordering of higher education to position it to contribute more substantially to the public good could in fact be seen as a constituent part of a multilayered struggle to make public values and public good goals prevail as part of larger processes of social transformation. This could involve the development of a new mix of policy priorities, rethinking funding allocations, reorienting curriculum, pedagogy, and research priorities, forging new or additional external partnerships, redefining graduate competencies, and redesigning evaluation systems and impact indicators. The question would, nevertheless, remain, whether, in the "long march" through higher education systems and institutions, some key publics and public interests, some almost nonnegotiable public value principles, and some clear limits on privatizing interests would have to be identified and asserted, together with a recognition of the structural limits of public good transformations in the current conjuncture.

The Public Good: Precarious Potential?

As indicated in the previous sections, the notion of the public good is a much invoked term, used across different structural locations and ideological positions (by governments as much as by their critics, by the World Social Forum as well as the World Bank). It is also an often-advocated alternative social imaginary posited as the basis on which to wrest higher education away from its neoliberal demons. The recuperation of the idea that higher education institutions have a public mission and that this mission is critical to thinking about the social accountability of higher education now features more strongly in discourses about the value and purposes of higher education. The analytical platform for conceptualizing and acting on public good goals in higher education is also more elucidated. However, the question about the potential of the notion to become hegemonic in the current contest of purposes, not only at a normative level but also in the structures, relationships, and operations of higher education, remains pressing. There are a host of challenges, difficulties, and limits in seeking to move from normative commitment or symbolic policy to a public good praxis. These include questions about the reality of dialogic processes of consensus formation on what the public good is in particular contexts, and the availability of resources and capacity to drive public good-oriented strategic and operational transformations in higher education. They also encompass questions about political will and the extent of the ideological spaces that exist for the reconfiguration of prevailing structural and systemic conditions. What the limits of the notion of the public good are, what its transgressive potential might be in the absence of radical structural change, and what potential dangers are inherent in the very processes of institutionalizing the public good are further considerations in translating notions of the public good into strategies and practices.

Questions have been posed about whose responsibility it is to translate the public good from a norm into a set of empirical possibilities for higher education transformations. Analysts have argued that the public good is a moral collective task not achievable by single effort (Calhoun, 2011; Chambers and Gopaul, 2008) and point to the necessary roles of both government (public authorities) and nongovernment actors in the pursuit and provision of public good benefits. What is the track record of different actors in advancing public good struggles? Despite increasing levels of analytical and policy attention to public good considerations in higher education, it does not appear to be the case that there is a systematic and substantial institutionalization and mainstreaming of public good values and orientations in different higher education systems and structures and within the core functions of higher education, beyond special projects and individual interventions. The reasons are many and varied. Governments are not driving a hard-nosed public good agenda in higher education with dedicated white papers, regulatory instruments, incentive funding, and strong steering as has been the case with other goals like economic competitiveness or innovation. It may also be the case that proponents of the public good have to wage more tenacious struggles, not only to expose analytically, but also to dislodge operationally a number of entrenched approaches that threaten public values in higher education (e.g., the corporatization and commodification of higher education). This undermining of public bads may be a necessary corollary of attempts to define and negotiate pathways toward the public good.

In the absence of a strong official public good framing of higher education, there remains a serious gap in giving sustained, large-scale, and integrated strategic attention to questions of system redesign in higher education in order to be able to translate public good norms into concrete requirements for funding, governance, and management and for rethinking research, teaching and learning, and external partnerships. Such a gap leaves a commitment to the public good only as a "good to have" symbolic position or a soft-edged oppositional discourse that is unable to displace currently hegemonic norms, practices, and structures of power. The notion of the public good appears to be a weak strategic and operational driver, not yet able to function as the basis for a new praxis in transforming higher education. It is even unclear whether it is in fact a shared value across different higher education systems and institutions.

The use of a public good framing to radically rethink and redesign higher education systems and institutions may very well face challenges from private interests that are both external and internal. The structural foundations and pathways shaped by the demands of a knowledge economy approach remain firmly entrenched in higher education, making many students, for example, focus on self-investment in acquiring qualifications for the purposes of upward financial and social mobility. The private interests of individual institutions and academics, seeking to position themselves more competitively in the reputational economy through participation in global, regional, and national ranking and assessment systems, may also impact on or divert attention from public good goals and initiatives (Marginson, 2007). In order for the public good to become rooted in the ethos and practices of higher education, key internal constituencies of students and academics have to accept the notion as fundamental to their work and professional ambitions. What kind of social and intellectual purchase do such constituencies have on the notion of the public good? There are, no doubt, countless examples of academics and students[11] who are actively involved in public good activities through formalized community engagement projects or through individual interventions within and outside their teaching, learning, and research responsibilities. However, academics and students are not uniformly and self-evidently on the side of public good norms and aspirations since both constituencies benefit from private positional goods availed by higher education. The public good may be a useful narrative to express discontent with and even opposition to higher education managers or neoliberal government policy. However, in order to get beyond commitment "noise" or *ad hoc* and special projects, quite concrete questions have to be confronted about what public good obligations and responsibilities accrue to different role-players in the core functions and activities of higher education.

Seeking to embed the normative ethos and the strategic requirements of the public good into the structures and operations of higher education institutions is clearly an important route to making the public good into more of an empirical reality. However, the process of institutionalizing the public good could bring its own difficulties and contradictions. One example of this relates to systems for demonstrating public good accountability. A shift to a public good dispensation assumes that a different state funding and regulatory dispensation would be sought. Even in contexts where public funding for higher education is limited or where private higher education is a significant part of the landscape, the public good question would still be pertinent, on the assumption that higher education remains the "proper business of the democratic state" (Jonathan, 2001, p. 41) What would be the appropriate parameters of state involvement in processes of institutionalizing the public good in higher education? Jonathan speaks of "democratic regulation and accountability" (Jonathan, 2001, p. 39) and the necessity for the transformation of higher education to be "steered and regulated by government" (2001, p. 76). Bergan, in seeking to clarify higher education as a public good and public responsibility (2005), provides examples of non-resourcing dimensions of the responsibility of government authorities for higher education, for example, the provision of enabling policy frameworks and regulatory oversight in facilitating qualifications frameworks, quality assurance systems, equal access provision, and ensuring protections for institutional autonomy and academic freedom through legal frameworks.

In these arguments about public good accountability, issues of state regulation and steering (even quality assurance systems) are not seen as antithetical to public good orientations in higher education. Relatedly, one assumes that it would be desirable to have publicly available information about the efficacy of public good orientations and initiatives in higher education. Information on what public good outcomes are being delivered in and through higher education, to which publics, how effectively, and with what impact may well be a requirement of a public good regime. However, it is not clear that a regulatory regime with a public good orientation in place of a private good one would remove the most serious concerns of critics about the nature, terms, and impact of external regulation on the academic project. What criteria and modalities could acceptably be used for higher education to be evaluated, monitored, and held to public account in a public good paradigm? Critics of performativity in neoliberal paradigms of accountability have often focused on state regulation in the form of measurement and evaluation systems like audit and accreditation as well as on monitoring and reporting systems in higher education. These systems are seen to buttress a narrow economically framed accountability to the private interests of students as consumers and of employers, and are argued to have entrenched an "audit culture" (Strathern, 2000) in higher education, whose consequences are increased surveillance, compliance, homogenization, and threats to academic freedom. Are such negative consequences unlikely or more tolerable if regulatory systems are premised on broader public good accountability to a wider variety of social partners and stakeholders?

In seeking to assess the effective insertion of public good goals into the operational strategies and activities of higher education institutions, the question is bound to arise about the kinds of measuring and evaluative systems and instruments that would be appropriate. This is likely to raise thorny policy and operational dilemmas about the kind of metrics that might be needed to plan for, steer, judge, and incentivize the institutionalization of public good goals, and the kinds of evidence that might count as indicators of public good achievement in conducting a public good "audit" of a higher education institution. It might be an unpalatable step to have to draw on "enemy tools" from new public management in the form of performance indicators and associated measuring, evaluating, and reporting instruments. Alternatively, one would have to investigate whether it might be possible to frame or fashion different regulatory tools, drawing on other literatures and practices of radical planning (Friedmann, 1987). The attempt to assess, evaluate, and monitor a public good orientation in higher education in the name of democratic regulation and accountability raises hard issues about regulatory values and cultures and regulatory system design and methodology. For democratic regulation not to tread too closely to the much-critiqued audit cultures of new public management, the notion of democratic regulation would itself have to be clarified as well as the nature of the relationship between external regulation and academic self-regulation.

The enlargement of the social accountability of higher education to include the public good could be a double-edged sword. A broader public good orientation (beyond the economic domain) would translate into many more significant publics and many more public good targets for higher education to address and deliver on. The emphasis on the dialogical and deliberative could restore to academe a greater space to engage with relevant publics on what it means to balance the relationship between what is valued in and deliverable through the academic project and what drives societal expectations of higher education, between the public and private interests of academia and the public responsibilities of higher education. However, this would require both academe and relevant publics to be persuaded that a conception of the public good in higher education could be reached that accommodates discourses of both academic freedom and social accountability or at least allows for the tensions between them to be consensually negotiated. The enlargement of social accountability could have repercussions that could enrich but also burden higher education with proliferating social demands, raising questions again about the core business of higher education and the limits of what higher education can deliver in respect of public good expectations.

A further example of the potentially contradictory effects of trying to institutionalize the public good stems from the possibility that some forms of institutionalization could close off the imaginative horizon for ongoing engagement with, and enlargement of, public good potential; produce a creeping fundamentalism and authoritarianism around preferred public good conceptualizations and approaches; curtail diversity in choice and agency in interpreting and acting on the public good; and result in the bureaucratization of "official" public good initiatives in higher education systems and institutions. Many of these contradictions revolve around vanguardist or exclusionary claims to power and authority in interpreting and enacting the public good in higher education. Such dangers raise questions as to the balances needed between close steering and surveillance of public good goals and modalities on the one hand and academic self-direction and diversity on the other in interpreting and acting on public good goals. Clearly, some broad framework coherence is needed but without the undue coercion of official models, templates, and criteria.

How full a conception of the public good can be realized under contemporary political and economic regimes? This question applies both to the dominance of global capital in shaping the limits and possibilities for states to fashion social policy, as well as to concerns about weak citizen participation in decision-making in the body politic. In higher education, the power of market ideologies and of private interests has not been displaced despite the destabilizations evident in recent socioeconomic crises. Official policy in many countries still reflects the dominance of knowledge economy and labor market discourses. The possibilities for rebalancing the weight of the public good and private interest dimensions within higher education are likely to be constrained by continuing socioeconomic trends at national and global levels, which have seen a concern for the public interest retreat in the face of the private interests of "consumer citizens" and markets. Despite these constraints of the conjuncture, the aspiration to claim higher education for the public good persists, often symbolically but also in the form of many context-specific strategies and practices.

Conclusion

In their reflections on public values, Benington and Moore speak of the need to address three sets of issues when embarking on public values transformations—clarity about definitional issues, having authorizing environments in place (enabling policy, partnerships, alliances), and developing the appropriate capacities to move to the next step (2011). The preceding analysis has attempted to indicate the complexities and difficulties of constructing a public good ethos in relation to all these three issues. Defining the public good as a basis for action has to contend with strong differences in personal and ideological interests and opposing views on how benefit is understood. Constructing the required "authorizing environments" has to traverse different layers of power and influence—from institutions and systems of higher education to state policy and global regimes. What public good capabilities are and how they are to be cultivated and evaluated in higher education is a very early and tentative debate. Without the effective presence of at least some of the requirements of these three sets of issues, prospects for a systematic deep-rooted shift toward a public good dispensation remain uncertain at best. Building the dialogical foundations on the basis of which consensual choices can be made in all three sets of areas may well be the first task in advancing the public good.

It has been argued earlier that the nature of the conjuncture could render precarious the possibility that the politics, values, policies, and practices of the public good will become hegemonic in higher education. Where does this leave those with strong political and normative commitments to the public good or those role-players (including governments) who are already undertaking a variety of public good initiatives and projects in different higher education contexts? In *The Idea of Justice*, Sen indicates that his aim in the book is "to clarify how we can proceed to address questions of justice and removing injustice, rather than to offer resolutions of questions about the nature of perfect justice" (2010, p. ix). This paradigm-changing approach is immensely valuable in providing a normative and pragmatic pointer for making choices and acting in contexts of public good struggle. Resisting, removing, or mediating public "bads," launching more bottom-up public good interventions in different layers and functions of higher education, and working toward making these initiatives more "joined up" within systems and institutions could all constitute elements of a credible and realistic public good praxis. Such an approach could help to steer between an overreaching search for a public good "grand narrative" on the one hand and a pessimism that public good-motivated resistance is futile in a totalizing knowledge economy regime on the other. In growing the public good in this long-haul fashion, much depends on increasing academic agency (Docherty, 2011; Dill, 2011) and fostering more dialogue and alliances among internal role-players and external publics.

Notes

1. See, for example, Jonathan (2001), Newman and Couturier (2002), Weber and Bergan (2005), Calhoun (2006), Docherty (2011), Nixon (2011), Rhoten and Calhoun (2011), and Leibowitz (2012).
2. See, for example, espousals of the importance of the connection between higher education and the "public good" in the policy documents and declarations of UNESCO, especially the 2009 Communiqué from the World Congress on

Higher Education, declaring higher education to *be* a public good and deserving of support from the public purse as well as a contributor to the public good (www.unesco.org); the 2001 Prague Communiqué in the Bologna Process, where ministers supported the idea that "higher education should be considered a public good and . . . a public responsibility" (www.ehea.info); the Association of African Universities' 2004 Accra Declaration on GATS [General Agreement on Trade in Services]and the Internationalization of Higher Education in Africa (www.aau.org), expressing the commitment to higher education as a "public mandate"; even the World Bank, which, in the report *Peril and Promise* of its Task Force on Higher Education and Society is seen to be putting public interest back into higher education (Post et al., 2004); and the 2009 call of the Higher Education Funding Council for England for micro-studies demonstrating the public benefits of UK universities (www.hefce.ac.uk).

3. See, for example, in the United States, the National Forum on Higher Education for the Public Good at the University of Michigan (www.soe.umich.edu) and the New York-based Social Science Research Council (SSRC) Transformations of the Public Sphere forum (http://publicsphere.ssrc.org); in the UK, the Beacons for Public Engagement project.
4. See, for example, essays on the SSRC Public Sphere forum website (http://publicsphere.ssrc.org).
5. See, for example, Walker (2012) on developing public good capabilities in professional education and training.
6. In this regard, Dill exempts the work of economists (2011, pp. 1–3).
7. In relation to strategic planning for the public good, it may be possible to draw on other literatures and approaches to planning besides the new public management framing of planning. See, for example, Friedmann (1987) on the notion of radical or oppositional planning.
8. In contrast, for example, to a position articulated by Fish (2008), who argues against the idea that universities and academics have social obligations of any kind that must be given effect through the core functions of higher education.
9. Already in 1963, Kerr had maintained that the modern American university was as "a new type of institution . . . not really private and . . . not really public" (1995, p. 1).
10. See, for example, funding provided by the Higher Education Funding Council for England in the United Kingdom to incentivize innovation as well as public engagement but with significant differences in allocations (www.hefce.ac.uk). See also some of the debates about the role of universities within the context of the "Europe of knowledge" in the special issue on the public role of the university in *Studies in Philosophy and Education* (2007), vol. 27, pp. 395–404.
11. Organized student formations have also signaled commitments to the public good. See, for example, European Students Union (*University World News*, July 2013, no. 280, www.universityworldnews.com); Canadian Federation of Students (*Public Education for the Public Good*, 2012, http://cfs-fcee.ca).

CHAPTER 15

Knowledge, Action, and Hope: A Call for Strengthening the Community-Based Research Movement

Budd Hall, Rajesh Tandon, Ronaldo Munck, and Lorraine McIlrath

Our Moment—Our Time

The purpose of knowledge is to enhance the well-being of all people and not just for economic growth or intellectual property rights.

We believe that there is a noninstrumental dimension to knowledge as a way of being, living, and learning.

Wherever in this remarkable, contradictory, and troubled planet that we live, work, love, struggle, resist, and survive, we face a number of persistent and complex common realities, including

- growing inequality between and within nations;
- the irreversible destruction of our biosphere;
- increasing levels of violence against women in all societies and all classes;
- loss of our global treasury of intangible cultural heritage of indigenous languages, stories, songs, and ways of knowing; and
- increased fear across social sectors for security and well-being.

Knowledge, Society, and Power

Cognizant that all knowledge is intimately linked with power and that the questions of whose knowledge counts and how knowledge can be linked with social change and enlarging the public good is critical to our shared future, we call for

- knowledge workers in social movements, civil society organizations, and higher education institutions to contribute to the progressive resolution of the critical challenges facing our communities, our nations, and the world;
- recognition of civil society and social movement structures and formations as sources of knowledge cocreation and repositories of valuable forms of knowledge;
- increased opportunities for all students to be able to learn about democratic approaches to research in theory and in practice;
- deepening of our understanding of knowledge democracy as a fundamental framework for transformative change.

Structures of Democratic Knowledge

Convinced that new forms of knowledge legitimation in pursuit of the public good require new support and enabling regimes, we urge the

- creation of university-wide and discipline-specific structures to facilitate community-university research partnerships;
- creation of policies and procedures within all higher education institutions to recognize excellence in community-based research as integral to an academic career;
- expansion of granting council and research funding agencies investment in civil society-led research and community-university partnership research;
- support for open access knowledge systems, respecting diversity and pluralism in sites, modes, and ways of knowledge production as a building block of open and inclusive societies;
- support to civil society for synthesizing its own practitioner knowledge and spaces for creative and respectful engagement with academic knowledge forms;
- strengthening of links between the spaces of democratic practice within universities such as community service learning, knowledge mobilization, and community-based research;
- decolonization of higher education academic programming through an explicit recognition of multiple epistemologies and multiple forms of representing knowledge.

Contributor Biographies

Avila, Maria is Assistant Professor in the Masters' of Social Work department at California State University. She was the Director of the Center for Community Based Learning at Occidental College from 2001 to June 2011 and led the development of the center's approach to civic engagement, based on community-organizing practices.

Barnett, Ronald is Emeritus Professor of Higher Education, Institute of Education, University of London, UK. In his scholarly work, he has been trying over the last 30 years to advance a social philosophy of higher education and the university. He is working on a trilogy, the first two books of which have been published, namely *Being a University* (2011) and *Imagining the University* (2013).

Bates, Catherine has coordinated the Programme for Students Learning with Communities since 2008 at Dublin Institute of Technology (DIT). She studied design for her degree and master's, and did her PhD in sociology. In 2006 she moved to the community sector, where she ran a second-chance education program for women drug users in rehabilitation, before taking up her current post in DIT.

Bawa, Ahmed C. is Vice-Chancellor and Principal of Durban University of Technology. He has previously worked at the University of Durban-Westville, University of Natal, University of KwaZulu-Natal, and the City University of New York. He is a physicist and a member of the Royal Society of South Africa and the Academy of Science of South Africa.

Burns, Kenneth is a lecturer, Deputy Director of the Master of Social Work course at University College Cork, Ireland, and a research associate with the Institute for Social Science in the 21st Century. He has authored research papers and books in the fields of child protection, child care and protection policy, staff retention and welfare, social work, and community-based research.

Cuthill, Michael holds a Chair in Regional Community Development at the University of Southern Queensland in Australia. His work focuses on community-engaged research that brings together diverse public, private, and community sector stakeholders in collaborative knowledge exchange processes. He is also a sailor.

Duncan, Sophie is deputy director of the National Coordinating Centre for Public Engagement (NCCPE), established to help to coordinate public engagement practice and to support innovation and strategic change in UK universities. A physicist by training, Sophie started her career at the Science Museum in London, where her work included exhibition development and public programs.

Gutberlet, Jutta is Associate Professor in the Department of Geography at the University of Victoria in Canada. She is also the director of the Community-Based Research Laboratory (CBRL) created in 2006. Her research focus is on local development, comanagement, social and ecoeconomy, and applying participatory action-oriented research with community groups.

Hall, Budd is the joint holder of the UNESCO Chair in Community-Based Research and Social Responsibility in Higher Education at the University of Victoria, Canada. He has been working in community-based research since 1973. He is also a poet.

Liston, Vanessa is Visiting Research Assistant in the Department of Political Science, Trinity College, the University of Dublin. Vanessa's work in international development has focused on the impact of participatory methodologies on the political attitudes and behavior of local NGO staff in Kenya. Her current research interests are in deliberative democracy and discursive knowledge system innovation.

Lyons, Ann is at the Community Knowledge Initiative, NUI Galway, Ireland, and works in close liaison with a wide range of individuals and groups, both inside and outside the university, to further community-university links and partnerships, with particular emphasis on community-based research and knowledge sharing and exchange.

Manners, Paul is Associate Professor in Public Engagement at the University of the West of England (UWE) and director of the UK's National Coordinating Centre for Public Engagement. Paul's whole career has been education related. Originally trained as an English teacher, then a BBC documentary producer, he is committed to developing innovative ways to engage people in learning.

McIlrath, Lorraine coordinates the Community Knowledge Initiative (CKI) at the National University of Ireland, Galway. There, she is responsible, with the CKI team, for developing and supporting civic engagement activities across the university, including service learning and student volunteering. She is Principal Investigator (PI) of Campus Engage, a national Irish network to support civic engagement within higher education in Ireland.

McKenna, Emma has coordinated The Science Shop at Queen's University Belfast in Northern Ireland since 2001, a public engagement initiative linking student researchers with communities to jointly create research. She is a Research Associate for the National Co-Ordinating Centre for Public Engagement in the UK and a member of the Public Engagement in Research and Research Engagement in Society project.

Moraes, Carmen is currently Head of the School for Administration and Economics of Education and Coordinator of the Centro de Memória da Educação, University of São Paulo. Her research focuses on labor relations and education in historical and sociological perspective.

Mullett, Jennifer is the Director of the Centre for Healthy Communities Research at Vancouver Island University, Canada. She has been engaged in collaborative community-based research with community members since 1992 and has developed the use of arts-based methods as a means of exploring and presenting social transformation.

Munck, Ronaldo is Head of Civic Engagement at Dublin City University, Ireland, and Co-Chair of Campus Engage, Ireland's national platform for civic engagement in higher education. He is a political sociologist who has written widely on globalization and its discontents, and has worked in South America and southern Africa, His outlook has always been one of critical engagement with the social movements for transformation.

Murphy, Pádraig is a Lecturer and Course Chair for MSc Science Communication at Dublin City University (DCU), Ireland, and Director of the DCU

Societal Impact Platform. He is author of *Biotechnology, Education and Life Politics: Debating Genetic Futures from School to Society* (2014). He is also coordinator of the Celsius research group at DCU and part of the Management Board of DCU Community Knowledge Exchange.

Peters, Scott J. is an associate professor of education at Cornell University in the United States. He has devoted his professional career to studying and strengthening higher education's public mission, purposes, and work. His research focuses on the connections between higher education and democracy, especially in the land-grant system.

Singh, Mala is Professor Extraordinaire in the Centre for Higher Education Research, Teaching and Learning, Rhodes University, South Africa. She has a doctorate in Philosophy and has published in the fields of philosophy, higher education, and quality assurance. She is a member of the Academy of Science of South Africa and serves on a number of international and South African academic boards and councils.

Steinhaus, Norbert is a board member of Wissenschaftsladen Bonn (Bonn Science Shop), Germany, since 1990. For the past 14 years he has cooperated in international projects, training and mentoring science shops, citizen participation in science and technology, and responsible research and innovation. Since 2007 he has acted as coordinator of Living Knowledge, the international science shop network.

Tandon, Rajesh is the founder President for Participatory Research in Asia (PRIA), a voluntary organization that provides support to grassroots initiatives in South Asia. Rajesh's research and advocacy initiatives straddle the issues of safe workplace, right to know, citizen leadership, accountable local self-governance, global solidarity, and responsive civil society in India, South Asia, and beyond.

Tremblay, Crystal is a post-Doctoral fellow at the Institute for Resources, Environment & Sustainability, University of British Columbia, and research Coordinator for the UNESCO Chair in Community-Based Research and Social Responsibility in Higher Education. Her research focuses on community development, resource management, and participatory governance.

Bibliography

Abreu, M., Grinevich, V., Hughes, A., and Kitson, M. 2009. *Knowledge Exchange between Academics and the Business, Public and Third Sectors*. http://www.cbr.cam.ac.uk/pdf/AcademicSurveyReport.pdf.
Advisory Council on Intellectual Property (ACIP). 2012. *Collaboration between the Public and Private Sectors: The Role of Intellectual Property Final Report*. Advisory Council on Intellectual Property, Canberra.
Alonso, V. 2005. *Argentina: Building a Solidarity Economy*. http://www.globenet3.org/Articles/Article_Argentina_Solidarity.shtml.
Altbach, P. G. 1999. What Higher Education Does Right: A Millennium Accounting. *International Higher Education* 18. http://www.bc.edu/bc_org/avp/soe/cihe/newsletter/News18/text1.html.
Angulo, N. 2007. Building the Solidarity Economy in Peru. In A. Allard, C. Davidson, and J. Matthaei (eds.) *Solidarity Economy: Building Alternatives for People and Planet*. Papers and Reports from the US. Social Forum 2007, Chicago: Changemaker Publications, pp. 277–281.
Aranda, D. 2011. Situación y perspectiva del MERCOSUR. Desafios para la economia solidaria. In M. C. Dutto (ed.) *Integracion Productiva; La economia social y solidaria en los procesos de integracion regional*, Agencia Española de Cooperación Internacional para el Desarrollo (aecidMontevideo), pp. 61–71.
Arruda, M. 2008. *Exchanging Visions on a Responsible, Plural and Solidarity-Based Economy*. Rio de Janeiro, ALOE—Workgroup Visions of a Responsible, Plural and Solidarity-Based Economy.
Ashforth, A. 2002. An Epidemic of Witchcraft? The Implications of AIDS for the Post-Apartheid State. *African Studies*, 61(1), pp. 121–143.
Ashforth, A. 2005. *Witchcraft, Violence, and Democracy in South Africa*. Chicago, IL: University of Chicago Press.
Association of Commonwealth Universities. 2001. *Engagement as a Core Value for the University: A Consultation Document*. http://www.viu.ca/integratedplanning/documents/Engagementasacorevalueoftheuniversity.pdf, accessed January 26, 2014.
Australian Academy of Technology Sciences and Engineering. 2013. *Translating Research into Economic Benefits for Australia: Rethinking Linkages*. http://www.

atse.org.au/Documents/Publications/position-paper/translating-research-into-productivity.pdf.
Australian Universities Community Engagement Alliance. 2006. Universities and Community Engagement: AUCEA Position Paper. http://traction.med.monash.edu.au:8080/traction/read?proj=Website&type=single&rec=290&side=1.
Australian University Quality Agency (AUQA). 2008. *Community Engagement and Inclusion in Australian Higher Education: A Thematic Analysis of AUDA's Cycle 1 Audits*. AUQA Occasional Publications No. 15. Melbourne.
Babbie, E. (Ed.). (2006). *The Practice of Social Research* (11th ed.). Wadsworth Publishing.
Bailey, M. and Freedman. D. (eds.). 2011. *The Assault on Universities: A Manifesto for Resistance*. London: Pluto Press.
Baldwin, R. J. 1934. Outlook Broadened. *Extension Service Review*, 5(6), pp. 89, 95.
Banthien, H., Jaspers, M., and Renner, A. 2003. *IFOK Interim Report: Governance of the European Research Area: The Role of Civil Society*. http://ec.europa.eu/research/science-society/pdf/final_report_study.pdf.
Barbier, R. 2002. *A pesquisa-ação*. Brasilia: Plano.
Barnett, R. 1994. *The Limits of Competence: Knowledge, Higher Education and Society*. Bristol: SRHE and Open University Press.
Barnett, R. 2000. *Realising the University in an Age of Supercomplexity*. Buckingham: Open University Press.
Barnett, R. 2013. *Imagining the University*. London and New York: Routledge.
Bauman, Z. 2000. *Liquid Modernity*. Cambridge: Polity.
Bawa, A. C., Mokoena, M. P., and Gqaleni, N. 2014. The importance of the mapping of non-traditional forms of science and technology. Unpublished.
Bawden, R. J. 1993. *"A Peri-Natal Journey—From Extension to Transactions," Evaluation Report on Kellogg Foundation Project University of Natal, South Africa* (March 1993).
Bawden, R. J. 2004. Sustainability as Emergence: The Need for Engaged Discourse. In P. B. Corcoran and A. E. J. Wals (eds.) *Higher Education and the Challenge of Sustainability: Problematics, Promise and Practice*. Dordrecht, Kluwer Academic Publishers, pp. 21–33.
Bebbington, T. and Mitlin, D. 1998. What Does Strengthening NGO Capacity Mean For Civil Society and Governance? Online Document. http://www.id21.org/society/8c6aAS1.html.
Beisiegel, C. 1974. *Estado e Educação Popular*. São Paulo: Pioneira.
Beisiegel, C. 1989. *Política e Educação Popular: a teoria e a prática de Paulo Freire no Brasil*. São Paulo: Ática.
Beisiegel, C. and Moraes, C. S. V. 2009. Oficina. História da Educação Popular. In G. N. M. de Barros (org.) *Celso de Rui Beisiegel: professor, administrador, pesquisador*. São Paulo: EDUSP, pp. 121–152.
Bell, P. T. Madew, A. M. and Kainulanen, S. 2012 Universities as agents of empowerment of local communities in Germany, Finland and Russia. In L. Goodson and J. Philmoore (eds.) *Community Research for Participation: From Theory to Method*. Bristol: The Policy Press.

Benington, J. and Moore, M. H. (eds.). 2011. *Public Value: Theory and Practice*. London: Palgrave Macmillan.
Benneworth, P. 2009. *The Challenges for 21st Century Science: A Review of the Evidence Base Surrounding the Value of Public Engagement by Scientists*. Centre for Higher Education Policy Studies (CHEPS) Working Paper.
Bergan, S. 2005. Higher Education as a "Public Good and Public Responsibility": What Does It Mean? In L. E. Weber and S. Bergan (eds.) *The Public Responsibility for Higher Education and Research*. Strasbourg: Council of Europe Publishing, pp. 13–28.
Berkes, F. 2004. Rethinking Community-Based Conservation. *Conservation Biology*, 18(3), pp. 621–630.
Bexley, E., James, R., and Arkoudis, S. 2011. *The Australian Academic Profession in Transition: Addressing the Challenge of Reconceptualising Academic Work and Regenerating the Academic Workforce*. Melbourne: Centre for the Study of Higher Education.
Bhaskar, R. 2002. *From Science to Emancipation: Journeys towards Meta-Reality*. New Delhi: Sage Publications.
Bhaskar, R. 2011. *Reclaiming Reality: A Critical Introduction to Contemporary Philosophy*. London and New York: Routledge.
B-HERT. 2006. Universities Third Mission: Communities Engagement. B-HERT Position Paper No. 11. http://www.bhert.com/publications_PolicyStatements.htm.
Biesta, G. 2007. Towards the Knowledge Democracy? Knowledge Production and the Civic Role of the University. *Studies in Philosophy and Education*, 26, pp. 467–479.
Biggs, Stephen D. 1989. *Resource-Poor Farmer Participation in Research: A Synthesis of Experiences from Nine National Agricultural Research Systems*. On-farm Client Orientated Research (OFCOR)-Comparative Study Paper, p. 3.
BIS (Department for Business, Innovation and Skills) (2009) 'The Future of Universities in a Knowledge Economy' http://webarchive.nationalarchives.gov.uk/+/http://www.bis.gov.uk/wp-content/uploads/publications/Higher-Ambitions.pdf, Accessed May 24, 2012.
BIS, 2011. *Innovation and Research Strategy for Growth, 2011*. http://www.bis.gov.uk/assets/biscore/innovation/docs/i/11-1387-innovation-and-research-strategy-for-growth.pdf, accessed March 16, 2012.
Blakeney, M. 2009. Protection of Traditional Knowledge by Geographical Indications. In C. Antons (ed.) *Traditional Knowledge, Traditional Cultural Expressions and Intellectual Property Law in the Asia-Pacific Region*. Alphen aan den Rijn, the Netherlands: Kluwer Law International, pp. 87–108.
Boal, A. 1979. *The Theatre of the Oppressed*. New York: Urizen Books.
Bohman, J. 2000. *Public Deliberation: Pluralism, Complexity and Democracy*. Cambridge, MA: The MIT Press.
Bok, D. 1984. *Beyond the Ivory Tower*. Cambridge, MA: Harvard University Press.
Boutang, Y. 2011. *Cognitive Capitalism*. Cambridge: Polity.
Boyer, E. L. 1996. The Scholarship of Engagement. *Journal of Public Service and Outreach*, 1(1), pp. 11–20.

Boyte, H. C. 2004. *Everyday Politics: Reconnecting Citizens and Public Life*. Philadelphia, PA: University of Pennsylvania Press.
Bradley, D., Noonan, P., Nugent, H., and Scales, B. 2008. *Review of Australian Higher Education: Final Report*. Canberra: Department of Education, Employment and Workplace Relations.
Brandão, C. R. 1984. *Saber e ensinar. Tres estudos de educação popular*. Campinas: Papirus.
Brandão, C. R. (org.) 1987. *Repensando a pesquisa participante*. São Paulo: Brasiliense.
Brandão, C. R. 2009. Trinta anos depois: alguns elementos de crítica atual aos projetos de cultura popular nos movimentos de cultura popular dos anos 1960. In P. Pontual and T. Ireland (orgs.) *Educação popular na América Latina: diálogos e perspectivas*. Brasilia: SECAD Secretaria de Educação Continuada, Alfabetização e Diversidade, and UNESCO, pp. 251–258.
Brennan, J. and Naidoo, R. 2007. Higher Education and the Achievement (or Prevention) of Equity and Social Justice. In *Higher Education Looking Forward: Relations between Higher Education and Society*. Strasbourg: European Science Foundation, pp. 25–38. http://www.esf.org.
Brown, L. D. 2001. *Practice-Research-Engagement and Civil Society in a Democratizing World*. Cambridge, MA: Harvard University Press/The Hauser Center.
Burawoy, M. 2011. *Redefining the Public University*. SSRC Public Sphere Forum. http://publicsphere.ssrc.org/burawoy, Berkeley, CA.
Calheiros, D. F., Seidl, A. F., and Ferreira, C. J. A. 2000. Participatory Research Methods in Environmental Science: Local and Scientific Knowledge of a Limnological Phenomenon in the Pantanal Wetland of Brazil. *Journal of Applied Ecology*, 37(4), pp. 684–696.
Calhoun, C.1998. The Public Good as a Social and Cultural Project. In W. W. Powell and E. S. Clemens (eds.) *Private Action and the Public Good*. New Haven, CT: Yale University Press, pp. 20–35.
Calhoun, C. 2006a. The University and the Public Good. *Thesis Eleven*, 84, pp. 7–43.
Calhoun, C. 2006b. Knowledge Production, Publicness, and the Structural Transformation of the University. Interview with M. McQuarrie. *Thesis Eleven*, 84, pp. 103–114.
Calhoun, C. 2009. Remaking America: Public Institutions and the Public Good. SSRC Public Sphere Forum. http://publicsphere.ssrc.org/calhoun., Berkeley, CA.
Calhoun, C. 2011. The Public Mission of the Research University. In D. Rhoten and C. Calhoun (eds.) *Knowledge Matters: The Public Mission of the Research University*. New York: Columbia University Press, pp. 1–33.
Campbell, C. 2004. Health Psychology and Community Action. In M. Murray (ed.) *Critical Health Psychology*. New York: Palgrave Macmillan., pp. 203–221.
Campus Compact. 1999. "Presidents' Declaration on the Civic Responsibility of Higher Education." http://www.compact.org/resources-for-presidents/presidents-declaration-on-the-civic-responsibility-of-higher-education/, accessed November 6, 2013.
Canadian Federation of Students. 2012. *Public Education for the Public Good*. http://cfs-fcee.ca.

Canning, D. and Reinsborough, P. 2010. *Re:Imagining Change: How to Use Story-Based Strategy to Win Campaigns, Build Movements, and Change the World.* Oakland, CA: PM Press.

CEP Alforja and CEAAL. 2012. *La sistematización de experiencias, práctica y teoría para otros mundos posibles.* San José: Oxfam.

Chakrabarty, D. 2007. *Provincializing Europe: Postcolonial Thought and Historical Difference,* Princeton: Princeton University Press.

Chambers, R. 1983. *Rural Development: Putting the Last First.* London: Longman.

Chambers, R. 1994. "Paradigm Shifts and the Practice of Participatory Research and Development." Working Paper. Brighton, UK: Institute of Development Studies.

Chambers, R. 1995. Rural Development: Whose Knowledge Counts. *IDS Bulletin,* 10(2).

Chambers, R. 1997. *Putting the Last First: Whose Reality Counts?* London: Intermediate Technology Publications.

Chambers, R. 2007. Who Counts: Quiet Revolution of Participation and Numbers. IDS Working Paper 296. Falmer, UK: IDS.

Chambers, R. 2010. Paradigms, Poverty and Adaptive Pluralism. *IDS Working Papers,* 2010(344), pp. 1–57.

Chambers, T. and Gopaul, B. 2008. Decoding the Public Good of Higher Education. *Journal of Higher Education Outreach and Engagement,* 12(4), pp. 59–91.

Clark, B. R. 1998. *Creating Entrepreneurial Universities: Organization Pathways of Transformation.* Guildford, UK: Pergamon.

Cleaver, F. 2001. Institutions, Agency and the Limitations of the Participatory Approaches to Development. In B. Cooke and U. Kothari (eds.) *Participation: The New Tyranny?* London: Zed Books, pp. 36–55.

Cloete, N., Muller, J., Makgoba, M. W., and Ekong, D. (eds.). 1997. *Knowledge, Identity and Curriculum Transformation in Africa.* Cape Town: Maskew Miller Longman.

Coaldrake, P. and Stedman, L. 2013. *Raising the Stakes: Gambling with the Future of Universities.* Brisbane: University of Queensland Press.

Coleman, James, S. 1984. The Idea of the Developmental University. In A. Hetland (ed.) *Universities and National Development.* Stockholm: Almquist & Wiksell International, pp. 85–104.

Collini, J. 2012. *What Are Universities For?* London: Penguin Books.

Common, R. and Flynn, N. 1992. *Contracting for Care.* New York: Joseph Rowntree Foundation.

Commonwealth of Australia. 2012. *Australia in the Asian Century.* Canberra: Commonwealth of Australia.

Cooke, B. (2004) Rules of Thumb for Participatory Change Agents. In S. Hickey and G. Moha (eds.) *Participation: From Tyranny to Transformation?: Exploring New Approaches to Participation in Development.* London: Zed Books, pp. 42–55.

Cooke, B. and Kothari, U. (eds.). 2001. The Case for Participation as Tyranny. In *Participation: The New Tyranny?* London: Zed Books, pp. 1–15.

Cornwall, A. and Jewkes, R. 1995. What Is Participatory Research? *Social Science and Medicine,* 41(12), pp. 1667–1676.

Crick, B. 1992. *Defense of Politics*, 4th ed. Chicago, IL: University of Chicago Press.
Crouch, C. 2011. Privates, Publics and Values. In J. Benington and M. H. Moore (eds.) *Public Value: Theory and Practice*. London: Palgrave Macmillan, pp. 52–73.
Cundill, G. N. R., Fabricius, C., and Marti, N. 2005. Foghorns to the Future: Using Knowledge and Transdisciplinarity to Navigate Complex Systems. *Ecology and Society*, 10(2), p. 8. http://www.ecologyandsociety.org/vol10/iss2/art8/.
Cuthill, M. 2008. A Quality Framework for University Engagement in Australia. *International Journal for Public Participation*, 2(2), pp. 22–41. http://www.iap2.org/displaycommon.cfm?an=1&subarticlenbr=307.
Cuthill, M. 2010. Working Together: A Methodological Case Study of Engaged Scholarship. *Gateways: International Journal of Community Research and Engagement*, 3, pp. 20–37.
Cuthill, M. 2011. Embedding Engagement in an Australian "Sandstone" University: From Community Service to University Engagement. *Metropolitan Universities*, 22(2), pp. 21–44.
Cuthill, M. 2012. A "Civic Mission" for the University: Engaged Scholarship and Community-Based Research. In L. McIlrath, A. Lyons, and R. Munck (eds.) *Higher Education and Civic Engagement: Comparative Perspectives*. Basingstoke, UK: Palgrave Macmillan, pp. 81–101.
Cuthill, M. and Brown, A. 2010. Sceptics, Utilitarians and Missionaries: Senior Managers Perceptions of Engagement in an Australian Research University. *Australasian Journal of University-Community Engagement*, 5(2), pp. 126–146.
Cuthill, M., O'Shea, E., Wilson, B., and Viljoen, P. 2014. Universities and the Public Good: A Review of "Knowledge Exchange" Policy and Related University Practice in Australia. *Australian Universities Review* (pending).
Cuthill, M., Warburton, J., Everingham, J., Petriwskyj, A., and Bartlett, H. 2011. Reflections on a Multi-Sector Action Research Collaboration: The Researchers' Perspective *Action Learning and Action Research Journal*, 17(1), pp. 92–118.
Davis, B. and Sumara, D. 2005. Complexity Science and Educational Action Research: Toward a Pragmatics of Transformation. *Educational Action Research*, 13(3), pp. 453–464.
Davis, G. 2013. National Press Club Address: Glyn Davis on a Smarter Australia. February 27, 2013. http://theconversation.com/national-press-club-address-glyn-davis-on-a-smarter-australia-12503.
De Bok, C. 2008. *TRAMS Training and Mentoring of Science Shops, Final Publishable Report*. http://www.livingknowledge.org/livingknowledge/wp-content/uploads/2012/02/TRAMS-final-report-120132711EN6.pdf.
DeBok, C. and Steinhaus, N. 2008. Breaking Out of the Local: International Dimensions of Science Shops. *Gateways International Journal of Community Based Research and Engagement*, 1, pp. 31–47.
Delanty, G. 2001. *Challenging Knowledge: The University in the Knowledge Society*. Buckingham: Open University Press.
DELNI. 2014. *Graduating to Success—A Higher Education Strategy for Northern Ireland*. http://www.delni.gov.uk/graduating-to-success-he-strategy-for-ni.pdf.

DELNI and Invest NI. 2010. *Evaluation of the Second Round of the Northern Ireland Higher Education Innovation Fund.* http://www.delni.gov.uk/review_of_ni_higher_education_innovation_fund_2_-_final_report.pdf.

Department of Education and Skills. 2010. *National Strategy for Higher Education to 2030.* Dublin: Government Publications Office.

Department of Education, Science and Training. 2006. *Knowledge Transfer and Australian Universities and Publicly Funded Research Agencies—A Report to the Department of Education, Science and Training.* Canberra: Commonwealth Department of Education, Science and Training.

De Sousa Santos, B. 2007. Beyond Abyssal Thinking: From Global Lines to Ecologies of Knowledge. *Eurozine*, 33, pp. 45–89.

Dewey, J. 1916. *Democracy and Education: An Introduction to the Philosophy of Education.* New York: The MacMillan Company.

DFID. 2005. *How to Leverage the Co-Operative Movement for Poverty Reduction.* http://www.caledonia.org.uk/papers/How-to-co-operatives-DFID-2005.pdf.

Dill, D. D. 2005. The Public Good, the Public Interest, and Public Higher Education. Background Paper, Public Policy for Academic Quality Research Program. Wilmington, University of North Carolina at Chapel Hill. http://www.unc.edu/ppag.

Dill, D. D. 2011. Assuring the Public Good in Higher Education: Essential Framework Conditions and Academic Values. Paper presented at SRHE seminar on Higher Education as a Public Good: Critical Perspectives, New College, Oxford, July 4–5.

Docherty, T. 2011. *For the University: Democracy and the Future of the Institution.* London: Bloomsbury.

Duke, C. 2010. Engaging with Difficulty: Universities in and with Regions. In P. Inman and H. Schuetze (eds.) *The Community Engagement and Service Mission of Universities.* Leicester, UK: NIACE, pp. 27–42.

Earle, L. 2014. Drawing the Line between State and Society: Social Movements, Participation and Autonomy in Brazil. *Journal of Development Studies*, 49(1), pp. 56–71.

Ehrlich, T. 2000. *Civic Responsibility and Higher Education.* Phoenix, AZ: Oryx Press.

Escobar, A. 1995. *Encountering Development: The Making and Unmaking of the Third World*, Princeton: Princeton University Press.

Escobar, A. and Alvarez, S. E. 1992. *The Making of Social Movements in Latin America: Identity, Strategy, and Democracy.* Boulder, CO: Westview.

Escrigas, C., Granados, J., Hall, B. L., and Tandon, R. (eds.). 2014. *Higher Education in the World 5: Knowledge, Engagement and Higher Education: Contributing to Social Change.* GUNI Series on the Social Commitment of Universities. London: Palgrave Macmillan.

European Commission. 2002. *Science and Society—Action Plan.* Communication from the Commission to the Council, the European Parliament, the Economic and Social Committee and the Committee of the Regions. http://ec.europa.eu/research/science-society/pdf/ss_ap_en.pdf.

European Commission. 2003a. *The Role of the Universities in the Europe of Knowledge*. Communication from the Commission. http://eur-lex.europa.eu/ LexUriServ/ LexUriServ.do?uri=COM:2003:0058:FIN:en:pdf.

European Commission. 2003b. *Science Shops—Knowledge for the Community*. http://ec.europa.eu/research/science-society/pdf/science_shop_en.pdf.

European Students Union. 2013. *University World News*, 280. http://www.university worldnews.com.

Facer, K., Manners, P., and Agusita, E. 2012. *Towards a Knowledge Base for University-Public Engagement: Sharing Knowledge, Building Insight, Taking Action*. Bristol: NCCPE. http://www.publicengagement.ac.uk/how-we-help/our-publications/towards-knowledge, accessed January 26, 2014.

Fals Borda, O. 1986. *Conocimiento y poder popular: lecciones con campesinos de Nicaragua, México, Colombia*. Mexico City: Siglo XXI.

Fals-Borda, O. 1987. The Application of Participatory Action-Research in Latin America. *International Sociology*, 2(4), pp. 329–347.

Fals Borda, O. 1988. Aspectos teóricos da pesquisa participante: considerações sobre o significado do papel da ciência na participação popular. In C. R. Brandão (ed.) *Pesquisa Participante*, 7th ed. São Paulo: Brasiliense, pp. 42–62.

Fals Borda, O. 1998. *People's Participation: Challenges Ahead*. Bogotá: Tercer Mundo.

Fals Borda, O. and Rahman, M. 1991. *Action and Knowledge*. Lanham, MD: Rowman and Littlefield.

Farkas, N. 1999. Dutch Science Shops: Matching Community Needs with University R&D. *Science Studies*, 12(2), pp. 33–47.

Farkas, N. 2002. Bread, Cheese, and Expertise: Dutch Science Shops and Democratic Institutions. Unpublished PhD thesis. Troy, NY: Rensselaer Polytechnic Institute.

Fetterman, D. F. 1994. Empowerment Evaluation. *Evaluation Practice*, 15(1), pp. 1–15.

Finnegan, R. 2005. *Participating in the Knowledge Society: Researchers beyond the University Walls*. Basingstoke, UK: Palgrave Macmillan.

Fischer, F. 1990. *Technocracy and the Politics of Expertise*. Newbury Park, CA: Sage Publications.

Fischer, F. 2000. *Citizens, Experts, and the Environment: The Politics of Local Knowledge*. Durham, NC: Duke University Press.

Fischer, C., Leydesdorff, L., and Schophaus, M. 2004. Science Shops in Europe: The Public as Stakeholder. *Science and Public Policy*, 31(3), pp. 199–211.

Fish, S. 2008. *Save the World on Your Own Time*. New York: Oxford University Press.

Fokkink, A. and Mulder, H. A. J. 2004. Curriculum Development through Science Shops. *Environmental Management and Engineering Journal*, 3(3), pp. 549–560.

Fonseca, M. 2007. Review of "From Movements to Parties in Latin America: The Evolution of Ethnic Politics" by Donna Lee Van Cott. *Canadian Journal of Political Science*, 40(2), pp. 558–560.

Forfás. 2012. *Report of the Research Prioritisation Steering Group*. Dublin: Forfás.

Foucault, M. 1980. *Power/Knowledge, Selected Interviews and Other Writings 1972–1977*, C. Gordon (ed.). Hemel Hempstead: Harvester.

Freire, P. 1970. *Pedagogy of the Oppressed*. New York: Seabury Press.
Freire, P. 1971. A Talk by Paulo Freire. In B. Hall (ed.) *Studies in Adult Education*. Dar es Salaam: Institute of Adult Education. pp. 1–14.
Freire, P. 1974. *Extension or Communication? Education for Critical Consciousness*. New York: Continuum.
Freire, P. 1982. Creating alternative research methods: Learning to do it by doing it, In B.L. Hall, A. Gilette, & R. Tandon (eds), *Creating Knowledge: A Monopoly? Participatory Research in Development*, New Dehli: Society for Participatory Research in Asia.
Freire, P. 2001. *Pedagogia da autonomia: saberes necessaries a pratica educativa*. Rio de Janeiro: Paz e Terra.
Freire, P. 2002. *Educação como prática da liberdade*, 26th ed. Rio de Janeiro: Paz e Terra.
Freire, P. 2011a. *Pedagogia do oprimido*, 50th ed. Rio de Janeiro: Paz e Terra.
Freire, P. 2011b. *Pedagogia da autonomia: saberes necessaries a pratica educativa*. Rio de Janeiro: Paz e Terra.
Friedmann, J. 1987. *Planning in the Public Domain*. Princeton, NJ: Princeton University Press.
Gadotti, M. and Torres, C. A. (orgs.) (1994). *Educação popular utopia Latino-Americana*. São Paulo: EDUSP and Cortez Editora.
Gall, É., Millot, G., and Neubauer, C. 2009. *Participation of Civil Society Organisations in Research: Science Technology and Civil Society (STACS)*. http://www.living knowledge.org/livingknowledge/wp-content/uploads/2011/12/STACS Final_Report-Partic.research.pdf.
Gaventa, J. and Bivens, F. 2014. Knowledge Democracy, Cognitive Justice and the Role of Universities. In C. Escrigas, J. Granados, B. L. Hall, and R. Tandon (eds.) *Higher Education in the World 5: Knowledge, Engagement and Higher Education: Contributing to Social Change*. GUNI Series on the Social Commitment of Universities. London, Palgrave Macmillan, pp. 69–74.
Gecan, M. 2002. *Going Public*. Boston, MA: Beacon Press.
Gellner, E. 1974. *Legitimation of Belief*. London: Cambridge University Press.
Gibbons, M. 2005. Engagement with the Community: The Emergence of a New Social Contract between Society and Science. Presentation to the Griffith University Community Engagement Workshop, South Bank campus, QLD.
Gibbons, M. 2006. *Engagement as a Core Value on a Mode 2 Society*. Cape Town: Council of Higher Education.
Gibbons, M., Limoges, C., Nowotny, H., Schwartzman, S., Scott, P., and Trow, M. 1994. *The New Production of Knowledge: The Dynamics of Science and Research in Contemporary Societies*. New York: Sage Publications.
Giroux, H. (2010). *On Critical Pedagogy*. New York: Continuum.
Goodin, L. and Phillimore, J. (eds.) 2012. *Community Research for Participation: From Theory to Method*. London: The Policy Press.
Gordon, P. and White, J. 1979. *Philosophers as Educational Reformers: The Influence of Idealism on British Educational Thought and Practice*. London: Routledge and Kegan Paul.

Gqaleni, N., Mbatha, N. and Mkhize, T. 2010. Education and Development of Traditional Health Practitioners in isiZulu to Promote Their Collaboration with Public Health Care Workers. *Alternation*, 17(1), pp. 295–311.

Grattan Institute. 2013. *Mapping Australian Higher Education*. http://grattan.edu.au/static/files/assets/28a92f8b/184_2013_mapping_higher_education.pdf.

Green, L. W., George, A., Daniel, M., Frankish, C. J., Herbert, C. P., Bowie, W. R., and O'Neill, M. 1995. *Study of Participatory Research in Health Promotion*. Ottawa, ON: Royal Society of Canada.

Guijt, I. and Shah, M. K. (eds.). 1998. *The Myth of Community: Gender Issues in Participatory Development*. London: Intermediate Technology Publications.

Gutberlet, J. 2008. Empowering Collective Recycling Initiatives: Video Documentation and Action Research with a Recycling Co-Op in Brazil. *Resources, Conservation and Recycling*, 52, pp. 659–670.

Gutberlet, J. 2009. Solidarity Economy and Recycling Co-Ops in Sao Paulo: Micro-Credit to Alleviate Poverty. *Development in Practice*, 19(6), pp. 737–751.

Gutberlet, J. 2012. Informal and Cooperative Recycling as a Poverty Eradication Strategy. *Geography Compass*, 6(1), pp. 19–34.

Gutberlet, J., Baeder, A. M., Pontuschka, N. N., Felipone, S. M. N., and dos Santos, T. L. F. 2013. Participatory Research Revealing the Work and Occupational Health Hazards of Cooperative Recyclers in Brazil. *International Journal of Environmental Research and Public Health*, 10, pp. 4607–4627.

Habermas, J. 1978. *Knowledge and Human Interests*. London: Heinemann.

Habermas, J. 1984. *The Theory of Communicative Action: Volume One: Reason and the Rationalization of Society*. Cambridge: Polity.

Habermas, J. 1987. *The Theory of Communicative Action: Volume Two: The Critique of Functionalist Reason*. Cambridge: Polity.

Habermas, J. 2006. Political Communication in Media Society: Does Democracy Still Enjoy an Epistemic Dimension? The Impact of Normative Theory on Empirical Research. *Communication Theory*, 16, pp. 411–426.

Hall, A. and Clark, N. 2010. What Do Complex Adaptive Systems Look Like and What Are the Implications for Innovation Policy? *Journal of International Development*, 22(3), pp. 308–324.

Hall, B. 1984. *Popular Knowledge and Power: Two Articles*. Toronto, ON: PRG, 39pp.

Hall, B. 2005. In from the Cold? Reflections on Participatory Research from 1970–2005. *Convergence*, 38(1), pp. 5–24.

Hall, B. and Bérubé, L. 2010. Towards a New Architecture of Knowledge: The Office of Community–Based Research at the University of Victoria. In P. Inman and H. Schuetze (eds.) *The Community Engagement and Service Mission of Universities*. Leicester, UK: NIACE, pp. 270–298.

Hall, B., Jackson, E., Tandon, R., Lall, N., and Fontan, J. M. (eds.). 2013. *Knowledge, Democracy and Action: Community University Research Partnerships in Global Perspectives*. Manchester: Manchester University Press.

Hall, B. and Kidd, J. R. 1978. *Adult Learning: A Design for Action*. Oxford: Pergamon.

Hall, D. and Hall, I. 2002. Country Report: United Kingdom. In C. Fischer and A. Wallentin (eds.) *INTERACTS: Improving Interaction between NGOs, Universities and Science Shops: Experiences and Expectations, State-of-the-Art Report*. http://wilawien.at/interacts/interacts-sar.pdf.

Hall, M. 2010. Community Engagement in South African Higher Education. *Kagisano*, 6(January), pp. 1–53.

Harding, S. 1990. Feminism, Science and the Anti-Enlightenment Critiques. In L. Nicholson (ed.) *Feminism/Postmodernism*. New York and London: Routledge. pp. 83–107.

Harnecker, C. P. 2005. *The New Co-Operative Movement in Venezuela's Bolivarian Process*. December 17, 2005. http://www.venezuelanalysis.com/analysis/1531.

Harris, E. M. 1992. Accessing Community Development Research Methodologies. *Canadian Journal of Public Health*, Supplement 1(March–April), pp. 62–66.

Hazelkorn, E. 2011. *Rankings and the Reshaping of Higher Education: The Battle for World-Class Excellence*. Basingstoke, UK: Palgrave Macmillan.

HEA. 2013. *Higher Education System Performance Framework 2014–2016*. http://www.education.ie/en/The-Education-System/Higher-Education/HEA-Higher-Education-System-performance-Framework-2014-2016.pdf.

HEFCE, 2014. *Beacons for Public Engagement: Invitation to Apply for Funds*. http://www.hefce.ac.uk/pubs/hefce/2006/06_49/06_49.pdf.

Hende, M. and Jørgensen, M. S. 2001. *The Impact of Science Shops on University Curricula and Research*. SCIPAS Report No. 6. Utrecht, Utrecht University.

Heron, J. 1996. *Cooperative Inquiry*. London: Sage Publications.

Heron, J. and Reason, P. 1997. A Participatory Inquiry Paradigm. *Qualitative Inquiry*, 3(3), pp. 274–294.

Hertzman, C. 2004. *Making Early Childhood Development a Priority: Lessons from Vancouver*. British Columbia, Canadian Centre for Policy Alternatives, BC Office. http://www.policyalternatives.ca.

Hickey, S. and Moha, G. (eds) 2004. *Participation: From Tyranny to Transformation?: Exploring New Approaches to Participation in Development*. London: Zed books.

Higgins, Michael. D. 2013. Remarks by President Higgins at the Conferral of Membership on him by the Royal Irish Academy. http://www.president.ie/speeches/remarks-by-president-higgins-at-the-conferral-of-membership-on-him-by-the-royal-irish-academy-tuesday-27th-november-2012/, accessed November 27, 2013.

Hilyard, N., Hegde, P., and Wolvekamp, P. 2001. Pluralism, Participation and Power: Joint Forest Management in India. In B. Cooke and U. Kothari (eds.) *Participation: The New Tyranny?* London: Zed Books, pp. 56–77.

Hind, D. 2010. *The Return of the Public*. London: Verso.

Hodges, R. A. and Dubb, S. 2012. *The Road Half-Traveled: University Engagement at a Crossroads*. East Lansing, MI: Michigan State University Press.

Hoyt, L. 2014. *Leaders in the Civic Engagement Movement: Maria Nieves Tapia, Founder and Director, Latin American Center for Service Learning*. http://talloiresnetwork.tufts.edu/wp-content/uploads/Nieves_Interview_final.pdf.

INSEA. 2013. *Seminário Reciclando Práticas e Transformando Vidas*, Luciano Marcos. Conference Proceedings. Rio de Janeiro.
Institute for Higher Education Policy (IHEP). 1998. *Reaping the Benefit: Defining the Public and Private Benefits of Going to College*. Washington, DC: IHEP. http://www.ihep.org.
INTERACTS. 2003. *The Final Report*. http://wilawien.at/interacts/interacts_report_final1.pdf and http://wilawien.at/interacts/interacts_report_final2.pdf.
Intzesiloglou, G., Kakderi, C., Komninos, N., and Zaharis, N. 2011. Identifying Successful Knowledge Exchange Practices between Academia & Industry in University-City Regions. *Proceedings of International Conference for Entrepreneurship, Innovation and Regional Development*. Knowledge Exchange in University City-Regions-ICEIRD-2011.
IPPR. 2013. *An Avalanche is Coming: Higher Education and the Revolution Ahead*. http://www.ippr.org/images/media/files/publication/2013/04/avalanche-is-coming_Mar2013_10432.pdf.
Irwin, A. 1995. *Citizen Science: A Study of People, Expertise and Sustainable Development*. London and New York: Routledge.
Israel, B. A., Coombe, C. M., Cheezum, R. R., Schulz, A. J., McGranaghan, R. J., Lichtenstein, R., and Burris, A. 2010. Community-Based Participatory Research: A Capacity-Building Approach for Policy Advocacy Aimed at Eliminating Health Disparities. *Journal Information*, 100(11), pp. 2094–2102.
Jacklin, H. and Vale, P. (eds.) 2009. *Re-Imagining the Social in South Africa: Critique, Theory and Post-Apartheid Sociey*. Scottsville, South Africa: University of KwaZulu-Natal Press.
Jonathan, R. 2001. Higher Education Transformation and the Public Good. *Kagisano* 1, pp. 36–89.
Jørgensen, M. S., Hall, I., Hall, D., Gnaiger, A., Schroffenegger, G., Brodersen, S., von der Heiden, K., Reimer, R., Strähle, M., Urban, C., Endler, W., Teodosiu, C., Rojo, T., and Leydesdorff, L. 2004. *Democratic Governance through Interaction between NGO's, Universities and Science Shops: Experiences, Expectations, Recommendations, Final Report of Interacts*. Lyngby: The Science Shop.
Judt, T. 2010. *Ill Fares the Land*. London: Penguin.
Kapoor, I. 2008. *The Postcolonial Politics of Development*. London: Routledge.
Kaul, I. 2001. Public Goods: Taking the Concept into the Twenty-First Century. In D. Drache (ed.) *The Market or the Public Domain: Global Governance and the Asymmetry of Power*. London and New York: Routledge, pp. 255–273.
Kaul, I., Grunberg, I., and Stern, M. A. (eds.). 1999. *Global Public Goods: International Co-Operation in the 21st Century*. New York: Oxford University Press.
Kay, J. J. and Schneider, E. D. 1994. Embracing Complexity, the Challenge of the Ecosystem Approach. *Alternatives*, 20(3), pp. 32–38.
Kelly, J. G. 1966. Ecological Constraints on Mental Health Services. *American Psychologist*, 21, pp. 535–539.
Kelly, J. G., Dassoff, N., Levin, I., Schreckengost, J., Stelzner, S. P., and Altman, E. 2000. A Guide to Conducting Prevention Research in the Community: First Steps. *Prev Human Services*, 6(1), 1–174.

Kerr, C. 2001. *The Uses of the University*, 5th ed. Cambridge, MA: Harvard University Press.

Kesby, M. 2000. Participatory Diagramming: Deploying Qualitative Methods through an Action Research Epistemology. *Area*, 32(4), pp. 423–435.

Keshavarz, N., Nutbeam, D., Rowling, L., and Khavarpour, F. 2010. Schools as Social Complex Adaptive Systems: A New Way to Understand the Challenges of Introducing the Health Promoting Schools Concept. *Social Science and Medicine*, 70(10), pp. 1467–1474.

Kezar, A. J., Chambers, A. C., and Burkhardt, J. (eds.) 2005. *Higher Education for the Public Good*. San Francisco, CA: Jossey-Bass.

King, M. and Gutberlet, J. 2013. Contribution of Cooperative Sector Recycling to Greenhouse Gas Emissions Reduction: A Case Study of Ribeirão Pires, Brazil. *Waste Management*, 33(12), pp. 2771–2780. http://dx.doi.org/10.1016/j.wasman.2013.07.031.

King, R. 2004. *The University in the Global Age*. London: Palgrave Macmillan.

Klerkx, L., van Mierlo, B., and Leeuwis, C. 2012. Evolution of Systems Approaches to Agricultural Innovation: Concepts, Analysis and Interventions. In I. Darnhofer, D. Gibbon, and B. Dedieu (eds.) *Farming Systems Research into the 21st Century: The New Dynamic*. The Netherlands: Springer, pp. 457–483.

Kotilla, W. 2012. *Youth Ecological Restoration Project Final Report*. http://youthecology.ca/category/youth-quotes/.

Kurtz, C. F. and Snowden, D. J. 2003. The New Dynamics of Strategy: Sense-Making in a Complex Complicated World. *IBM System Journal*, 42(3), pp. 462–483.

Langworthy, A. 2009. *Benchmarking Community Engagement: The AUCEA Pilot Project Report*. http://rur.pascalobservatory.org/sites/default/files/AUCEA%20Benchmarking%20Project%20Institutional%20Benchmarking%20Report%5B2%5D.pdf.

Laurell, A. C. 2000. Structural Adjustment and the Globalization of Social Policy in Latin America. *International Sociology*, 15(2), pp. 306–325.

Laverack, G. and Wallerstein, N. 2001. Measuring Community Empowerment: A Fresh Look at Organizational Domains. *Health Promotion International*, 16(2), pp. 179–185.

Laws, S. 2003. *Research for Development: A Practical Guide*. London: Sage Publications.

Ledwith, M. 2005. *Community Development: A Critical Approach*. Bristol: Policy Press.

Leibowitz, B. (ed.) 2012. *Higher Education for the Public Good: Views from the South*. Stoke-on-Trent, UK: Trentham Books.

Lewin, K. 1946. Action Research and Minority Problems. *Journal of Social Issues*, 2(4), pp. 34–46.

Leydesdorff, L. and Besselaar, P. 1987. What We Have Learned from the Amsterdam Science Shop. In S. Blume, J. Bunders, L. Leydesdorff, and R. D. Whitley (eds.) *The Social Direction of the Public Sciences. Sociology of the Sciences Yearbook* (Vol. XI). Dordrecht, the Netherlands: Reidel, pp. 135–160.

Leydesdorff, L. and Ward, J. 2004. *Communication of Science Shop Mediation: A Kaleidoscope of University-Society Relations*. INTERACTS: Improving Interaction between NGOs, Universities, and Science Shops: Experiences and Expectations,

Lyngby, http://www.leydesdorff.net/scishop/ communication%20of%20science%20shop%20mediation.pdf.
Leydesdorff, L. and Ward, M. 2005. Science Shops: A Kaleidoscope of Science. Society Collaborations in Europe. *Public Understanding of Science*, 14, pp. 353–372.
Lidskog, R. 2008. Scientised Citizens and Democratised Science: Re-Assessing the Expert-Lay Divide. *Journal of Risk Research*, 11(1–2), pp. 69–86.
Living Knowledge. 2013. *Living Knowledge Newsletter* 40. http://www.livingknowledge.org/livingknowledge/wp-content/uploads/2013/04/40-LK-Newsletter-April-20131.pdf.
Living Knowledge Network. 2013. About Living Knowledge—The International Science Shop Network. http://www.livingknowledge.org/livingknowledge/.
Lord, R. 1939. *The Agrarian Revival: A Study of Agricultural Extension*. New York: George Grady Press.
Lyotard, J. F. 1984. *The Postmodern Condition: A Report on Knowledge*. Manchester: Manchester University Press.
Macpherson, I. 2009. *A Century of Cooperation*. Ottawa, ON: Canadian Cooperative Association.
Mahony, N., Newman, J., and Barnett, C (eds.). 2010. *Rethinking the Public: Innovations in Research, Theory and Politics*. Bristol: Policy Press.
Manchester 2020. 2014. *The Strategic Plan for the University of Manchester*. http://documents.manchester.ac.uk/display.aspx?DocID=11953, accessed January 26, 2014.
Mansuri, G. and Rao, V. 2004. Community-Based and -Driven Development: A Critical Review. *World Bank Research Observer*, 19(1), pp. 1–39.
Marginson, S. 2007. The Public/Private Divide in Higher Education: A Global Revision. *Higher Education*, 53, pp. 307–333.
Marks, M., Erwin, K., and Mosavel, M. 2014. Community engagement, service learning and reflexivity: Knowledge building in practice through the Building Global Bridges project (pending).
Martin, E. and McKenna, E. 2013. Handbook of models of community engagement strategies in higher education institutions: Policy and curriculum development. PERARES Deliverable Report D7.1. Queen's University Belfast (pending).
Martin, E., McKenna, E., and Treasure, K. 2011. *Embedding Community and Public Engagement within Regional and National Policy and Higher Education Institutions*. Milestone Report 7.2 in the PERARES project. Queen's University Belfast. http://www.livingknowledge.org/livingknowledge/wp-content/uploads/2012/09/WP7-PERARES-Milestone-7-2-rpt-Final-Dublin.pdf.
Maurrasse, D. J. 2001. *Beyond the Campus: How Colleges and Universities form Partnerships with their Communities*. New York, NY: Routledge.
Mayoux, L. 2001. *Participatory Methods*. http://library.uniteddiversity.coop/Measuring_Progress_and_Eco_Footprinting/ParticipatoryMethods.pdf.
McCarthy, D. D., Whitelaw, G. S., Anderson, S., Cowan, D., McGarry, F., Robins, A., and Tsuji, L. J. 2012. Collaborative Geomatics and the Mushkegowuk

Cree First Nations: Fostering Adaptive Capacity for Community-Based Sub-Arctic Natural Resource Management. *Geoforum*, 43(2), pp. 305–314.
Mc Carthy, I. 2010. The Fifth Province: Imagining a Space of Dialogical Co-Creations! *Context*, December, pp. 6–11.
McDonald, M. A. 2009. *Practicing Community-Engaged Research*. https://www.dtmi.duke.edu/about-us/organization/duke-center-for-community-research/training-center/PracticingCommunityEngagedResearch.pdf/view.
McIlrath, L., Lyons, A., and Munck, R. 2012. *Higher Education and Civic Engagement—Comparative Perspectives*. New York: Palgrave Macmillan.
McKenna, B. 2013. Paulo Freire's Blunt Challenge to Anthropology: Create a Pedagogy of the Oppressed for Your Times *Critique of Anthropology*, 33(4), pp. 447–475.
McQuoid-Mason, D. 2002. Interview. http://www.wmd.org/resources/whats-being-done/civic-education-democracy/interview-david-mcquoid-mason.
Mead, G. H. 1956. *The Social Psychology of George Herbert Mead*. Chicago, IL: The University of Chicago Press.
Mills, C. W. 1959. *The Sociological Imagination*. London: Oxford University Press.
Ministry of Education. 1997. White Paper 3: A Programme for the Transformation of Higher Education. Pretoria: Ministry of Education.
Ministry of Higher Education and Training. 2014. White Paper on Post School Education and Training. Pretoria: Ministry of Higher Education and Training.
Minkler, M. 2004. Ethical Challenges for the "Outside" Researcher in Community-Based Participatory Research. *Health Education and Behavior*, 31(6), pp. 684–697.
Minkler, M. 2005. Community-Based Research Partnerships: Challenges and Opportunities. *Journal of Urban Health*, 82(2), pp. ii3–ii12.
Minkler, M. and Wallerstein, N. (eds.) 2003. *Community Based Participatory Research for Health*. San Francisco, CA: Jossey-Bass.
Mojab, S. 2000. Civilizing the State: The University in the Middle East. In S. Inayatullah and J. Gidley (eds.) *The University in Transformation: Global Perspectives on the Futures of the University*. Westport, CT: Bergin and Garvey, pp. 137–148.
Moore, B. 1966. *Social Origins of Dictatorship and Democracy*. Boston, MA: Beacon Press.
Morley, L. 2003. *Quality and Power in Higher Education*. Maidenhead, UK: SRHE and Open University Press.
Morris, G. P. 2010. Ecological Public Health and Climate Change Policy. *Perspectives in Public Health*, 130(1), pp. 34–40.
Mosse, D. 2001. Peoples' Knowledge, Participation and Patronage: Operations and Representations in Rural Development. In B. Cooke and U. Kothari (eds.) *Participation: The New Tyranny?* London: Zed Books, pp. 16–35.
Muirhead, B. and Woolcock, G. 2008. Doing what we know we should: engaged scholarship and community development, *Gateways, International Journal of Community Research and Engagement*, 1, pp. 8–30.
Mulder, H. 2000. *Final Evaluation Report, Science Shops in Romanian Moldavia*. Matra Project RO/97/04, 1-9-1998–31-12-2000.

Mulder, H., Auf Der Heyde, T., Goffer, R., and Teodosiu, C. 2001. *Success and Failure in Starting Science Shops*. SCIPAS Report No. 2. Utrecht, Utrecht University. http://www.livingknowledge.org/livingknowledge/wp-content/uploads/2012/02/wp2-so.pdf.

Mulder, H., Jørgensen, M. S., Pricope, L., Steinhaus, N., and Valentin, A. 2006. Science Shops as Science-Society Interfaces. In A. G. S. Pereira, S. Guedes Vaz, and S. Tognetti (eds) *Interfaces between Science and Society*. Sheffield, UK: Greenleaf Publishing, pp. 276–298.

Muller, J. 2010. Engagements with Engagement: A Response to Martin Hall. *Kagisano*, 6(January).

NCCPE. 2012 (a). *Concordat for Engaging the Public with Research*. http://www.nuffieldfoundation.org/sites/default/files/files/Grants%20for%20research%20and%20innovation%20%202012(1).pdf.

NCCPE. 2012 (b). *The Engaged University: A Manifesto for Public Engagement*. http://www.publicengagement.ac.uk/why-does-it-matter/manifesto.

NCCPE. 2013. *Catalyst Projects*. http://www.publicengagement.ac.uk/about/catalyst-projects.

Neave, G. 1998. The Evaluative State Reconsidered. *European Journal of Education*, 33(3), pp. 265–284.

Nelson, G. and Prilleltensky, I. 2005. *Community Psychology: In Pursuit of Liberation and Well-Being*. New York: Palgrave Macmillan.

Newfield, C. 2008. *Unmaking the Public University*. Cambridge, MA: Harvard University Press.

Newman, F. and Couturier, L. 2002. *Trading Public Good in the Higher Education Market*. London: The Observatory on Borderless Higher Education. http://www.obhe.ac.uk.

Nixon, J. 2011. *Higher Education and the Public Good: Imagining the University*. London: Continuum.

Nowotny, H., Scott, P., and Gibbons, M. 2001. *Re-Thinking Science: Knowledge and the Public in an Age of Uncertainty*. Cambridge: Polity.

Nunez, H. C. 2009. Contribuições para o debate Latino-Americano sobre a vigência e a projeção da educação popular. In P. Pontual and T. Ireland (orgs.) *Educação popular na América Latina: diálogos e perspectivas*. Brasilia: SECAD Secretaria de Educação Continuada, Alfabetização e Diversidade, and UNESCO, pp. 147–156.

Nunn, N. and Gutberlet, J. 2013. Cooperative Recycling in São Paulo, Brazil: Towards an Emotional Consideration of Empowerment. *Area*, 45(4), pp. 452–458.

Ochocka, J., Moorlag, E., and Janzen, R. 2010. A Framework for Entry: PAR Values and Engagement Strategies in Community Research. *Gateways: International Journal of Community Research and Engagement*, 3, pp. 2–19.

O'Connor, R. 2013. *Online Cancer Support: A Pilot Study to Implement and Evaluate a Support Blog at ARC Cancer Support House*. http://www.ucc.ie/en/scishop/rr/, accessed October 30, 2013.

Odora-Hoppers, C. A. (ed.). 2002. *Indigenous Knowledge and the Integration of Knowledge Systems: Towards a Philosophy of Articulation*. Cape Town: New Africa Books.

PACEC. 2012. *Strengthening the Contribution of English HEIs to the Innovation System: Knowledge Exchange and HEIF Funding*. https://secure.pacec.co.uk/documents/HEIF11-15-FullReport.pdf.

Pain, R., and Francis, P. (2003) Reflections on participatory research, *Area*, 35(1), 46–54.

Pandor, N. 2008. Remarks by the Minister of Education, Naledi Pandor MP, at the Handing Over of the Community-Higher Education Service Partnership (CHESP) from JET to the Council on Higher Education (CHE), Johannesburg. September 9, 2008.

Patton, M. Q. 2011. *Developmental Evaluation: Applying Complexity Concepts to Enhance Innovation and Use*. New York: The Guilford Press.

Peters, M. A. 2011. *The Last Book of Postmodernism: Apocalyptic Thinking, Philosophy and Education in the Twenty-First Century*. New York: Peter Lang.

Peters, S. J. 2008. Reconstructing a Democratic Tradition of Public Scholarship in the Land-Grant System. In D. Brown and D. Witte (eds.) *Agent of Democracy: Higher Education and the HEX Journey*. Dayton, OH: Kettering Foundation Press, pp. 79–102.

Peters, S. J. 2010. *Democracy and Higher Education, Traditions and Stories of Civic Engagement*. East Lansing, MI: Michigan State University Press.

Peters, S. J. 2013. Storying and Restorying the Land-Grant Mission. In R. L. Geiger and N. M. Sorber (eds.) *The Land-Grant Colleges and the Reshaping of American Higher Education*. Perspectives on the History of Higher Education (Vol. 30). New Brunswick, NJ: Transaction Publishers, pp. 335–353.

Peters, S. J., Jordan, N. R., Adamek, M., and Alter, T. R. (eds.). 2005. *Engaging Campus and Community: The Practice of Public Scholarship in the State and Land-Grant University System*. Dayton, OH: Kettering Foundation Press.

Peters, S. J., O'Connell, D. J., Alter, T. R., and Jack, A. (eds.). 2006. *Catalyzing Change: Profiles of Cornell Cooperative Extension Educators from Greene, Tompkins, and Erie Counties, New York*. Ithaca, NY: Cornell Cooperative Extension.

Pinto, J. B. 1989. *Pesquisa-ação: detalhamento de sua sequência*. Recife, Brazil: SUDENE/PNUD.

Pinto, J. B., Angel, M. A., and Reyes, V. 1973. *Metodología de investigación temática. Taller de metodología de investigación para capacitación campesina*. Caracas: IICA/OEA/CIARA.

Platteau, J. P. 2004. Monitoring Elite Capture in Community-Driven Development. *Development and Change*, 35(2), pp. 223–246.

Pontual, P. and Ireland, T. (orgs.). 2009. Educação popular na América Latina: diálogos e perspectivas. Brasilia: SECAD Secretaria de Educação Continuada, Alfabetização e Diversidade, and UNESCO.

Post, D., Clipper, L., Enkhbaatar, D., Manning, A., Riley, T., and Zaman, H. 2004. World Bank Okays Public Interest in Higher Education. *Higher Education*, 48, pp. 213–229.

PRIA. 2000. *Doing Research with People: Approaches to Participatory Research*. New Delhi: PRIA.

Puntasen, T., Kleiman, F., Taylor, P., and Boothroyd, P. 2008. *Higher Education and Participatory Development: Opportunities for Strengthening the Linkage*. Presented to Asia Pacific Sub-Regional Preparatory Conference for the 2009 World Conference on Higher Education "Facing Global and Local Challenges: The New Dynamics for Higher Education." September 24–26, 2008, Macao SAR, PR China.

Rappoport, J. 1981. In Praise of Paradox: A Social Policy of Empowerment over Prevention. *American Journal of Community Psychology*, 9, pp. 1–25.

RCUK. 2011. Impact Requirements: Frequently Asked Questions. http://www.rcuk.ac.uk/documents/impacts/RCUKImpactFAQ.pdf.

RCUK. 2014. *Concordat for Engaging the Public with Research*. http://www.rcuk.ac.uk/pe/concordat/date, accessed January 26, 2014.

Reading, P. 1994. *Community Care and the Voluntary Sector: The Role of Voluntary Organizations in a Changing World*. Birmingham: Venture Press.

Readings, B. 1996. *The University in Ruins*. Cambridge, MA: Harvard University Press.

Reason, P. 1988. *Human Inquiry in Action*. London: Sage Publications.

Reason, P. 1994. *Participation in Human Inquiry*. London: Sage Publications.

REF 2014. (2012). Panel Criteria and Working Methods. http://www.ref.ac.uk/media/ref/content/pub/panelcriteriaandworkingmethods/01_12_2D.pdf/

REF 2014. (2013). Assessment Criteria and Level Definitions. http://www.ref.ac.uk/panels/assessmentcriteriaandleveldefinitions/, accessed February 16, 2014.

Regional Universities Network. 2013. Regional Universities Network Contribution to Regions and the Nation. A proposal developed by the RUN Engagement Working Group (not publically available).

Research Council Economic Impact Group. 2006. *Increasing the Economic Impact of Research Councils*. http://www.bis.gov.uk/files/file32802.pdf, accessed January 26, 2014.

Research Councils UK. 2012(a). *Excellence with Impact*. http://www.rcuk.ac.uk/kei/impacts/Pages/home.aspx, accessed May 24, 2012.

Research Councils UK. 2012(b). *Bridging the Gap between Higher Education and the Public*. http://www.rcuk.ac.uk/documents/scisoc/beaconslaunch.pdf, accessed May 24, 2012.

Research Councils UK. 2012(c). *Public Engagement with Research Catalysts*. http://www.rcuk.ac.uk/per/Pages/catalysts.aspx, accessed June 24, 2012.

Resnicow, K. and Page, S. E. 2008. Embracing Chaos and Complexity: A Quantum Change for Public Health. *American Journal of Public Health*, 98(8), pp. 1382–1389.

Rolfe, G. 2013. *The University in Dissent. Scholarship in the Corporate University*. London: Routledge.

Rhoades, G. 1987. Higher Education in a Consumer Society. *Journal of Higher Education*, 58(1), pp. 1–24.

Rhoten, D. and Calhoun, C. (eds.). 2011. *Knowledge Matters: The Public Mission of the Research University*. New York: Columbia University Press.

Riggirozzi, P. and Tussie, D. 2012. *The Rise of Post-Hegemonic Regionalism*. London and New York: Springer.
Roux, A. V. D. 2011. Complex Systems Thinking and Current Impasses in Health Disparities Research. *American Journal of Public Health*, 101(9), p. 1627.
Royal Society. 2006. *Survey of Factors Affecting Science Communication by Scientists and Engineers*. http://royalsociety.org/uploadedFiles/Royal_Society_Content/Influencing_Policy/Themes_and_Projects/Themes/Governance/Final_Reporton_website_and_amended_by_SK_no_navigation.pdf.
Saguier, M. and Brent, Z. 2013. *Regional Policy Frameworks of Social and Solidarity Economy in South America*. Prepared for United Nations Research Institute for Social Development.
Said, E. 1996. *Culture and Imperialism*. New York: Random House.
Sall, E., Lebeau, Y., and Kassimir, R. 2003. The Public Dimensions of the University in Africa. *Journal of Higher Education in Africa* 1(1), pp. 126–148.
Sandoval, J. A., Lucero, J., Oetzel, J., Avila, M., Belone, L., Mau, M., and Wallerstein, N. 2012. Process and Outcome Constructs for Evaluating Community-Based Participatory Research Projects: A Matrix of Existing Measures. *Health Education Research*, 27(4), pp. 680–690.
Santos, B de S., Arriscado Nunes, J. and Meneses, M. P. 2007 Opening up the canon of knowledge and recognition of difference. in B de S Santos (ed.) *Another knowledge is possible: beyond northern epistemologies*. New York: Verso pp. xviv–lxii.
Saxby, J. 2004. *COEP—Comitê de Entidades no Combate à Fome e pela Vida, Mobilising against Hunger and for Life: An Analysis of Capacity and Change in a Brazilian Network*. A case study prepared for the project "Capacity, Change and Performance." Brussels, European Centre for Development Policy Management.
Schnell, S. and Saxby, J. 2010. Mobilizing against Hunger and Poverty: Capacity and Change in a Brazilian Social Solidarity Network. *Public Administration and Development*, 1(30), pp. 38–48.
Schuetze, H. G. and Inman, P. 2010 *The Community Engagement and Service Mission of Universities*. Leicester, UK: NIACE, 2011.
Schut, M., van Paassen, A., Leeuwis, C., and Klerkx, L. 2013. Towards Dynamic Research Configurations: A Framework for Reflection on the Contribution of Research to Policy and Innovation Processes. *Science and Public Policy*, 36, pp. 255–270.
Sciencewise Expert Resource Centre. http://www.sciencewise-erc.org.uk/, accessed January 26, 2014.
Sclove, R. E. 1995. *Democracy and Technology*. New York and London: The Guildford Press.
Scocuglia, A. C. and de Melo Neto, J. F. (orgs.). 1999. *Educação popular outros caminhos*. João Pessoa, Brazil: Editora Universitária.
Scriven, M. A. 2008. Summative Evaluation of RCT Methodology: & An Alternative Approach to Causal Research. *Journal of Multidisciplinary Evaluation*, 5(9), pp. 11–24.
Sen, A. 2010. *The Idea of Justice*. London: Penguin Books.

Sharma, Y. 2012. Fast Pace of Higher Education Enrolment Growth Predicted to Slow. *University World News*, February 25.
Shattock, M. (ed.) 2009. *Entrepreneurialism in Universities and the Knowledge Economy—Diversification and Organizational Change in European Higher Education*. Maidenhead, UK: SRHE/Open University Press.
Shavit, Y., Arum, R., and Gamoran, A. (eds.) 2007. *Stratification in Higher Education: A Comparative Study*. Stanford, CA: Stanford University Press.
Sidaway, R. 2005. *Resolving Environmental Disputes: From Conflict to Consensus*. London: Earthscan.
Sivanandan, A. 2013. The Market State vs. the Good Society. *Race and Class*, 54, pp. 1–9.
Slaughter, S. and Leslie, L. L. 1997. *Academic Capitalism: Politics, Policies, and the Entrepreneurial University*. Baltimore, MD: The Johns Hopkins University Press.
Small, A. 1896. Scholarship and Social Agitation. *American Journal of Sociology*, 1(5), pp. 564–582.
Smith, R. G. 2013 [1949]. *The People's Colleges: A History of the New York State Extension Service in Cornell University and the State, 1876–1948*. Ithaca, NY: Cornell University Press.
Sorlin, S. and Vessuri, H. (eds.). 2007. *Knowledge Society vs. Knowledge Economy: Knowledge, Power and Politics*. Paris: Palgrave Macmillan/UNESCO/IAU.
Souza, J. F. 2009. A vigência da educação popular. In P. Pontual and T. Ireland (orgs.) *Educação popular na América Latina: diálogos e perspectivas*. Brasilia: SECAD Secretaria de Educação Continuada, Alfabetização e Diversidade, and UNESCO.
Stanton, T. K., Giles, D. E., Cruz, J. R., and Nadine I. 1999. *Service-Learning: A Movement's Pioneers Reflect on Its Origins, Practices, and Future*. San Francisco, CA: Jossey-Bass.
Steinhaus, N. 1999. Dialog jenseits von Expertensprachen. Das Konzept der Wissenschaftsläden. *WechselWirkung*, 99.
Steinhaus, N. 2013. Editorial. *Living Knowledge Magazine*, 11. http://www.living knowledge.org/livingknowledge/wp-content/uploads/2013/05/LK-Magazine-11-May-2013.pdf, p.2.
Sterman, J. 2000. *Business Dynamics: Systems Thinking and Modeling for a Complex World*. Boston, MA: McGraw Hill.
Stifterverband für die Deutsche Wissenschaft. 2013. *Sozial und engagiert. Das Programm "Mehr als Forschung und Lehre."* http://www.stifterverband.de/mafl/mehr_als_forschung_und_lehre.pdf, accessed November 28, 2013.
Stiftung Mercator. 2011.Global Young Facility Report, http://www.stiftung-mercator.de/kompetenzzentren/wissenschaft/mehr-als-forschung-und-lehre.html, accessed November 28, 2013.
Stiglitz, J. E. 1999. Knowledge as a Global Public Good. In I. Kaul, I. Grunberg, and M. A. Stern (eds.) *Global Public Goods: International Co-Operation in the 21st Century*. New York: Oxford University Press, pp. 308–325.
Stilgoe, J. 2009. *Citizen Scientists—Reconnecting Science with Civil Society*. London: Demos.

Strand, K. J., Cutforth, N., Stoecker, R., Marullo, S., and Donohue, P. 2003. *Community-Based Research and Higher Education: Principles and Practices*. San Francisco, CA: John Wiley & Co.
Strathern, M. 2000. *Audit Cultures*. London: Routledge.
Stringer, L. C., Dougill, A. J., Fraser, E., Hubacek, K., Prell, C., and Reed, M. S. 2006. Unpacking "Participation" in the Adaptive Management of Social-Ecological Systems: A Critical Review. *Ecology and Society*, 11(2), p. 39.
Stufflebeam, D. L. 1994. Empowerment Evaluation, Objectivist Evaluation, and Evaluation Standards: Where the Future of Evaluation Should Not Go and Where It Needs to Go. *American Journal of Evaluation*, 15(3), pp. 331–338.
Sturm, S., Eatman, T., Saltmarsh, J., and Bush, A. 2011. Full Participation: Building the Architecture for Diversity and Public Engagement in Higher Education. White paper, New York, Center for International and Social Change, Columbia University Law School. http://imaginingamerica.org/wp-content/uploads/2011/04/Catalyst-Paper_Final.pdf.
Swantz, M. L. 1975. Research as an Educational Tool for Development. *Convergence*, viii (2), pp. 44–53.
Tandon, R. 1978. Impact of Organisations Development in Under Organised Communities. PhD thesis, Case Western Reserve University.
Tandon, R. 1998. Struggle for Knowledge: A Personal Journey. *Studies in Culture, Organisations and Societies*, 4, pp. 187–195.
Teodosiu, C. and Teleman, D. 2003. *Interacts, Improving Interaction between NGO's, Universities and Science Shops: Experiences and Expectations*. Romanian case studies report. Iaşi, Romania: Intermediu, Gh. Asachi University.
Thériault, L., Skibbens, R., and Brown, L. 2008. *A Portrait of Co-Operatives and Credit Unions in Atlantic Canada: Preliminary Analysis*. Working Paper 2008-01, Nova Scotia, The Social Economy and Sustainability Research (SES/ÉSD) Network.
Thiollent, M. 1988. *Metodologia da pesquisa-ação*, 4th ed. São Paulo: Cortez.
Thiollent, M. 2005. *Metodologia da pesquisa-ação*, 14th ed. São Paulo: Cortez.
Thiollent, M. 2011a. *Metodologia da pesquisa-ação*, 18th ed. São Paulo: Cortez.
Thiollent, M. 2011b. Action Research and Participatory Research: An Overview. *International Journal of Action Research*, 7(2), pp. 160–174.
Torres, R. M. 2007. Incidir en la educación. *Polis*, 5(16). http://firgoa.usc.es/drupal/taxonomy/term/313, accessed January 17, 2014.
Tremblay, C. and Gutberlet, J. 2011. Empowerment through Participation: Assessing the Voices of Leaders from Recycling Cooperatives in São Paulo, Brazil. *Community Development Journal*, 46(3), pp. 282–302.
UNEP. 2009. *Gap Analysis for the Purpose of Facilitating the Discussion on How to Improve and Strengthen the Science-Policy Interface on Biodiversity and Ecosystems*. http://www.ipbes.net/meetings/Documents/IPBES_2_1_INF_1%282%29.pdf, retrieved November 15, 2012.
UNESCO. 2009. *Communiqué of 2009 World Conference on Higher Education: The New Dynamics of Higher Education and Research for Societal Change and Development*. Paris, July 5–8, 2009.

United States Statutes. 1862. *Morrill Act.* http://www.loc.gov.
Universities Australia. 2013. *Universities Australia Response to the DIICCSRTE Discussion Paper—Assessing the Wider Benefits Arising from University-Based Research.* Universities Australia. http://www.universitiesaustralia.edu.au/resources/858/1659.
University College Cork. 2013. *UCC Strategic Plan 2013–2017.* http://www.ucc.ie/en/strategicplanning/2013/, accessed October 21, 2013.
UUK. 2012. *Futures for Higher Education: Analysing Trends.* http://www.universitiesuk.ac.uk/highereducation/Documents/2012/FuturesForHigherEducation.pdf, accessed January 26, 2014.
Uyarra, E. and Flanagan, K. 2013. Reframing Regional Innovation Systems: Evolution, Complexity and Public Policy. In P. N. Cooke (ed.) *Re-Framing Regional Development: Evolution, Innovation and Transition.* Regions and Cities. Abingdon, UK: Routledge, pp.146–163.
Valle, E. and Queirós, J. J. (orgs.). 1988a. Apresentação. In *A Cultura do Povo.* São Paulo: Cortez/Instituto de Estudos Especiais, p. 7.
Valle, E. and Queirós, J. J. (orgs.). 1988b. *A Cultura do Povo.* São Paulo: Cortez/Instituto de Estudos Especiais.
van Olphen, J., Schulz, A., and Israel, B. 2003. Religious Involvement, Social Support, and Health among African-American Women on the East Side of Detroit. *Journal of General Internal Medicine,* 18, pp. 548–556.
Visvanathan, S. 2009. *The Search for Cognitive Justice.* http://bit.ly/3ZwMD2, accessed on September 8, 2012.
Vygotsky, L. 1934. *Thought and Language.* Moscow and Leningrad: Sozekgiz. (Translation in English published in 1962. Cambridge, MA: The MIT Press and Wiley.)
Wachelder, J. 2003. Democratizing Science: Various Routes and Visions of Dutch Science Shops. *Science, Technology, Human Values,* 28(2), pp. 244–273.
Walker, M. 2012. Universities, Professional Capabilities and Contributions to the Public Good in South Africa: *COMPARE. A Journal of Comparative and International Education,* 42(6), pp. 819–838.
Wallerstein, N. and Duran, B. 2008. Theoretical, Historical and Practical Roots of CBPR. In M. Minkler and N. Wallerstein (eds.) *Community-Based Participatory Research for Health: From Process to Outcomes.* San Francisco, CA: John Wiley & Co, pp. 25–39.
Wallerstein, N. and Duran, B. 2010. Community-Based Participatory Research Contributions to Intervention Research: The Intersection of Science and Practice to Improve Health Equity. *American Journal of Public Health,* 100(1), pp. 40–46.
Wallerstein, N., Oetzel, J. G., and Duran, B. 2008. CBPR: What Predicts Outcomes? In M. Minkler and N. Wallerstein (eds.) *Community-Based Participatory Research for Health: From Process to Outcomes.* San Francisco, CA: John Wiley & Co, pp. 371–394.
Wallerstein, N. B. and Duran, B. 2006. Using Community-Based Participatory Research to Address Health Disparities. *Health Promotion Practice,* 7(3), pp. 312–323.

Waltner-Toews, D. and Kay, J. 2005. The Evolution of an Ecosystem Approach: the Diamond Schematic and an Adaptive Methodology for Ecosystem Sustainability and Health. *Ecology and Society*, 10(1), p. 38.
Wangoola, P. 2002. Mpambo, the African Multiversity: A Philosophy to Rekindle the African Spirit. In G. Dei, B. Hall, and D. Goldin-Rosenberg (eds.) *Indigenous Knowledges in the Global Contexts: Multiple Readings of the World*. Toronto, ON: University of Toronto Press, pp. 265–279.
Warry, P. 2006. *Increasing the Economic Impact of the Research Councils* (The Warry Report). Swindon, Research Council UK.
Watkins, M. 2003. Dialogue, Development and Liberation. In I. E. Joseph (ed.) *Dialogicality in Development*. Westport, CT: Praeger Publishers, pp. 127–149.
Watson, D. 2007. *Managing Civic and Community Engagement*. Maidenhead, UK: Open University Press.
Watson, D., Hollister, R. Stroud, S. E., and Babcock, E. 2011. *The Engaged University: International Perspectives on Civic Engagement*. London and New York: Routledge.
Webb, S. A. 2001. Some Considerations on the Validity of Evidence-Based Practice in Social Work. *British Journal of Social Work*, 31(1), pp. 57–79.
Weber, L. E. and Bergan, S. (eds.) 2005. *The Public Responsibility for Higher Education and Research*. Strasbourg: Council of Europe Publishing.
Wertsch, J. V. 1985. *Vygotsky and the Social Formation of Mind*. Cambridge, MA: Harvard University Press.
Wethington, E. and Dunifo, R. E. (eds.). 2012. *Research for the Public Good: Applying Methods of Translational Research to Improve Human Health and Well-Being*. Washington, DC: American Psychological Association.
WHO. 1986. *Ottawa Charter for Health Promotion*. First International Conference on Health Promotion, Ottawa. Geneva: World Health Organization.
Williams, B. 2002. *Truth and Truthfulness: An Essay in Genealogy*. Princeton, NJ: Princeton University Press.
Wilson, T. 2012. *A Review of Business-University Collaboration* (The Wilson Review). UK: Crown Copyright, Department for Business, Innovation and Skills, London,. https://www.gov.uk/.
Winter, A., Wiseman, J., and Muirhead, B. 2005. *Beyond Rhetoric: University Community Engagement in Victoria*. Brisbane: EIDOS Publications.
Wistow, G., Knapp, M., Hardy, B., and Allen, C. 1994. *Social Care in a Mixed Economy*. Buckingham: Open University Press.
World Bank. 1996. Participation Handbook <http://www.worldbank.org/wbi/source book/sbhome.htm>
World Bank. 2002. *Constructing Knowledge Societies: New Challenges for Tertiary Education*. Washington DC: the World Bank.
Yates, J. S. and Gutberlet, J. 2011. Enhancing Livelihoods and the Urban Environment: The Local Political Framework for Integrated Organic Waste Management in Diadema, Brazil. *Journal of Development Studies*, 47(4), pp. 639–656.

Young, M. 2008. *Bringing Knowledge Back In*. Abingdon, UK: Routledge.
Young, M. and Muller, J. 2007. Truth and Truthfulness in the Sociology of Educational Knowledge. *Theory and Research in Education*, 5(2), pp. 173–201.
Zublena, J. 2013. *North Carolina State University: Cooperative Extension Measuring Excellence in Extension Implementation Team*. Washington DC: ECOP.

Index

'academic capitalism', 20, 22, 189
action research, 15–16, 29, 58, 59, 171
activist scholars, *see individual names or countries*
adult education
  development of, 1
  Director of Adult Education, UNESCO, 55
  International Council for Adult Education, 57, 58
  Latin American Council for Adult Education, 173
  Ontario Institute for Studies in Education, 58
  participatory research, involvement in, 57
Africa
  Chambers' work in, 13
  indigenous knowledge, 54, 158, 160, 161–2, 164–5
  participatory rural appraisal (PRA), 13, 30, 63, 171
  rural extension reform program, 16
  Tanzania and participatory research, 55–7
Al-Azhar University (Cairo), 54
Albo, Xavier, 58
Amsterdam, University of, 73
Argentina
  Latin American Centre for Service-Learning, 179
  solidarity economy, 175
Arraes, Miguel, 169
Arruda, Marcos, 174
Ashforth, Adam, 156, 157, 158

Association of Commonwealth Universities, 99, 118
Australia
  Australian Universities Community Engagement Alliance, 120, 123
  Australian University Quality Agency, 121
  university–community engagement, 5, 117–31
Avila, Maria, 133, 219

Baldwin, R.J., 138, 139
Barnett, Ronald, 183, 219
Bates, Catherine, 101, 219
Bauman, Zygmunt, 187
Bawa, Ahmed C., 149, 219
Bawden, Richard, 152
Beacons for Public Engagement initiative (UK), 4, 75, 92–3
Beisiegel, Celso, 168, 171
Bhaskar, Ray, 23–4
Boal, Augusto, 171–2
Bolivia
  Albo's work in, 58
  Bolivian Centre for Multidisciplinary Studies, 178
Boyer, Ernest, 65
Brandão, Carlos Rodrigues, 171, 173
Brazil
  Committee of Entities in the Struggle against Hunger and for a Full Life (COEP), 177–8
  Freire's work in, 13, 29–30, 168–71

Brazil—*continued*
    Participatory Sustainable Waste Management (PSWM) project, 176–7
    popular education and participatory research, 171
    solidarity economy, 174–5
Burns, Kenneth, 101, 219–20

Calhoun, Craig, 86, 96, 203
Callaway, Helen, 57
Campus Engage (Ireland), 5, 102, 114
Canada
    community evaluation research plans, 47–9
    early childhood learning project, 42–7
    health and social interventions, 39–52
    Office of Community Based Research, University of Victoria, 64
    Ontario Institute for Studies in Education, 58
    Social Sciences and Humanities Research Council, 75
    Youth and Ecological Restoration Project, 49–51
Cartagena Conference
    First (April 1977), 58–9, 172
    Second (June 1997), 63
Case Western Reserve University (Cleveland), 61
Chambers, Robert, 3, 13, 30, 33, 38, 63
Chile, Vio Grossi's work in, 57
civic engagement, 5, 15, 22–3, 75, 107, 109
Coady International Institute (Canada), 68
cognitive justice, 4, 67
Colombia
    Cartagena Conferences (1977 and 1997), 58–9, 63, 172
    community-based participatory research, 12
    Fals Borda's work in, 12, 59, 172

Committee on the Public Understanding of Science (COPUS), 91
community-based learning, 1
community-based participatory research (CBPR), 11, 12–15
community-based research
    benefits of, 1–2, 20, 21, 27–8, 104
    'bottom-up' or grassroots approach, 4, 5, 14, 30
    community organizing, 140–5
    community practices, 3, 39–52
    community research/local knowledge approach, 21
    complex systems research approach, 35–8
    context of, 20
    culture change, 5, 133–47
    definitions of, 28–9, 103
    land-grant universities (USA), 5, 15, 16, 136–40
    Latin American influences on, 167–80
    limitations of, 22, 28
    North/South models of, 15, 23
    origins and development of, 2, 3, 11–26, 29–31, 53–68, 183–98
    participatory approach, 2–3, 13–14, 19, 27–38, 51, 103
    participatory methodologies, 29, 30–3
    policy and support at European level, 110–13
    politics of, 17–18
    principles of, 40–1, 103
    science shops, 4, 16–17, 71–83, 105–6, 107, 108, 110, 112, 113
    social sciences, 15–16, 173
    techniques used in, 29
    see also individual countries/case studies; university–community engagement
Community Health Scholars Program, 103

Community Higher Education Service Partnerships (CHESP) Program, 153
Community Knowledge Initiative (Ireland), 109
community, notion of, 19–20, 31–2, 103, 190
community practices
health systems and social services, 3, 39–52
Community University Exposition (CUExpo, 2008), 64
complex systems research approach, 35–8
conscientização concept in critical thinking, *see* Freire
Convergence journal, 57
Cornell University, 136, 138
Council for the Defence of British Universities (CDBU), 95
Cuba and national literacy plan, 169
culture change through community-based research, 5, 133–47
Cuthill, Michael, 117, 220

Dar es Salaam, University of, 55, 56
dependency theory, 13
De Schutter, Anton, 173
De Sousa Santos, Boaventura, 66–7
De Souza, Herbert, 177
De Souza, João Francisco, 171, 173
development research (research for development), 23
De Vries, Jan, 60
Dublin City University, 108–9
Dublin Institute of Technology, 106–7
Duncan, Sophie, 85, 220
Durban Moment, *see* Trade Union Research Project (South Africa)
Durban University of Technology, 161

education
humanist approach to, 13
networks of, 173
popular learning movements, 13, 30, 168–71, 172

and the public good, 7, 199–216
see also adult education
Engagement Australia (EA), 123
Escrigas, Cristina, 66
Essen, University of, 76
Europe
EU Horizon 2020 Programme, 83, 112
EU research funding strategy for science shops, 4, 74–5, 78
EU Seventh Framework Programme (FP7), 75
Public Engagement with Research and Research Engagement with Society (PERARES), 75, 79, 106, 113, 114
Science & Society Action Plan (European Commission), 78, 112
science shops, 16–17, 71–83, 112, 113
evaluation, new methods of, 41
Extension Service, Cooperative (USA), 16, 136–40

Fals Borda, Orlando, 12, 58–9, 63, 171, 172
Fifth Province initiative (Ireland), 24
Fish, Stanley, 25–6
Ford Foundation, 153
France, science shops, 76
Freire, Paulo, 6, 13, 29–30, 41, 48, 50, 51, 56, 168–71, 173, 176
conscientização concept, 170, 176
influences on, 169–70

Gandhi, Mahatma, 54
Gaventa, John, 68
Gellner, Ernest, 184
genetically modified (GM) food debate, 91
Germany, science shops, 76
Gerold, Rainer, 17, 78
Gianotten, Vera, 58
Gibbons, Michael, 22, 155, 159–60

250 • Index

Global Alliance on
  Community-Engaged Research
  (GACER), 64
Global University Network for
  Innovation, 66
Gramsci, Antonio, 168
Gujarat Vidyapith, University of
  (India), 54
Gutberlet, Jutta, 167, 220

Habermas, Jürgen, 190, 206
Hall, Budd, 1, 53, 56, 57–9, 64, 65,
  172, 217, 220
Hall, Martin, 154–5
Harkavy, Ira, 164
health and social interventions
  role of community-based research,
  39–52
Higgins, Michael D., 101, 116
Higher Education Authority (Ireland),
  5, 106
Higher Education Funding Council for
  England, 89
higher education and research
  and the public good, 199–216
  science shops, 77–81
  see also universities
Highlander Center (USA), 68
Huizer, Gerrit, 173
humanist approach to education and
  research, 13
Hunt Report (Ireland), 75, 102, 110–11

Improving Science Shop Networking
  (ISSNET), 78
India, Tandon's work in, 57, 61–2
Industrial Areas Foundation (IAF),
  140, 141
Institute for Public Policy Research
  (UK), 86
INTERACTS case studies, 73, 78,
  80, 81
International Council for Adult
  Education
  First World Assembly (1976), 57
  Officers of, 58

International Participatory Research
  Network, 57, 59–61, 65
International Sociological
  Association, 58
Ireland (Republic of)
  Community-Academic Research
  Links (CARL) at University
  College Cork, 107–8
  community engagement in research
  and learning, 4–5, 75, 101–16
  Community Knowledge Exchange
  (CKE) at Dublin City
  University, 108–9
  Engaging People in Communities
  (EPIC) at National University of
  Ireland, Galway, 109–10
  Fifth Province initiative, 24
  Irish Network for
  Community-Engaged Research
  and Learning (INCERL), 114
  Irish Universities Association, 114
  national community engagement
  strategy, 5
  National Strategy for Higher
  Education to 2030 (Hunt
  Report), 75, 102, 110–11
  science shops, 113
  Students Learning with Communities
  (SLWC) at Dublin Institute of
  Technology, 106–7
  see also Northern Ireland
Islamic scholarship, 54

Jackson, Ted, 57, 58
Jamia Millia Islamia, University of
  (India), 54
Judt, Tonyt, 66

Kassam, Yusuf, 60
Kerr, Clark, 95, 199
Kidd, Roby, 58
knowledge
  application for social transformation,
  8, 21, 68, 168, 217–18
  commodification of, 2, 8
  community knowledge exchange, 7,
  108–9

democratization of, 3, 7, 51, 64, 66, 68, 149, 218
ecologies of, 67
exchange, principles of, 119–20
indigenous African, 54, 158, 160, 161–2, 164–5
knowledge-constitutive interests, 190
legitimation by universities, 7, 184–5
local community-based, 21, 176
Modes 1 and 2 of knowledge production, 5, 22, 24, 103, 155, 159–61
subaltern, 66
types of, 2, 18–19, 66, 156
wissenschaft, 107
KwaZulu-Natal, University of, 158, 162

Lammerink, Marc, 173
land-grant universities (USA), 5, 15, 16, 136–40
Latin America
community-based participatory research, 12–15
community-based research tradition, 6, 167–80
Latin American Centre for Service-Learning, 179
Latin American Council for Adult Education, 173
participatory action research (PAR), 12–13
solidarity economies and regional integration, 173–6
Le Boterf, Guy, 173
Lewin, Kurt, 15, 29, 171
Liston, Vanessa, 27, 220
Living Knowledge Network, international, 113
London School of Economics, 86
Lyons, Ann, 101, 220
Lyotard, 189

majority-world foundations of community-based research, 53–68
Manchester, University of, 90
Manners, Paul, 85, 221

Maranhão, Djalma, 169
Marino, Dian, 58
Marks, Monique, 162
Mayo, Elton, 16
McIlrath, Lorraine, 1, 101, 217, 221
McKenna, Emma, 101, 221
McQuoid-Mason, David, 151
Mead, George Herbert, 41, 51
Mexico, Núñez Hurtado's work in, 173
Mhaiki, Paul, 55
Millennium Ecosystem Assessment, 36
Mills, C. Wright, 16
Mode 1 knowledge production, 22, 103, 159, 160
Mode 2 knowledge production, 5, 22, 24, 103, 159–61
Mokoena, Paul Mduduzi, 161–2
Moore, Barrington, 12
Moraes, Carmen, 167, 221
Mullett, Jennifer, 39, 221
Munck, Ronaldo, 1, 11, 217, 221
Murphy, Pádraig, 101, 221–2
Mustapha, Kemal, 56

Natal, University of, 151–3
National Coordinating Centre for Public Engagement (UK), 86
National Research Foundation (South Africa), 158
National University of Ireland, Galway, 109–10
Netherlands, science shops, 73–4, 76–7
Ngcobo, Chief Nkosi, 162
Nicaragua, Fals Borda's work in, 172
Northern Ireland
community engagement in research and learning, 101–16
A Higher Education Strategy for Northern Ireland, 102, 112
Queen's University Belfast science shop, 105–6
science shops, 113
see also Ireland (Republic of)
North/South models of community-based research, 15, 23
Nuffield Foundation (UK), 74

Núñez Hurtado, Carlos, 173
Nyerere, Julius K., 55

Occidental College (Los Angeles), Center for Community Based Learning, 141
Ontario Institute for Studies in Education, 58
Open University, 4
oppression, determinants of, 29
Oquist, Paul, 58, 173
Ottawa Charter (1986), 40

Pandor, Naledi, 153
Partenariats Institutions-Citoyens pour la Recherche et l'Innovation (PICRI), 75
participation in community-based research, 2–3, 13–14, 19, 27–38
participatory action research (PAR), 12–13, 59, 172
participatory appraisal (PA), 30
participatory learning and action (PLA), 30
participatory methodologies
 aim of, 30–1
 critiques of, 31–3
 principles of, 29
 types of, 29, 30
participatory research (PR)
 academia's initial rejection of concept, 62, 63
 building of academia–civil society partnerships, 64–6
 Cartagena Conference (1977), 58–9, 172
 Cartagena Conference (1997), 63
 first use of term (Budd Hall), 57
 founding of Global Alliance on Community-Engaged Research (GACER), 64
 founding of International Participatory Research Network, 59–61, 65
 founding of Participatory Research in Asia (PRIA), 61–2
 Latin American influences on, 171–3
 origins and development of, 53–68
 Participatory Research (PR) Project (Hall *et al*), 58
 practice research engagement (PRE), 63
 principles of, 59–61
Participatory Research in Asia (PRIA), 61–2
participatory rural appraisal (PRA), 13, 30, 63, 171
Pedagogy of the Oppressed (Freire), 13, 56, 170
peer review, 155, 196
performativity, principle of, 189
Peru, solidarity economy, 175
Peters, Scott J., 133, 222
Pinto, João Bosco, 173
power relationships, 14, 18, 28, 29, 31, 32, 159, 160–1, 163
practice research engagement (PRE), 63
Public Engagement with Research and Research Engagement with Society (PERARES), 75, 79, 106, 113, 114
public good, education and the, 7, 199–216

Queensland, University of
 Boilerhouse, Community Engagement Centre, 125–7
 engagement typology, 122–3
Queen's University Belfast, 105–6

Reading, Bill, 149, 156
REFLECT approach, 14
reform programs
 agricultural modernization (USA), 16, 136–40
 rural extension (Africa), 16
Research Councils UK (RCUK), 115
Rockhill, Kathleen, 57

Said, Edward, 68
São Paulo, University of, 176
science shops, 4, 16–17, 71–83, 105–6, 107, 108, 110, 112, 113
science and society, *see* science shops

Sciencewise Expert Resource Centre (UK), 91
SCIPAS study, 78
service learning, 16, 106, 109, 179
Service Learning Academy (Ireland), 113
Shantiniketan, University of (India), 55
Singh, Mala, 199, 222
Sitas, Ari, 152
Small, Albion, 15
Smith-Lever Act (1914), 136, 137
Smith, Ruby Green, 136, 138, 139
social reality, 60
social science
  Chicago school's concept of, 15
  development in North America, 15
  initial rejection of participatory research, 65
  relationship to community-based research, 11, 61
Social Sciences and Humanities Research Council (Canada), 75
sociocultural theories, 41
solidarity economies in Latin America, 173–6
South Africa
  university–community engagement, 6, 150–65
Stanford University, 65
Steinhaus, Norbert, 71, 222
Street Law Project (South Africa), 151–2
student volunteering, 109
Sussex, University of, 57
Swantz, Marja-Liisa, 56–7

Tagore, Rabindranath, 55
Tandon, Rajesh, 1, 53, 57, 59, 60, 61–2, 64, 217, 222
Tanzania, participatory research in, 55–7
Taxila, University of (former India), 54
Taylorism, 16
'third mission' of universities (social engagement/responsibility/service), 20, 89, 90, 102, 150
time–motion study, *see* Taylorism
Toronto Participatory Research Group, 59

Toronto, University of, 58
Trade Union Research Project (South Africa), 152
Training and Mentoring of Science Shops (TRAMS), 78
translational research, 19, 140
Tremblay, Crystal, 167, 222

ujamaa (African philosophy), 55
UNESCO
  Chair in Community-Based Research, 54
  Chair in Community Based Research and Social Responsibility in Higher Education, 64
  Director of Adult Education, 55
United Kingdom (UK)
  Beacons for Public Engagement initiative, 4, 75, 92–3
  university–community research engagement, 4, 85–99, 111–12, 115
United Nations Research Institute for Social Development, 180
Universidad Nacional Experimental Simón Rodríguez (Caracas), 59
universities
  'academic capitalism', 20, 22, 189
  commercialization of, 2, 4, 7, 8, 20, 22, 189
  competition between, 22
  culture change within, 134–5
  'ecological university', 7, 186, 191–4, 196–7
  'engaged university, the', 1, 93
  'entrepreneurial university', 24
  funding crisis, 8
  future role of, 24–6, 66, 86–7, 149–50, 156
  'imaginative university', 24
  knowledge legitimation, 7, 184–5
  land-grant (USA), 5, 15, 16, 136–40
  leadership crisis, 8
  mission crisis, 21, 24
  societal (civic) engagement, 4, 5, 22–3, 24, 25, 89–95, 186

universities—*continued*
   three missions of, 20, 89, 90, 102, 150
   translational research, 19, 140
   see also science shops; university–community engagement
Universities UK (UUK), 88
University College Cork, 107–8
university–community engagement
   academia's initial rejection of participatory research concept, 62, 63
   in Australia, 5, 117–31
   benefits of community-based research, 1–2, 27–8, 104
   building of academia–civil society partnerships, 64–6
   in Canada, 39–52, 75
   'ecological university' concept, 191–4, 196–7
   in Europe, 16–17, 75
   in France, 75
   in Germany, 76
   in Ireland (Republic of), 4–5, 75, 101–16
   in Latin America, 6, 12–15, 167–80
   in Netherlands, 77
   in Northern Ireland, 101–16
   in South Africa, 6, 150–65
   in UK, 4, 75, 85–99, 111–12, 115

UNESCO Chair in Community Based Research and Social Responsibility in Higher Education, 64
   in USA, 5, 15, 16, 136–47
   see also community-based research; science shops
USA
   community organizing and culture change, 140–5
   land-grant universities, 5, 15, 16, 136–40
   university–community engagement, 136–47
US Agency for International Development (USAID), 168

Vancouver Island Health Authority, 42
Venezuela, solidarity economy, 175
Victoria, University of (Canada), 64, 65, 176
Vio Grossi, Francisco, 57, 59, 60
Virginia Commonwealth University (South Africa), 162
Visvanathan, Shiv, 67
Vygotsky, Lev, 41, 45

Warry Report, 93
Wit, Ton, 58
Workers' Educational Association (UK), 4
World Bank, 13, 14, 209
World Social Forum, 209

GPSR Compliance
The European Union's (EU) General Product Safety Regulation (GPSR) is a set of rules that requires consumer products to be safe and our obligations to ensure this.

If you have any concerns about our products, you can contact us on

ProductSafety@springernature.com

In case Publisher is established outside the EU, the EU authorized representative is:

Springer Nature Customer Service Center GmbH
Europaplatz 3
69115 Heidelberg, Germany

www.ingramcontent.com/pod-product-compliance
Lightning Source LLC
LaVergne TN
LVHW011811060526
838200LV00053B/3741